Microsoft® Office Excel® 2007

ILLUSTRATED COURSE GUIDE

BASIC

Elizabeth Eisner Reding/Lynn Wermers

THOMSON
★
COURSE TECHNOLOGY ™

Australia • Canada • Mexico • Singapore • Spain • United Kingdom • United States

THOMSON

™

COURSE TECHNOLOGY

Illustrated Course Guide: Microsoft® Office Excel® 2007 Basic

Elizabeth Eisner Reding/Lynn Wermers

Senior Acquisitions Editor:
Marjorie Hunt

Senior Product Manager:
Christina Kling Garrett

Associate Product Manager:
Rebecca Padrick

Editorial Assistant:
Michelle Camisa

Marketing Coordinator:
Jennifer Hankin

Developmental Editors:
MT Cozzola, Barbara Clemens

Content Project Manager:
Daphne Barbas

Copy Editor:
Gary Michael Spahl

QA Manuscript Reviewers:
Nicole Ashton, John Freitas,
Jeff Schwartz, Susan Whalen

Cover Designer:
Marissa Falco

Cover Artist:
Mark Hunt

Composition:
GEX Publishing Services

About The Illustrated Course Guides

Welcome to the Microsoft Office 2007 Illustrated Course Guides! The books in this series are ideally suited for a wide range of learners who need to gain skill proficiency at a particular level for Word, Excel, Access, PowerPoint or Windows Vista. The highly visual and full-color lesson material is extremely approachable for learners of all levels, and the wealth of reinforcement exercises ensures skills retention. To maximize skills retention and measure proficiency, use Illustrated Course Guides in conjunction with SAM 2007, our robust assessment and training system.

As you probably have heard by now, Microsoft completely redesigned this latest version of Office from the ground up. No more menus! No more toolbars! The software changes Microsoft made were based on years of research during which they studied users' needs and work habits. The result is a phenomenal and powerful new version of the software that will make you and your learners more productive and help you get better results faster.

Before we started working on the Illustrated Course Guides for Microsoft Office 2007, we also conducted our own research. We reached out to nearly 100 instructors like you who have used previous editions of our Microsoft Office texts. Some of you responded to one of our surveys, others of you generously spent time with us on the phone, telling us your thoughts. Seven of you agreed to serve on our Advisory Board and guided our decisions.

As a result of all the feedback you gave us, we have preserved the features that you love, and made improvements that you suggested and requested. And of course we have covered all the key features of the new software. (For more details on what's new, please read the Preface.) We are confident that the Illustrated Course Guides for Microsoft Office 2007 and all their available resources will help any type of learner master Microsoft Office 2007.

Advisory Board

We thank our Advisory Board who enthusiastically gave us their opinions and guided our every decision on content and design from beginning to end. They are:

Kristen Callahan, Mercer County Community College

Paulette Comet, Assistant Professor, Community College of Baltimore County

Barbara Comfort, J. Sargeant Reynolds Community College

Margaret Cooksey, Tallahassee Community College

Rachelle Hall, Glendale Community College

Hazel Kates, Miami Dade College

Charles Lupico, Thomas Nelson Community College

Author Acknowledgments

Elizabeth Eisner Reding Creating a book of this magnitude is a team effort. I would like to thank my husband, Michael, as well as Christina Kling Garrett, the project manager, and my development editor, MT Cozzola, for her suggestions and corrections. I would also like to thank the production and editorial staff for all their hard work that made this project a reality.

Lynn Wermers I would like to thank Barbara Clemens for her insightful contributions, great humor, and patience. I would also like to thank Christina Kling Garrett for her encouragement and support in guiding and managing the project.

Preface

Welcome to *Illustrated Course Guide: Microsoft Office Excel 2007 Basic*. If this is your first experience with the Illustrated Course Guides, you'll see that this book has a unique design: each skill is presented on two facing pages, with steps on the left and screens on the right. The layout makes it easy to digest a skill without having to read a lot of text and flip pages to see an illustration.

This book is an ideal learning tool for a wide range of learners—the "rookies" will find the clean design easy to follow and focused with only essential information presented, and the "hotshots" will appreciate being able to move quickly through the lessons to find the information they need without reading a lot of text. The design also makes this a great reference after the course is over! Note that the combined content in the Basic, Intermediate and Advanced Course Guides for Microsoft Excel 2007 maps to the MCAS objectives, making the books an ideal preparation tool for the MCAS exam. See the illustration on the right to learn more about the pedagogical and design elements of a typical lesson.

What's New

We've made many changes and enhancements to the Microsoft Office 2007 Illustrated Course Guides. Here are some highlights of what's new:

- **New Getting Started with Microsoft Office 2007 Unit**—This unit begins every Basic level Course Guide book and gets learners up to speed on features of Office 2007 that are common to all the applications, such as the Ribbon, the Office button, and the Quick Access toolbar.

- **Real Life Independent Challenge**—The new Real Life Independent Challenge exercises offer learners the opportunity to create projects that are meaningful to their lives, such as spreadsheets that calculate loan payments, or track personal expenses.

Each two-page spread focuses on a single skill.

Concise text introduces the basic principles in the lesson and integrates a real-world case study.

UNIT A
Excel 2007

Editing Cell Entries

You can change, or **edit**, the contents of an active cell at any time. To do so, double-click the cell, click in the formula bar, or just start typing. Excel switches to Edit mode when you are making cell entries. Different pointers, shown in Table A-3, guide you through the editing process. ▨▨▨ You noticed some errors in the worksheet and want to make corrections. The first error is in cell A5, which contains a misspelled name.

STEPS

QUICK TIP
Pressing [Enter] also accepts the cell entry, but moves the cell pointer down one cell.

1. **Click cell A5, then click to the right of P in the formula bar**
   As soon as you click in the formula bar, a blinking vertical line called the **insertion point** appears on the formula bar at the location where new text will be inserted. See Figure A-9. The mouse pointer changes to I when you point anywhere in the formula bar.

2. **Press [Delete], then click the Enter button ☑ on the formula bar**
   Clicking the Enter button accepts the edit, and the spelling of the employee's first name is corrected. You can also press [Enter] or [Tab] to accept an edit.

QUICK TIP
On some keyboards, you might need to press an "F Lock" key to enable the function keys.

3. **Click cell B6, then press [F2]**
   Excel switches to Edit mode, and the insertion point blinks in the cell. Pressing [F2] activates the cell for editing directly in the cell instead of the formula bar. Some people prefer editing right in the cell instead of using the formula bar, but it's simply a matter of preference; the results in the worksheet are the same.

QUICK TIP
The Undo button allows you to reverse up to 100 previous actions, one at a time.

4. **Press [Backspace], type 8, then press [Enter]**
   The value in the cell changes from 35 to 38, and cell B7 becomes the active cell. Did you notice that the calculations in cells B15 and E15 also changed? That's because those cells contain formulas that include cell B6 in their calculations. If you make a mistake when editing, you can click the Cancel button ☒ on the formula bar *before* pressing [Enter] to confirm the cell entry. The Enter and Cancel buttons appear only when you're in Edit mode. If you notice the mistake *after* you have confirmed the cell entry, click the Undo button ▨ on the Quick Access toolbar.

5. **Click cell A9, press [F2], press and hold [Shift], press [Home], then release [Shift]**
   Pressing and holding [Shift] lets you select text using the keyboard. Pressing [Home] moves the cursor to the beginning of the cell; pressing [End] would move the cursor to the end or the cell.

6. **Type Maez, Javier, then press [Enter]**
   When text is selected, typing deletes it and replaces it with the new text.

7. **Double-click cell C12, press [Delete], type 4, then click ☑**
   Double-clicking a cell activates it for editing directly in the cell. Compare your screen to Figure A-10.

8. **Save your work**
   Your changes to the workbook are saved.

Recovering a lost workbook file

Sometimes while you are using Excel, you may experience a power failure or your computer may "freeze," making it impossible to continue working. If this type of interruption occurs, Excel has a built-in recovery feature that allows you to open and save files that were open at the time of the interruption. When you restart Excel after an interruption, File Recovery mode automatically starts and tries to make any necessary repairs. If you need to use a corrupted workbook, you can try and repair it manually by clicking the Office button, then clicking Open. Select the workbook file you want to repair, click the Open list arrow, then click Open and Repair.

Excel 10   Getting Started with Excel 2007

Hints as well as troubleshooting advice appear right where you need them—next to the step itself.

Clues to Use boxes provide concise information that either expands on the major lesson skill or describes an independent task that in some way relates to the major lesson skill.

iv

Every lesson features large, full-color representations of what the screen should look like as learners complete the numbered steps.

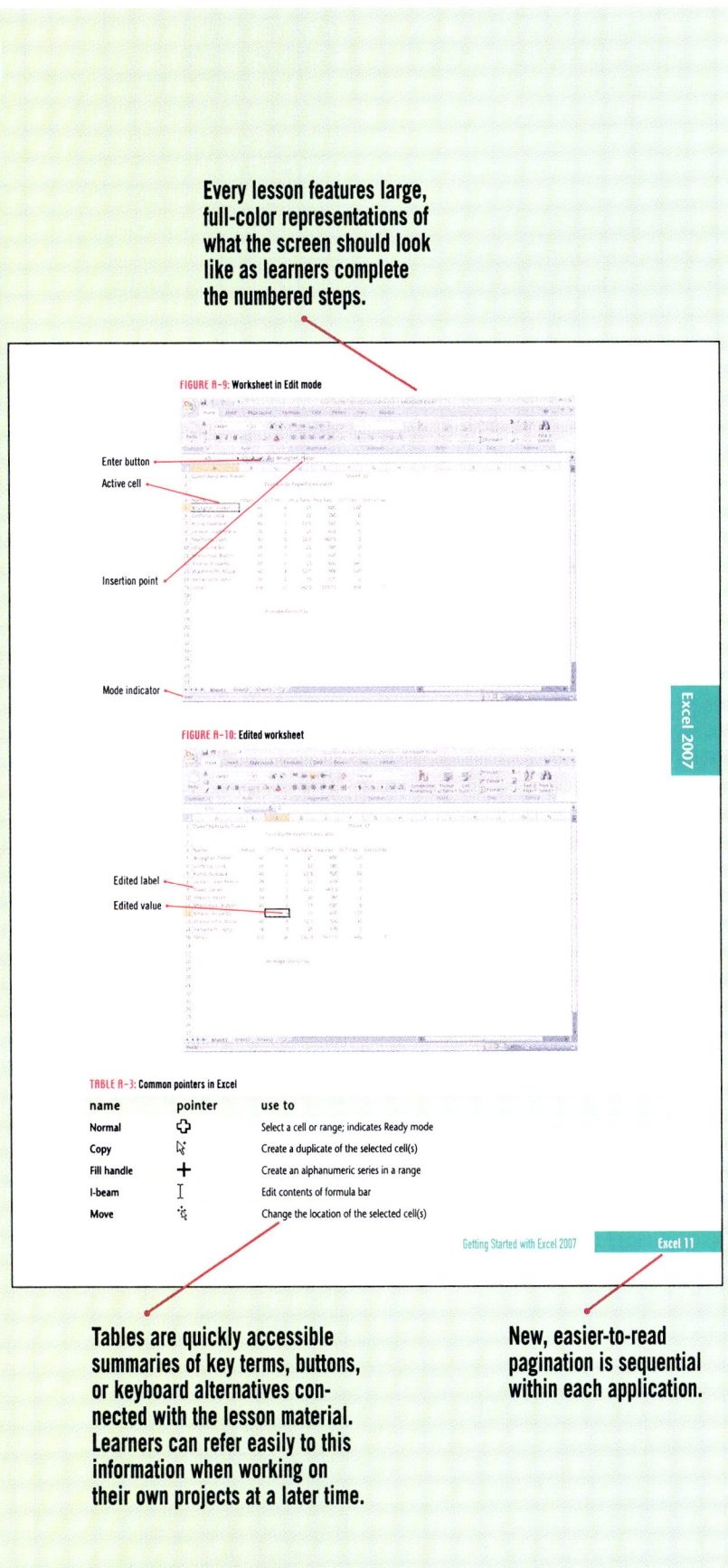

FIGURE A-9: Worksheet in Edit mode

Enter button

Active cell

Insertion point

Mode indicator

Excel 2007

FIGURE A-10: Edited worksheet

Edited label

Edited value

TABLE A-3: Common pointers in Excel

name	pointer	use to
Normal		Select a cell or range; indicates Ready mode
Copy		Create a duplicate of the selected cell(s)
Fill handle	+	Create an alphanumeric series in a range
I-beam	I	Edit contents of formula bar
Move		Change the location of the selected cell(s)

Getting Started with Excel 2007   Excel 11

Tables are quickly accessible summaries of key terms, buttons, or keyboard alternatives connected with the lesson material. Learners can refer easily to this information when working on their own projects at a later time.

New, easier-to-read pagination is sequential within each application.

- **New Case Study**—A new case study featuring Quest Specialty Travel provides a practical scenario that learners can relate to as they learn skills and promote skills retention. This fictional company offers a wide variety of tours around the world.

- **Content Improvements**—All of the content in the every Illlustrated Course Guide has been updated to cover Office 2007 and also to address customer feedback.

Assignments

The lessons use Quest Specialty Travel, a fictional adventure travel company, as the case study. The assignments on the light purple pages at the end of each unit increase in difficulty. Data Files and case studies provide a variety of interesting and relevant business applications to help reinforce learning and retain skills. Assignments include:

- **Concepts Reviews** consist of multiple choice, matching, and screen identification questions.

- **Skills Reviews** provide additional hands-on, step-by-step reinforcement.

- **Independent Challenges** are case projects requiring critical thinking and application of the unit skills. The Independent Challenges increase in difficulty, with the first one in each unit being the easiest. Independent Challenges 2 and 3 become increasingly open-ended, requiring more independent problem solving.

- **Real Life Independent Challenges** are practical exercises in which learners create projects to help them with their every day lives.

- **Advanced Challenge Exercises** set within the Independent Challenges provide optional steps for more advanced learners.

- **Visual Workshops** are practical, self-graded capstone projects that require independent problem solving.

v

Assessment & Training Solutions

SAM 2007

SAM 2007 helps bridge the gap between the classroom and the real world by allowing learners to train and test on important computer skills in an active, hands-on environment.

SAM 2007's easy-to-use system includes powerful interactive exams, training, or projects on critical applications such as Word, Excel, Access, PowerPoint, Outlook, Windows, the Internet, and much more. SAM simulates the application environment, allowing learners to demonstrate their knowledge and think through the skills by performing real-world tasks.

Designed to be used with the Illustrated Course Guides, SAM 2007 includes built-in page references so learners can print helpful study guides that match the Illustrated textbooks used in class. Powerful administrative options allow instructors to schedule exams and assignments, secure tests, and run reports with almost limitless flexibility.

Online Content   Blackboard

Blackboard is the leading distance learning solution provider and class-management platform today. Thomson Course Technology has partnered with Blackboard to bring you premium online content. Instructors: Content for use with this title is available in a Blackboard Course Cartridge and may include topic reviews, case projects, review questions, test banks, practice tests, custom syllabi, and more.

Thomson Course Technology also has solutions for several other learning management systems. Please visit *www.course.com* today to see what's available for this title.

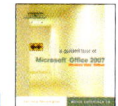

A Guided Tour of Microsoft Office 2007, Windows Vista Edition

This CD of movie tutorials helps learners get exposed to the new features of Microsoft Office 2007 quickly. Dynamic and engaging author Corinne Hoisington presents the highlights of the new features of Word, Excel, Access, and PowerPoint plus a bonus movie tutorial on Windows Vista. This CD is a great supplement to this book, offering a fun overview of the software to inspire learners and show them what is possible.

Instructor Resources

The Instructor Resources CD is Thomson Course Technology's way of putting the resources and information needed to teach and learn effectively into your hands. With an integrated array of teaching and learning tools that offer you and your learners a broad range of technology-based instructional options, we believe this CD represents the highest quality and most cutting edge resources available to instructors today. Many of these resources are available at *www.course.com*. The resources available with this book are:

- **Instructor's Manual**—Available as an electronic file, the Instructor's Manual includes detailed lecture topics with teaching tips for each unit.

- **Sample Syllabus**—Prepare and customize your course easily using this sample course outline.

- **Course Outline**—Available online, the Course Outline includes suggested times for each unit (as well as time for breaks and lunch), to complete the Basic, Intermediate, or Advanced skills in one training day. You can customize it to suit your needs or provide it as a hand out.

- **PowerPoint Presentations**—Each unit has a corresponding PowerPoint presentation that you can use in lecture, distribute to your learners, or customize to suit your course.

- **Figure Files**—The figures in the text are provided on the Instructor Resources CD to help you illustrate key topics or concepts. You can create traditional overhead transparencies by printing the figure files. Or you can create electronic slide shows by using the figures in a presentation program such as PowerPoint.

- **Solutions to Exercises**—Solutions to Exercises contains every file learners are asked to create or modify in the lessons and end-of-unit material. Also provided in this section, there is a document outlining the solutions for the end-of-unit Concepts Review, Skills Review, and Independent Challenges. An Annotated Solution File and Grading Rubric accompany each file and can be used together for quick and easy grading.

- **Data Files**—To complete most of the units in this book, learners will need Data Files. You can post the Data Files on a file server for learners to copy. The Data Files are available on the Instructor Resources CD, the Review Pack, and can also be downloaded from *www.course.com*. In this edition, we have included a lesson on downloading the Data Files for this book, see page xvi.

Instruct learners to use the Data Files List included on the Review Pack and the Instructor Resources CD. This list gives instructions on copying and organizing files.

- **ExamView**—ExamView is a powerful testing software package that allows you to create and administer printed, computer (LAN-based), and Internet exams. ExamView includes hundreds of questions that correspond to the topics covered in this text, enabling learners to generate detailed study guides that include page references for further review. The computer-based and Internet testing components allow learners to take exams at their computers, and also saves you time by grading each exam automatically.

CourseCasts—Learning on the Go. Always Available...Always Relevant.

Want to keep up with the latest technology trends relevant to you? Visit our site to find a library of podcasts, CourseCasts, featuring a "CourseCast of the Week," and download them to your mp3 player at *http://coursecasts.course.com*.

Our fast-paced world is driven by technology. You know because you're an active participant—always on the go, always keeping up with technological trends, and always learning new ways to embrace technology to power your life.

Ken Baldauf, a faculty member of the Florida State University Computer Science Department, is responsible for teaching technology classes to thousands of FSU learners each year. He knows what you know; he knows what you want to learn. He's also an expert in the latest technology and will sort through and aggregate the most pertinent news and information so you can spend your time enjoying technology, rather than trying to figure it out.

Visit us at *http://coursecasts.course.com* to learn on the go!

Brief Contents

Preface   **iv**

OFFICE 2007   **Unit A: Getting Started with Microsoft Office 2007**   **1**

EXCEL 2007   **Unit A: Getting Started with Excel 2007**   **1**

EXCEL 2007   **Unit B: Working with Formulas and Functions**   **25**

EXCEL 2007   **Unit C: Formatting a Worksheet**   **51**

EXCEL 2007   **Unit D: Working with Charts**   **79**

EXCEL 2007   **Unit E: Analyzing Data Using Formulas**   **105**

Appendix   **1**

Glossary   **9**

Index   **20**

Contents

Preface iv

OFFICE 2007

Unit A: Getting Started with Microsoft Office 2007   1

Understanding the Office 2007 Suite 2
      Deciding which program to use

Starting and Exiting an Office Program 4
      Using shortcut keys to move between Office programs

Viewing the Office 2007 User Interface 6
      Customizing the Quick Access toolbar

Creating and Saving a File...8
      Using the Office Clipboard

Opening a File and Saving it with a New Name..10
      Exploring File Open options
      Working in Compatibility mode

Viewing and Printing Your Work 12
      Using the Print Screen feature to create a screen capture

Getting Help and Closing a File 14
      Recovering a document

Concepts Review 16

Independent Challenge...16

EXCEL 2007

Unit A: Getting Started with Excel 2007   1

Understanding Spreadsheet Software 2

Touring the Excel 2007 Window...4

Understanding Formulas..6

Entering Labels and Values and Using AutoSum 8
      Navigating a worksheet

Editing Cell Entries 10
      Recovering a lost workbook file

Entering and Editing a Simple Formula 12
      Understanding named ranges

Switching Worksheet Views 14

Choosing Print Options 16
    Printing worksheet formulas
    Scaling to fit
Concepts Review 18
Skills Review 19
Independent Challenges 20
Visual Workshop 24

Unit B: Working with Formulas and Functions   25

Creating a Complex Formula..26
    Reviewing the order of precedence
Inserting a Function 28
Typing a Function 30
    Using the COUNT and COUNTA functions
Copying and Moving Cell Entries..32
    Inserting and deleting selected cells
Understanding Relative and Absolute Cell References.....................................34
    Using a mixed reference
Copying Formulas with Relative Cell References 36
    Using Auto Fill options
Copying Formulas with Absolute Cell References 38
    Using the fill handle for sequential text or values
Rounding a Value with a Function 40
    Creating a new workbook using a template
Concepts Review 42
Skills Review 44
Independent Challenges 46
Visual Workshop 50

Unit C: Formatting a Worksheet   51

Formatting Values..52
    Formatting as a table
Changing Font and Font Size 54
    Inserting and adjusting clip art and other images
Changing Attributes and Alignment 56
    Rotating and indenting cell entries
Adjusting Column Width 58
    Changing row height

Inserting and Deleting Rows and Columns 60
  Hiding and unhiding columns and rows
  Adding and editing comments
Applying Colors, Patterns, and Borders 62
  Saving time with themes and cell styles
Applying Conditional Formatting 64
  Managing conditional formatting rules
Naming and Moving a Sheet 66
  Copying worksheets
Checking Spelling 68
  E-mailing a workbook
Concepts Review 70
Skills Review 71
Independent Challenges 73
Visual Workshop 78

EXCEL 2007　　　**Unit D: Working with Charts**　　　**79**

Planning a Chart 80
Creating a Chart 82
  Using the contextual Chart Tools tabs
Moving and Resizing a Chart 84
  Moving an embedded chart to a sheet
Changing the Chart Design 86
  Creating a Combination Chart
  Working with a 3-D chart
Changing the Chart Layout 88
  Adding data labels to a chart
Formatting a Chart 90
  Changing alignment in axis text and titles
Annotating and Drawing on a Chart 92
  Adding SmartArt graphics
Creating a Pie Chart 94
  Using the Page Setup dialog box for a chart
Concepts Review 96
Skills Review 97
Independent Challenges 99
Visual Workshop 104

EXCEL 2007　　　**Unit E: Analyzing Data Using Formulas**　　　**105**

Formatting Data Using Text Functions...106
  Using text functions

Summing a Data Range Based on Conditions 108

Consolidating Data Using a Formula 110
  Linking data between workbooks

Checking Formulas for Errors 112
  Correcting circular references

Constructing Formulas Using Named Ranges 114
  Managing workbook names

Building a Logical Formula with the IF Function.............................116

Building a Logical Formula with the AND Function 118
  Using the OR and NOT logical functions

Calculating Payments with the PMT Function.............................120
  Calculating future value with the FV function

Concepts Review 122

Skills Review 123

Independent Challenges 125

Visual Workshop 128

Appendix   1

Glossary   9

Index   20

Read This Before You Begin

Frequently Asked Questions

What are Data Files?

A Data File is a partially completed Excel spreadsheet, or another type of file that you use to complete the steps in the units and exercises to create the final document that you submit to your instructor. Each unit opener page lists the Data Files that you need for that unit.

Where are the Data Files?

Your instructor will provide the Data Files to you or direct you to a location on a network drive from which you can download them. Alternatively, you can follow the instructions on page xvi to download the Data Files from this book's Web page.

What software was used to write and test this book?

This book was written and tested using a typical installation of Microsoft Office 2007 installed on a computer with a typical installation of Microsoft Windows Vista. The browser used for any steps that require a browser is Internet Explorer 7.

If you are using this book on Windows XP, please see the "Important Notes for Windows XP Users" on the next page. If you are using this book on Windows Vista, please see the Appendix at the end of this book.

Do I need to be connected to the Internet to complete the steps and exercises in this book?

Some of the exercises in this book assume that your computer is connected to the Internet. If you are not connected to the Internet, see your instructor for information on how to complete the exercises.

What do I do if my screen is different from the figures shown in this book?

This book was written and tested on computers with monitors set at a resolution of 1024 × 768. If your screen shows more or less information than the figures in the book, your monitor is probably set at a higher or lower resolution. If you don't see something on your screen, you might have to scroll down or up to see the object identified in the figures.

The Ribbon (the blue area at the top of the screen) in Microsoft Office 2007 adapts to different resolutions. If your monitor is set at a lower resolution than 1024 × 768, you might not see all of the buttons shown in the figures. The groups of buttons will always appear, but the entire group might be condensed into a single button that you need to click to access the buttons described in the instructions. For example, the figures and steps in this book assume that the Editing group on the Home tab in Word looks like the following:

1024 × 768 Editing Group

Editing Group on the Home Tab of the Ribbon at 1024 × 768

If your resolution is set to 800 × 600, the Ribbon in Word will look like the following figure, and you will need to click the Editing button to access the buttons that are visible in the Editing group.

800 × 600 Editing Group

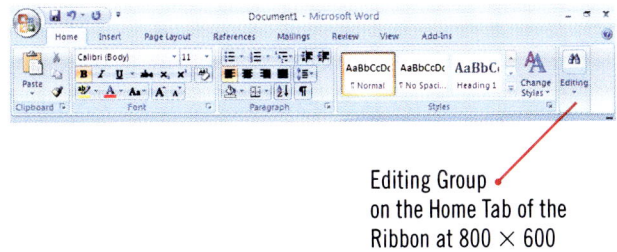

Editing Group on the Home Tab of the Ribbon at 800 × 600

800 × 600 Editing Group Clicked

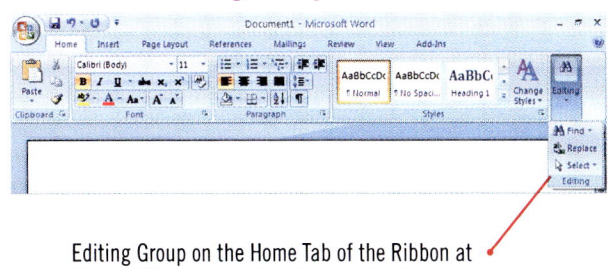

Editing Group on the Home Tab of the Ribbon at 800 × 600 is selected to show available buttons

Important Notes for Windows XP Users

The screen shots in this book show Microsoft Office 2007 running on Windows Vista. However, if you are using Microsoft Windows XP, you can still use this book because Office 2007 runs virtually the same on both platforms. There are a few differences that you will encounter if you are using Windows XP. Read this section to understand the differences.

Dialog boxes

If you are a Windows XP user, dialog boxes shown in this book will look slightly different than what you see on your screen. Dialog boxes for Windows XP have a blue title bar, instead of a gray title bar. However, beyond this difference in appearance, the options in the dialog boxes across platforms are the same. For instance, the screen shots below show the Font dialog box running on Windows XP and the Font dialog box running on Windows Vista.

FIGURE 1: Dialog box in Windows XP

FIGURE 2: Dialog box in Windows Vista

Alternate Steps for Windows XP Users

Nearly all of the steps in this book work exactly the same for Windows XP users. However, there are a few tasks that will require you to complete slightly different steps. This section provides alternate steps for a few specific skills.

Starting a program

1. Click the **Start button** on the taskbar
2. Point to **All Programs**, point to **Microsoft Office**, then click the application you want to use

FIGURE 3: Starting a program

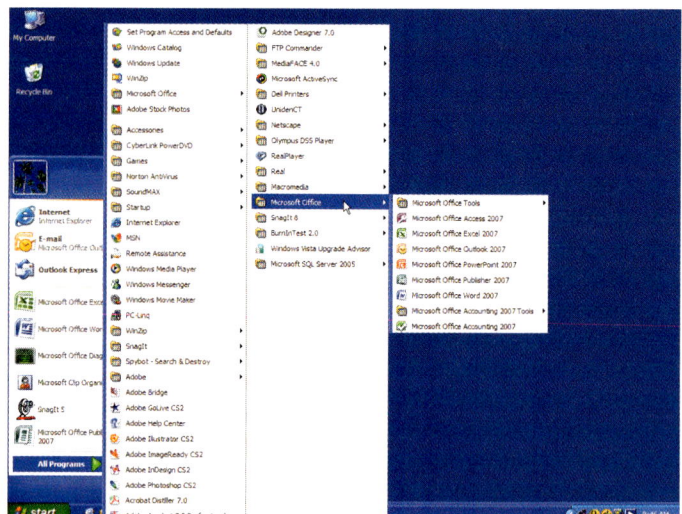

Saving a file for the first time

1. Click the **Office button**, then click **Save As**
2. Type a name for your file in the File name text box
3. Click the **Save in list arrow**, then navigate to the drive and folder where you store your Data Files
4. Click **Save**

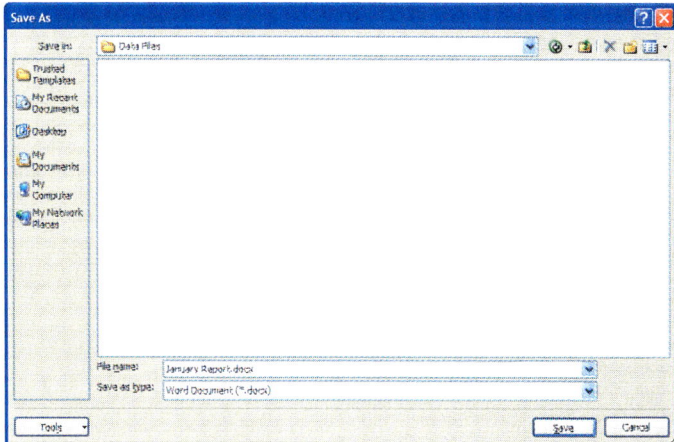

FIGURE 4: Save As dialog box

Opening a file

Saving a file for the first time

1. Click the **Office button**, then click **Open**
2. Click the **Look in list arrow**, then navigate to the drive and folder where you store your Data Files
3. Click the file you want to open
4. Click **Open**

FIGURE 5: Open dialog box

Downloading Data Files for This Book

In order to complete many of the lesson steps and exercises in this book, you are asked to open and save Data Files. A **Data File** is a partially completed file that you use as a starting point to complete the steps in the units and exercises. The benefit of using a Data File is that it saves you the time and effort needed to create a file; you can simply open a Data File, save it with a new name (so the original file remains intact), then make changes to it to complete lesson steps or an exercise. Your instructor will provide the Data Files to you or direct you to a location on a network drive from which you can download them. Alternatively, you can follow the instructions in this lesson to download the Data Files from this book's Web page.

1. Start Internet Explorer, type www.course.com in the address bar, then press [Enter]

2. When the Course.com Web site opens, click the Student Downloads link

3. On the Student Downloads page, click in the Search text box, type this book's ISBN, 9781423905349, then click Go

QUICK TIP
You can also click Student Downloads on the right side of the product page.

4. When the page opens for this textbook, in the left navigation bar, click the Download Student Files link, then, on the Student Downloads page, click the Data Files link

5. If the File Download – Security Warning dialog box opens, click Save. (If no dialog box appears, skip this step and go to Step 6)

TROUBLE
If a dialog box opens telling you that the download is complete, click Close.

6. If the Save As dialog box opens, click the Save in list arrow at the top of the dialog box, select a folder on your USB drive or hard disk to download the file to, then click Save

7. Close Internet Explorer and then open My Computer or Windows Explorer and display the contents of the drive and folder to which you downloaded the file

8. Double-click the file 905349.exe in the drive or folder, then, if the Open File – Security Warning dialog box opens, click Run

QUICK TIP
By default, the files will extract to C:\ CourseTechnology\ 905349

9. In the WinZip Self-Extractor window, navigate to the drive and folder where you want to unzip the files to, then click Unzip

10. When the WinZip Self-Extractor displays a dialog box listing the number of files that have unzipped successfully, click OK, click Close in the WinZip Self-Extractor dialog box, then close Windows Explorer or My Computer

You are now ready to open the required files.

Getting Started with Microsoft Office 2007

Microsoft Office 2007 is a group of software programs designed to help you create documents, collaborate with co-workers, and track and analyze information. Each program is designed so you can work quickly and efficiently to create professional-looking results. You use different Office programs to accomplish specific tasks, such as writing a letter or producing a sales presentation, yet all the programs have a similar look and feel. Once you become familiar with one program, you'll find it easy to transfer your knowledge to the others. This unit introduces you to the most frequently used programs in Office, as well as common features they all share.

OBJECTIVES

Understand the Office 2007 Suite

Start and exit an Office program

View the Office 2007 user interface

Create and save a file

Open a file and save it with a
   new name

View and print your work

Get Help and close a file

Understanding the Office 2007 Suite

Microsoft Office 2007 features an intuitive, context-sensitive user interface, so you can get up to speed faster and use advanced features with greater ease. The programs in Office are bundled together in a group called a **suite** (although you can also purchase them separately). The Office suite is available in several configurations, but all include Word and Excel. Other configurations include PowerPoint, Access, Outlook, Publisher, and/or others. Each program in Office is best suited for completing specific types of tasks, though there is some overlap in terms of their capabilities.

DETAILS

The Office programs covered in this book include:

• **Microsoft Office Word 2007**

When you need to create any kind of text-based document, such as memos, newsletters, or multi-page reports, Word is the program to use. You can easily make your documents look great by inserting eye-catching graphics and using formatting tools such as themes. **Themes** are predesigned combinations of color and formatting attributes you can apply, and are available in most Office programs. The Word document shown in Figure A-1 was formatted with the Solstice theme.

• **Microsoft Office Excel 2007**

Excel is the perfect solution when you need to work with numeric values and make calculations. It puts the power of formulas, functions, charts, and other analytical tools into the hands of every user, so you can analyze sales projections, figure out loan payments, and present your findings in style. The Excel worksheet shown in Figure A-1 tracks personal expenses. Because Excel automatically recalculates results whenever a value changes, the information is always up-to-date. A chart illustrates how the monthly expenses are broken down.

• **Microsoft Office PowerPoint 2007**

Using PowerPoint, it's easy to create powerful presentations complete with graphics, transitions, and even a soundtrack. Using professionally designed themes and clip art, you can quickly and easily create dynamic slideshows such as the one shown in Figure A-1.

• **Microsoft Office Access 2007**

Access helps you keep track of large amounts of quantitative data, such as product inventories or employee records. The form shown in Figure A-1 was created for a grocery store inventory database. Employees use the form to enter data about each item. Using Access enables employees to quickly find specific information such as price and quantity, without hunting through store shelves and stockrooms.

Microsoft Office has benefits beyond the power of each program, including:

• **Common user interface: Improving business processes**

Because the Office suite programs have a similar **interface**, or look and feel, your experience using one program's tools makes it easy to learn those in the other programs. Office documents are **compatible** with one another, meaning that you can easily incorporate, or **integrate**, an Excel chart into a PowerPoint slide, or an Access table into a Word document.

• **Collaboration: Simplifying how people work together**

Office recognizes the way people do business today, and supports the emphasis on communication and knowledge-sharing within companies and across the globe. All Office programs include the capability to incorporate feedback—called **online collaboration**—across the Internet or a company network.

Word document

Excel worksheet

PowerPoint presentation

Access database form

Deciding which program to use

Every Office program includes tools that go far beyond what you might expect. For example, although Excel is primarily designed for making calculations, you can use it to create a database. So when you're planning a project, how do you decide which Office program to use? The general rule of thumb is to use the program best suited for your intended task, and make use of supporting tools in the program if you need them. Word is best for creating text-based documents, Excel is best for making mathematical calculations, PowerPoint is best for preparing presentations, and Access is best for managing quantitative data. Although the capabilities of Office are so vast that you *could* create an inventory in Excel or a budget in Word, you'll find greater flexibility and efficiency by using the program designed for the task. And remember, you can always create a file in one program, and then insert it in a document in another program when you need to, such as including sales projections (Excel) in a memo (Word).

Starting and Exiting an Office Program

The first step in using an Office program is of course to open, or **launch**, it on your computer. You have a few choices for how to launch a program, but the easiest way is to click the Start button on the Windows taskbar, or to double-click an icon on your desktop. You can have multiple programs open on your computer simultaneously, and you can move between open programs by clicking the desired program or document button on the taskbar or by using the [Alt][Tab] keyboard shortcut combination. When working, you'll often want to open multiple programs in Office, and switch among them throughout the day. Begin by launching a few Office programs now.

STEPS

QUICK TIP

You can also launch a program by double-clicking a desktop icon or clicking an entry on the Recent Items menu.

1. **Click the Start button 🔵 on the taskbar**

   The Start menu opens, as shown in Figure A-2. If the taskbar is hidden, you can display it by pointing to the bottom of the screen. Depending on your taskbar property settings, the taskbar may be displayed at all times, or only when you point to that area of the screen. For more information, or to change your taskbar properties, consult your instructor or technical support person.

2. **Point to All Programs, click Microsoft Office, then click Microsoft Office Word 2007**

   Microsoft Office Word 2007 starts and the program window opens on your screen.

QUICK TIP

It is not necessary to close one program before opening another.

3. **Click 🔵 on the taskbar, point to All Programs, click Microsoft Office, then click Microsoft Office Excel 2007**

   Microsoft Office Excel 2007 starts and the program window opens, as shown in Figure A-3. Word is no longer visible, but it remains open. The taskbar displays a button for each open program and document. Because this Excel document is **active**, or in front and available, the Microsoft Excel – Book1 button on the taskbar appears in a darker shade.

4. **Click Document1 – Microsoft Word on the taskbar**

   Clicking a button on the taskbar activates that program and document. The Word program window is now in front, and the Document1 – Microsoft Word taskbar button appears shaded.

QUICK TIP

If there isn't room on your taskbar to display the entire name of each button, you can point to any button to see the full name in a Screentip.

5. **Click 🔵 on the taskbar, point to All Programs, click Microsoft Office, then click Microsoft Office PowerPoint 2007**

   Microsoft Office PowerPoint 2007 starts, and becomes the active program.

6. **Click Microsoft Excel – Book1 on the taskbar**

   Excel is now the active program.

QUICK TIP

As you work in Windows, your computer adapts to your activities. You may notice that after clicking the Start button, the name of the program you want to open appears in the Start menu; if so, you can click it to start the program.

7. **Click 🔵 on the taskbar, point to All Programs, click Microsoft Office, then click Microsoft Office Access 2007**

   Microsoft Office Access 2007 starts, and becomes the active program.

8. **Point to the taskbar to display it, if necessary**

   Four Office programs are open simultaneously.

9. **Click the Office button 🔵, then click Exit Access, as shown in Figure A-4**

   Access closes, leaving Excel active and Word and PowerPoint open.

FIGURE A-2: Start menu

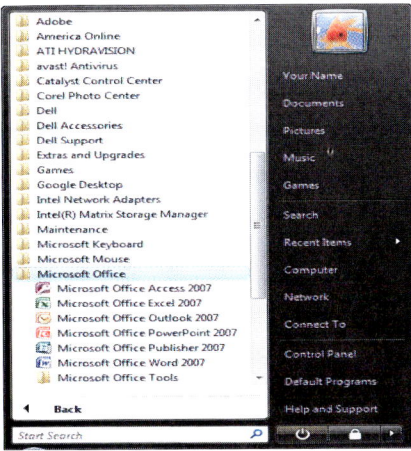

FIGURE A-3: Excel program window and Windows taskbar

Excel button
on taskbar

Word button
on taskbar

Your icons in the notification
area will differ

FIGURE A-4: Exiting Microsoft Office Access

Microsoft
Office button

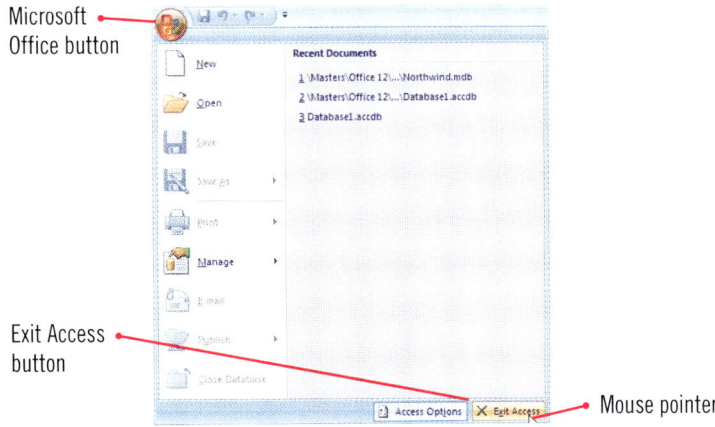

Exit Access
button

Mouse pointer

Using shortcut keys to move between Office programs

As an alternative to the Windows taskbar, you can use a keyboard shortcut to move among open Office programs. The [Alt][Tab] keyboard combination lets you either switch quickly to the next open program, or choose one from a palette. To switch immediately to the next open program, press [Alt][Tab]. To choose from all open programs, press and hold [Alt], then press and release [Tab] without releasing [Alt]. A palette opens on screen, displaying the icon and filename of each open program and file. Each time you press [Tab] while holding [Alt], the selection cycles to the next open file. Release [Alt] when the program/file you want to activate is selected.

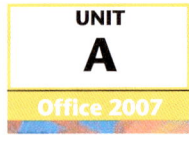
Viewing the Office 2007 User Interface

One of the benefits of using Office is that the programs have much in common, making them easy to learn and making it simple to move from one to another. Individual Office programs have always shared many features, but the innovations in the Office 2007 user interface mean even greater similarity among them all. That means you can also use your knowledge of one program to get up to speed in another. A **user interface** is a collective term for all the ways you interact with a software program. The user interface in Office 2007 includes a more intuitive way of choosing commands, working with files, and navigating in the program window. Familiarize yourself with some of the common interface elements in Office by examining the PowerPoint program window.

STEPS

1. **Click** Microsoft PowerPoint – [Presentation1] **on the taskbar**

   PowerPoint becomes the active program. Refer to Figure A-5 to identify common elements of the Office user interface. The **document window** occupies most of the screen. In PowerPoint, a blank slide appears in the document window, so you can build your slide show. At the top of every Office program window is a **title bar**, which displays the document and program name. Below the title bar is the **Ribbon**, which displays commands you're likely to need for the current task. Commands are organized into **tabs**. The tab names appear at the top of the Ribbon, and the active tab appears in front with its name highlighted. The Ribbon in every Office program includes tabs specific to the program, but all include a Home tab on the far left, for the most popular tasks in that program.

2. **Click the** Office button

   The Office menu opens. This menu contains commands common to most Office programs, such as opening a file, saving a file, and closing the current program. Next to the Office button is the **Quick Access toolbar**, which includes buttons for common Office commands.

3. **Click** again to close it, then point to the Save button **on the Quick Access toolbar, but do not click it**

   You can point to any button in Office to see a description; this is a good way to learn the available choices.

4. **Click the** Design tab **on the Ribbon**

   To display a different tab, you click its name on the Ribbon. Each tab arranges related commands into **groups** to make features easy to find. The Themes group displays available themes in a **gallery**, or palette of choices you can browse. Many groups contain a **dialog box launcher**, an icon you can click to open a dialog box or task pane for the current group, which offers an alternative way to choose commands.

5. **Move the mouse pointer** over the Aspect theme **in the Themes group as shown in Figure A-6, but do not click the mouse button**

   Because you have not clicked the theme, you have not actually made any changes to the slide. With the **Live Preview** feature, you can point to a choice, see the results right in the document, and then decide whether you want to make the change.

6. **Move** away from the Ribbon and towards the slide

   If you clicked the Aspect theme, it would be applied to this slide. Instead, the slide remains unchanged.

7. **Point to the** Zoom slider **on the status bar, then drag to the right until the Zoom percentage reads** 166%

   The slide display is enlarged. Zoom tools are located on the status bar. You can drag the slider or click the plus and minus buttons to zoom in/out on an area of interest. The percentage tells you the zoom effect.

8. **Drag the** Zoom slider **on the status bar to the left until the Zoom percentage reads** 73%

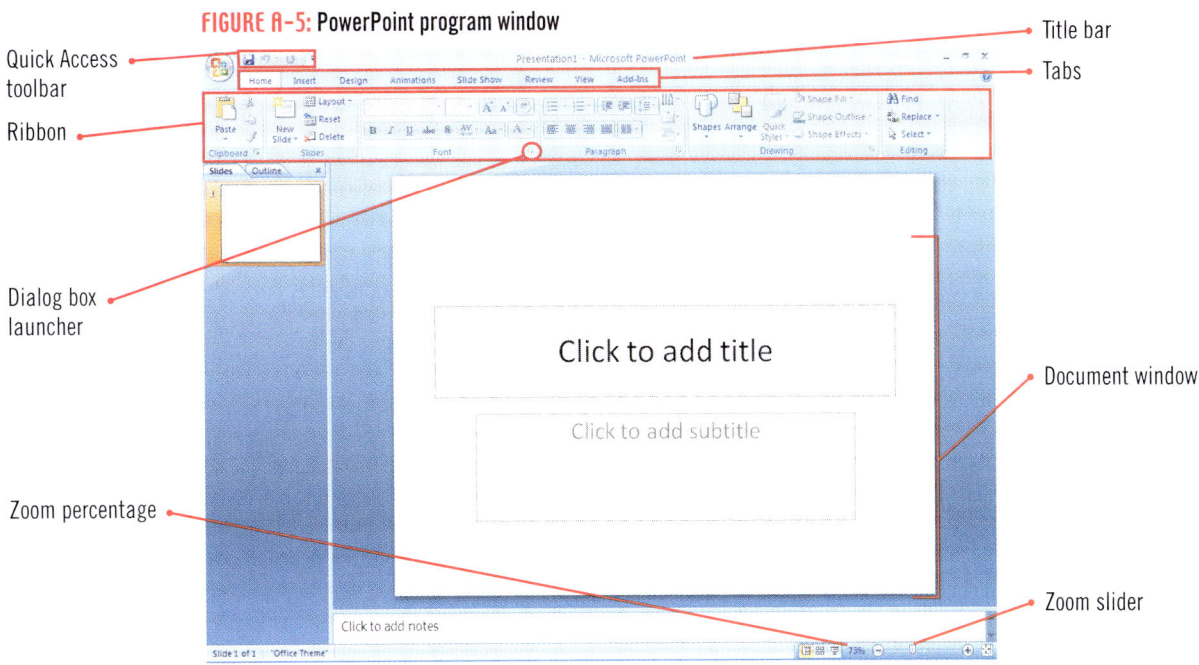

FIGURE A-5: PowerPoint program window

Quick Access toolbar

Ribbon

Dialog box launcher

Zoom percentage

Title bar

Tabs

Document window

Zoom slider

FIGURE A-6: Viewing a theme with Live Preview

Aspect theme

Mouse pointer

ScreenTip

Current zoom percentage

Zoom slider

Customizing the Quick Access toolbar

You can customize the Quick Access toolbar to display your favorite commands. To do so, click the Customize Quick Access Toolbar button in the title bar, then click the command you want to add. If you don't see the command in the list, click More Commands to open the Customize tab of the Options dialog box. In the Options dialog box, use the Choose commands from list to choose a category, click the desired command in the list on the left, click Add to add it to the Quick Access toolbar, then click OK. To remove a button from the toolbar, click the name in the list on the right, then click Remove. To add a command to the Quick Access toolbar on the fly, simply right-click the button on the Ribbon, then click Add to Quick Access Toolbar on the shortcut menu. You can also use the Customize Quick Access Toolbar button to move the toolbar below the ribbon, by clicking Show Below the Ribbon, or to minimize the Ribbon so it takes up less space onscreen. If you click Minimize the Ribbon, the Ribbon is minimized to display only the tabs. When you click a tab, the Ribbon opens so you can choose a command; once you choose a command, the Ribbon closes again, and only the tabs are visible.

Creating and Saving a File

When working in a program, one of the first things you need to do is to create and save a file. A **file** is a stored collection of data. Saving a file enables you to work on a project now, then put it away and work on it again later. In some Office programs, including Word, Excel, and PowerPoint, a new file is automatically created when you start the program, so all you have to do is enter some data and save it. In Access, you must expressly create a file before you enter any data. You should give your files meaningful names and save them in an appropriate location, so they're easy to find. 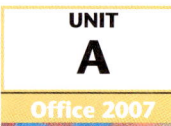 Use Microsoft Word to familiarize yourself with the process of creating and saving a document. First you'll type some notes about a possible location for a corporate meeting, then you'll save the information for later use.

STEPS

1. **Click Document1 – Microsoft Word on the taskbar**

2. **Type Locations for Corporate Meeting, then press [Enter] twice**

   The text appears in the document window, and a cursor blinks on a new blank line. The cursor indicates where the next typed text will appear.

3. **Type Las Vegas, NV, press [Enter], type Orlando, FL, press [Enter], type Chicago, IL, press [Enter] twice, then type your name**

   Compare your document to Figure A-7.

   > **QUICK TIP**
   > A filename can be up to 255 characters, including a file extension, and can include upper- or lowercase characters and spaces, but not ?, ", /, \, <, >, *, |, or :.

4. ► **Click the Save button 🖫 on the Quick Access toolbar**

   Because this is the first time you are saving this document, the Save As dialog box opens, as shown in Figure A-8. The Save As dialog box includes options for assigning a filename and storage location. Once you save a file for the first time, clicking 🖫 saves any changes to the file *without* opening the Save As dialog box, because no additional information is needed. In the Address bar, Office displays the default location for where to save the file, but you can change to any location. In the File name field, Office displays a suggested name for the document based on text in the file, but you can enter a different name.

   > **QUICK TIP**
   > You can create a desktop icon that you can double-click to both launch a program and open a document, by saving it to the desktop.

5. **Type Potential Corporate Meeting Locations**

   The text you type replaces the highlighted text.

6. ► **In the Save As dialog box, use the Address bar or Navigation pane to navigate to the drive and folder where you store your Data Files**

   Many students store files on a flash drive or Zip drive, but you can also store files on your computer, a network drive, or any storage device indicated by your instructor or technical support person.

   > **QUICK TIP**
   > To create a new blank file when a file is open, click the Office button, click New, then click Create.

7. ► **Click Save**

   The Save As dialog box closes, the new file is saved to the location you specified, then the name of the document appears in the title bar, as shown in Figure A-9. (You may or may not see a file extension.) See Table A-1 for a description of the different types of files you create in Office, and the file extensions associated with each. You can save a file in an earlier version of a program by choosing from the list of choices in the Save as type list arrow in the Save As dialog box.

TABLE A-1: Common filenames and default file extensions

File created in	is called a	and has the default extension
Excel	workbook	.xlsx
Word	document	.docx
Access	database	.accdb
PowerPoint	presentation	.pptx

FIGURE A-7: Creating a document in Word

Save button

Your name should appear here

Insertion point

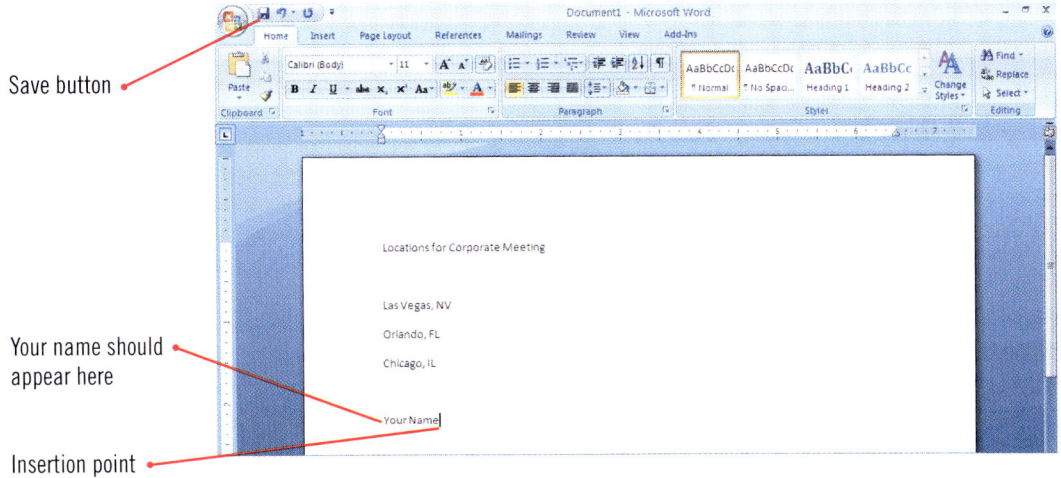

FIGURE A-8: Save As dialog box

Address bar

Navigation pane; your links and Folders setting may differ

File name field; your computer may not be set to display file extensions

Previous Locations list arrow

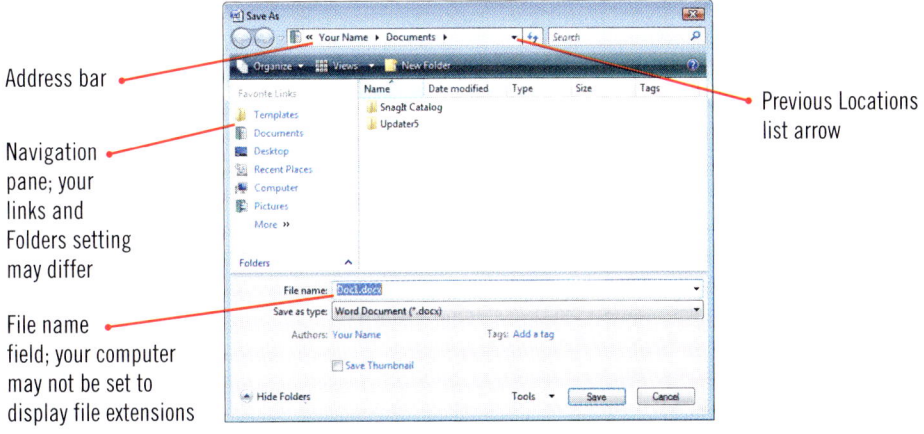

FIGURE A-9: Named Word document

Name appears in title bar

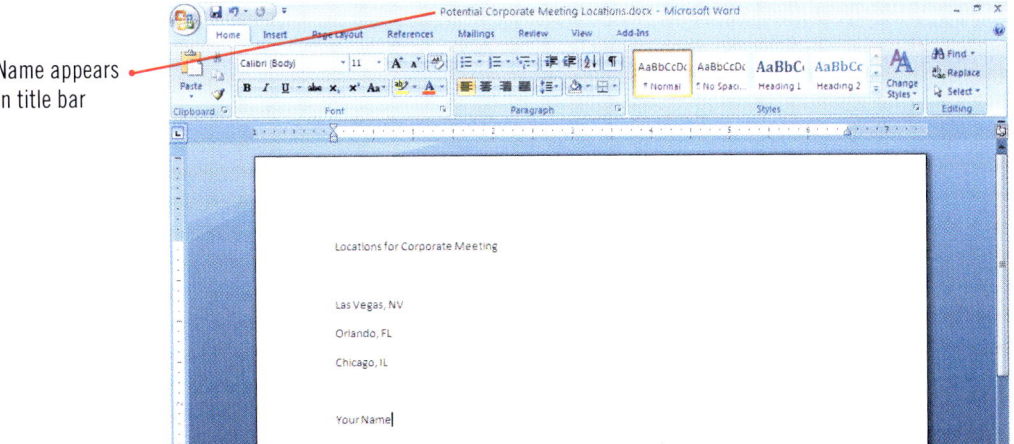

Using the Office Clipboard

You can use the Office Clipboard to cut and copy items from one Office program and paste them into others. The Clipboard can store a maximum of 24 items. To access it, open the Office Clipboard task pane by clicking the launcher in the Clipboard group in the Home tab. Each time you copy a selection, it is saved in the Office Clipboard. Each entry in the Office Clipboard includes an icon that tells you the program in which it was created. To paste an entry, click in the document where you want it to appear, then click the item in the Office Clipboard. To delete an item from the Office Clipboard, right-click the item, then click Delete.

Opening a File and Saving it with a New Name

In many cases as you work in Office, you start with a blank document, but often you need to use an existing file. It might be a file you or a co-worker created earlier as a work-in-progress, or it could be a complete document that you want to use as the basis for another. For example, you might want to create a budget for this year using the budget you created last year; you could type in all the categories and information from scratch, or you could open last year's budget, save it with a new name, and just make changes to update it for the current year. By opening the existing file and saving it with the Save As command, you create a duplicate that you can modify to your heart's content, while the original file remains intact. ▄▄▄▄▄ Use Excel to open an existing workbook file, and save it with a new name so the original remains unchanged.

STEPS

QUICK TIP

If you point to a command on the Office menu that is followed by an arrow, a submenu opens displaying additional, related commands.

1. **Click Microsoft Excel – Book1 on the taskbar, click the Office button 🗔, then click Open**

   The Open dialog box opens, where you can navigate to any drive or folder location accessible to your computer to locate a file.

2. **In the Open dialog box, navigate to the drive and folder where you store your Data Files**

   The files available in the current folder are listed, as shown in Figure A-10. This folder contains one file.

3. **Click OFFICE A-1.xlsx, then click Open**

   The dialog box closes and the file opens in Excel. An Excel file is an electronic spreadsheet, so it looks different from a Word document or a PowerPoint slide.

QUICK TIP

The Recent Items list on the Office menu displays recently opened documents; you can click any file to open it.

4. **Click 🗔, then click Save As**

   The Save As dialog box opens, and the current filename is highlighted in the File name text box. Using the Save As command enables you to create a copy of the current, existing file with a new name. This action preserves the original file, and creates a new file that you can modify.

QUICK TIP

The Save As command works identically in all Office programs, except Access; in Access, this command lets you save a copy of the current database object, such as a table or form, with a new name, but not a copy of the entire database.

5. **Navigate to the drive and folder where your Data Files are stored if necessary, type Budget for Corporate Meeting in the File name text box, as shown in Figure A-11, then click Save**

   A copy of the existing document is created with the new name. The original file, Office A-1.xlsx, closes automatically.

6. **Click cell A19, type your name, then press [Enter], as shown in Figure A-12**

   In Excel, you enter data in cells, which are formed by the intersection of a row and a column. Cell A19 is at the intersection of column A and row 19. When you press [Enter], the cell pointer moves to cell A20.

7. **Click the Save button 🖫 on the Quick Access toolbar**

   Your name appears in the worksheet, and your changes to the file are saved.

Exploring File Open options

You might have noticed that the Open button on the Open dialog box includes an arrow. In a dialog box, if a button includes an arrow you can click the button to invoke the command, or you can click the arrow to choose from a list of related commands. The Open button list arrow includes several related commands, including Open Read-Only and Open as Copy. Clicking Open Read-Only opens a file that you can only save by saving it with a new name; you cannot save changes to the original file. Clicking Open as Copy creates a copy of the file already saved and named with the word "Copy" in the title. Like the Save As command, these commands provide additional ways to use copies of existing files while ensuring that original files do not get inadvertently changed.

FIGURE A-10: Open dialog box

Available files
in this folder

Files of type
list arrow

FIGURE A-11: Save As dialog box

New filename

FIGURE A-12: Adding your name to the worksheet

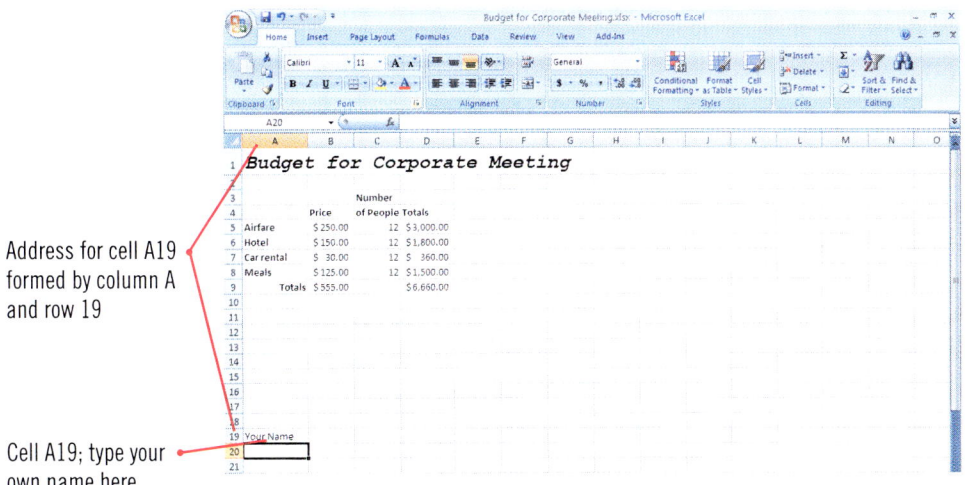

Address for cell A19
formed by column A
and row 19

Cell A19; type your
own name here

Working in Compatibility mode

Not everyone upgrades to the newest version of Office. As a general rule, new software versions are **backward-compatible**, meaning that documents saved by an older version can be read by newer software. The reverse is not always true, so Office 2007 includes a feature called Compatibility mode. When you open a file created in an earlier version of Office, "Compatibility Mode" appears in the title bar, letting you know the file was created in an earlier, but usable version of the program. If you are working with someone who may not be using the newest version of the software, you can avoid possible incompatibility problems by saving your file in

another, earlier format. To do this, click the Office button, point to the Save As command, then click a choice on the Save As submenu. For example, if you're working in Excel, click Excel 97-2003 Workbook format. When the Save As dialog box opens, you'll notice that the Save as type box reads "Excel 97-2003 Workbook" instead of the default "Excel Workbook." To see more file format choices, such as Excel 97-2003 Template or Microsoft Excel 5.0/95 Workbook, click Other Formats on the Save As submenu. In the Save As dialog box, click the Save as type button, click the choice you think matches what your co-worker is using, then click Save.

Viewing and Printing Your Work

If your computer is connected to a printer or a print server, you can easily print any Office document. Printing can be as simple as clicking a button, or as involved as customizing the print job by printing only selected pages or making other choices, and/or **previewing** the document to see exactly what a document will look like when it is printed. (In order for printing and previewing to work, a printer must be installed.) In addition to using Print Preview, each Microsoft Office program lets you switch among various **views** of the document window, to show more or fewer details or a different combination of elements that make it easier to complete certain tasks, such as formatting or reading text. You can also increase or decrease your view of a document, so you can see more or less of it on the screen at once. Changing your view of a document does not affect the file in any way, it affects only the way it looks on screen. Experiment with changing your view of a Word document, and then preview and print your work.

STEPS

1. **Click Potential Corporate Meeting Locations – Microsoft Word on the taskbar**

   Word becomes the active program, and the document fills the screen.

2. **Click the View tab on the Ribbon**

   In most Office programs, the View tab on the Ribbon includes groups and commands for changing your view of the current document. You can also change views using the View buttons on the status bar.

3. **Click Web Layout button in the Document Views group on the View tab**

   The view changes to Web Layout view, as shown in Figure A-13. This view shows how the document will look if you save it as a Web page.

   > **QUICK TIP**
   > You can also use the Zoom button in the Zoom group of the View tab to enlarge or reduce a document's appearance.

4. **Click the Zoom in button ⊕ on the status bar eight times until the zoom percentage reads 180%**

   Zooming in, or choosing a higher percentage, makes a document appear bigger on screen, but less of it fits on the screen at once; **zooming out**, or choosing a lower percentage, lets you see more of the document but at a reduced size.

5. **Drag the Zoom slider ▽ on the status bar to the center mark**

   The Zoom slider lets you zoom in and out without opening a dialog box or clicking buttons.

6. **Click the Print Layout button on the View tab**

   You return to Print Layout view, the default view in Microsoft Word.

7. **Click the Office button ⦿, point to Print, then click Print Preview**

   The Print Preview presents the most accurate view of how your document will look when printed, displaying the entire page on screen at once. Compare your screen to Figure A-14. The Ribbon in Print Preview contains a single tab, also known as a **program** tab, with commands specific to Print Preview. The commands on this tab facilitate viewing and changing overall settings such as margins and page size.

   > **QUICK TIP**
   > You can open the Print dialog box from any view by clicking the Office button, then clicking Print.

8. **Click the Print button on the Ribbon**

   The Print dialog box opens, as shown in Figure A-15. You can use this dialog box to change which pages to print, the number of printed copies, and even the number of pages you print on each page. If you have multiple printers from which to choose, you can change from one installed printer by clicking the Name list arrow, then clicking the name of the installed printer you want to use.

9. **Click OK, then click the Close Print Preview button on the Ribbon**

   A copy of the document prints, and Print Preview closes.

FIGURE A-13: Web Layout view

Web Layout button

View tab

View buttons on status bar

Current zoom percentage

Zoom Out button

Zoom slider at center mark

Zoom In button

FIGURE A-14: Print Preview screen

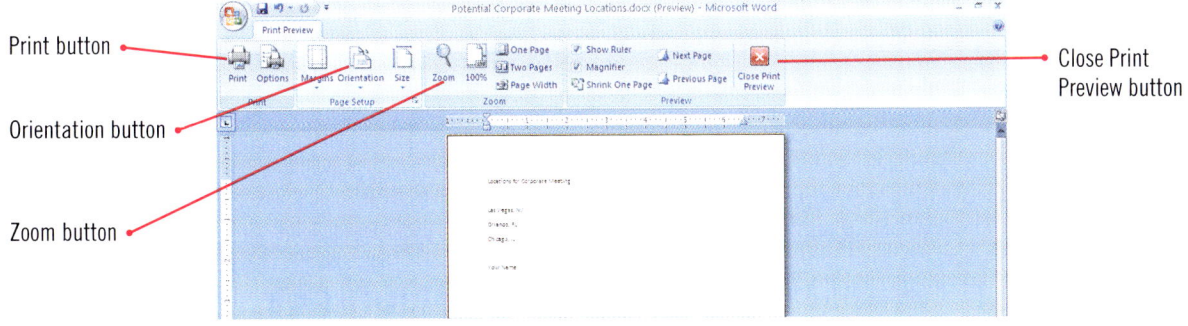

Print button

Orientation button

Zoom button

Close Print Preview button

FIGURE A-15: Print dialog box

Your selected printer will be different

Print range options let you choose which pages to print

Number of copies to print

OK button

Using the Print Screen feature to create a screen capture

At some point you may want to create a screen capture. A **screen capture** is a snapshot of your screen, as if you took a picture of it with a camera. You might want to take a screen capture if an error message occurs and you want Technical Support to see exactly what's on the screen. Or perhaps your instructor wants to see what your screen looks like when you create a particular document. To create a screen capture, press [PrtScn]. (Keyboards differ, but you may find the [PrtScn] button on the Insert key in or near your keyboard's function keys. You may have to press the [F Lock] key to enable the Function keys.) Pressing this key places a digital image of your screen in the Windows temporary storage area known as the **Clipboard**. Open the document where you want the screen capture to appear, click the Home tab on the Ribbon (if necessary), then click Paste on the Home tab. The screen capture is pasted into the document.

Getting Help and Closing a File

You can get comprehensive help at any time by pressing [F1] in an Office program. You can also get help in the form of a ScreenTip by pointing to almost any icon in the program window. When you're finished working in an Office document, you have a few choices regarding ending your work session. You can close a file or exit a program by using the Office button or by clicking a button on the title bar. Closing a file leaves a program running, while exiting a program closes all the open files in that program as well as the program itself. In all cases, Office reminds you if you try to close a file or exit a program and your document contains unsaved changes. 🎨 Explore the Help system in Microsoft Office, and then close your documents and exit any open programs.

STEPS

1. **Point to the Zoom button on the View tab of the Ribbon**
   A ScreenTip appears that describes how the Zoom button works.

2. **Press [F1]**
   The Word Help window opens, as shown in Figure A-16, displaying the home page for help in Word. Each entry is a hyperlink you can click to open a list of related topics. This window also includes a toolbar of useful Help commands and a Search field. The connection status at the bottom of the Help window indicates that the connection to Office Online is active. Office Online supplements the help content available on your computer with a wide variety of up-to-date topics, templates, and training.

3. **Click the Getting help link in the Table of Contents pane**
   The icon next to Getting help changes and its list of subtopics expands.

4. **Click the Work with the Help window link in the topics list in the left pane**
   The topic opens in the right pane, as shown in Figure A-17.

5. **Click the Hide Table of Contents button 📖 on the Help toolbar**
   The left pane closes, as shown in Figure A-18.

6. **Click the Show Table of Contents button 📗 on the Help toolbar, scroll to the bottom of the left pane, click the Accessibility link in the Table of Contents pane, click the Use the keyboard to work with Ribbon programs link, read the information in the right pane, then click the Help window Close button**

7. **Click the Office button 🔵, then click Close; if a dialog box opens asking whether you want to save your changes, click Yes**
   The Potential Corporate Meeting Locations document closes, leaving the Word program open.

8. **Click 🔵, then click Exit Word**
   Microsoft Office Word closes, and the Excel program window is active.

9. **Click 🔵, click Exit Excel, click the PowerPoint button on the taskbar if necessary, click 🔵, then click Exit PowerPoint**
   Microsoft Office Excel and Microsoft Office PowerPoint both close.

FIGURE A-16: Word Help window

Help toolbar

Search field

Hide Table of
Contents
button

The colors
of your links
may differ

Connection status

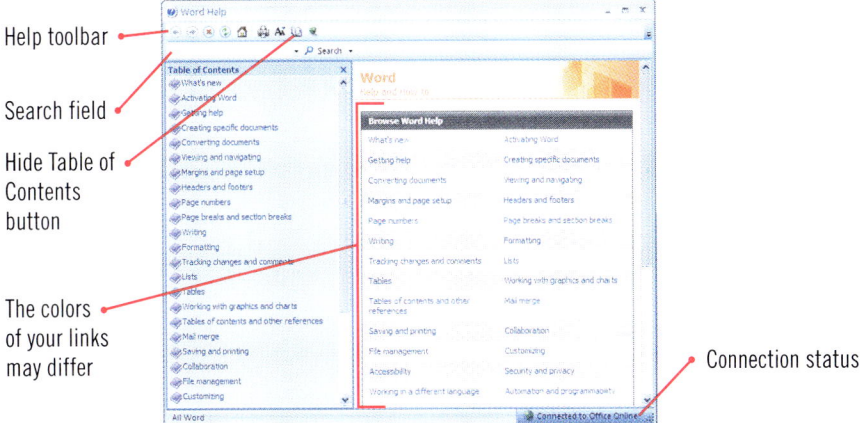

FIGURE A-17: Work with the Help window

Print button

Icon indicates
expanded topic

Work with
the Help
window link

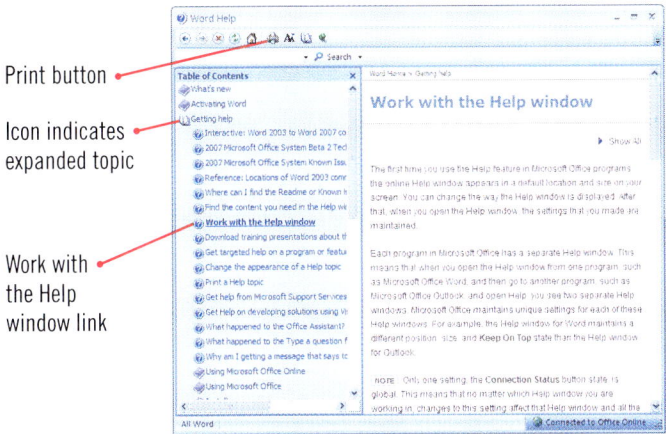

FIGURE A-18: Help window with Table of Contents closed

Show Table of
Contents button

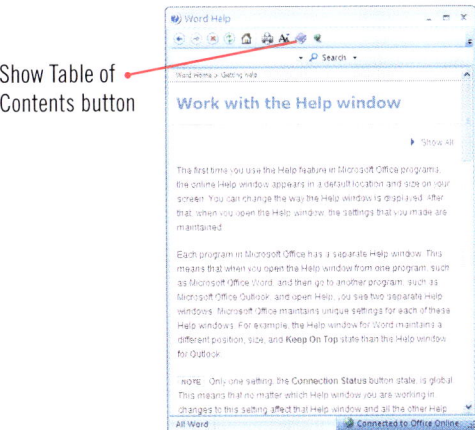

Recovering a document

Sometimes while you are using Office, you may experience a power failure or your computer may "freeze," making it impossible to continue working. If this type of interruption occurs, each Office program has a built-in recovery feature that allows you to open and save files that were open at the time of the interruption. When you restart the program(s) after an interruption, the Document Recovery task pane opens on the left side of your screen displaying both original and recovered versions of the files that were open. If you're not sure which file to open (original or recovered), it's usually better to open the recovered file because it will contain the latest information. You can, however, open and review all versions of the file that were recovered and save the best one. Each file listed in the Document Recovery task pane displays a list arrow with options that allow you to open the file, save it as is, delete it, or show repairs made to it during recovery.

Practice

▼ CONCEPTS REVIEW

Label the elements of the program window shown in Figure A-19.

FIGURE A-19

Match each project with the program for which it is best suited.

8. Microsoft Office PowerPoint d   a. Corporate expansion budget with expense projections
9. Microsoft Office Excel a   b. Business résumé for a job application
10. Microsoft Office Word b   c. Auto parts store inventory
11. Microsoft Office Access c   d. Presentation for Board of Directors meeting

▼ INDEPENDENT CHALLENGE 1

You just accepted an administrative position with a local car dealership that's recently invested in computers and is now considering purchasing Microsoft Office. You are asked to propose ways Office might help the dealership. You produce your proposal in Microsoft Word.

a. Start Word, then save the document as **Microsoft Office Proposal** in the drive and folder where you store your Data Files.

b. Type **Microsoft Office Word**, press [Enter] twice, type **Microsoft Office Excel**, press [Enter] twice, type **Microsoft Office PowerPoint**, press [Enter] twice, type **Microsoft Office Access**, press [Enter] twice, then type your name.

c. Click the line beneath each program name, type at least two tasks suited to that program, then press [Enter].

d. Save your work, then print one copy of this document.

Advanced Challenge Exercise

- Press the [PrtScn] button to create a screen capture, then press [Ctrl][V].
- Save and print the document.

e. Exit Word.

Getting Started with Excel 2007

Files You Will Need:

EX A-1.xlsx
EX A-2.xlsx
EX A-3.xlsx
EX A-4.xlsx
EX A-5.xlsx

In this unit, you will learn how spreadsheet software helps you analyze data and make business decisions, even if you aren't a math pro. You'll become familiar with the different elements of a spreadsheet and learn your way around the Excel program window. You will also work in an Excel worksheet and make simple calculations. You have been hired as an assistant at Quest Specialty Travel (QST), a company offering tours that immerse travelers in regional culture. You report to Grace Wong, the vice president of finance. As Grace's assistant, you create worksheets to analyze data from various divisions of the company, so you can help her make sound decisions on company expansion and investments.

OBJECTIVES

Understand spreadsheet software

Tour the Excel 2007 window

Understand formulas

Enter labels and values and use AutoSum

Edit cell entries

Enter and edit a simple formula

Switch worksheet views

Choose print options

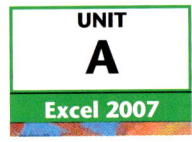

Understanding Spreadsheet Software

Microsoft Excel is the electronic spreadsheet program within Microsoft Office. An **electronic spreadsheet** is an application you use to perform numeric calculations and to analyze and present numeric data. One advantage of spreadsheet programs over pencil and paper is that your calculations are updated automatically, so you can change entries without having to manually recalculate. Table A-1 shows some of the common business tasks people accomplish using Excel. In Excel, the electronic spreadsheet you work in is called a **worksheet**, and is contained in a file called a **workbook**, which has the file extension .xlsx. At Quest Specialty Travel, you use Excel extensively to track finances and manage corporate data.

DETAILS

When you use Excel, you have the ability to:

- ### Enter data quickly and accurately
  With Excel, you can enter information faster and more accurately than with pencil and paper. Figure A-1 shows a payroll worksheet created using pencil and paper. Figure A-2 shows the same worksheet created using Excel. Equations were added to calculate the hours and pay. You can copy the payroll deductions that don't change from quarter to quarter, then use Excel to calculate the gross and net payroll by supplying unique data and formulas for each quarter. You can also quickly create charts and other elements to help visualize how the payroll is distributed.

- ### Recalculate data easily
  Fixing typing errors or updating data is easy in Excel. In the payroll example, if you receive updated hours for an employee, you just enter the new hours and Excel recalculates the pay.

- ### Perform what-if analysis
  The ability to change data and quickly view the recalculated results gives you the power to make informed business decisions. For instance, if you're considering raising the hourly rate for an entry-level tour guide from $12.50 to $15.00, you can enter the new value in the worksheet and immediately see the impact on the overall payroll as well as on the individual employee. Any time you use a worksheet to ask the question "what if?" you are performing **what-if analysis**. Excel also includes a Scenario Manager where you can name and save different what-if versions of your worksheet.

- ### Change the appearance of information
  Excel provides powerful features for making information visually appealing and easier to understand. You can format text and numbers in different fonts, colors, and styles to make it stand out.

- ### Create charts
  Excel makes it easy to create charts based on worksheet information. Charts are updated automatically in Excel whenever data changes. The worksheet in Figure A-2 includes a 3-D pie chart.

- ### Share information
  It's easy for everyone at QST to collaborate in Excel, using the company intranet, the Internet, or a network storage device. For example, you can complete the weekly payroll that your boss, Grace Wong, started creating. You can also take advantage of collaboration tools such as shared workbooks, so that multiple people can edit a workbook simultaneously.

- ### Build on previous work
  Instead of creating a new worksheet for every project, it's easy to modify an existing Excel worksheet. When you are ready to create next week's payroll, you can open the file for last week's payroll, save it with a new filename, and modify the information as necessary. You can also use predesigned, formatted files called **templates** to create new worksheets quickly. Excel comes with many templates, that you can customize.

FIGURE A-1: Traditional paper worksheet

Quest Specialty Travel
Tour Guide Payroll Calculator

Name	Hours	O/T Hrs	Hrly Rate	Reg Pay	O/T Pay	Gross Pay
Brueghel, Pieter	40	4	15–	600–	120–	720–
Cortona, Livia	35	0	10–	350–	0–	350–
Klimt, Gustave	40	2	12⁵⁰	500–	50–	550–
Le Pen, Jean-Marie	29	0	15–	435–	0–	435–
Martinez, Juan	37	0	12⁵⁰	462.50	0–	462.50
Mioshi, Keiko	39	0	20–	780–	0–	780–
Sherwood, Burton	40	0	15–	600–	0–	600–
Strano, Riccardo	40	8	15–	600–	240–	840–
Wadsworth, Alicia	40	5	12⁵⁰	500–	125–	625–
Yamamoto, Johji	38	0	15–	570–	0–	570–

FIGURE A-2: Excel worksheet

Corporate logo

3-D pie chart

TABLE A-1: Business tasks you can accomplish using Excel

you can use spreadsheets to	by
Perform calculations	Adding formulas and functions to worksheet data; for example, adding a list of sales results or calculating a car payment
Represent values graphically	Creating charts based on worksheet data; for example, creating a chart that displays expenses
Generate reports	Creating workbooks that combine information from multiple worksheets, such as summarized sales information from multiple stores
Organize data	Sorting data in ascending or descending order; for example, alphabetizing a list of products or customer names, or prioritizing orders by date
Analyze data	Creating data summaries and short lists using PivotTables or AutoFilters; for example, making a list of the top 10 customers based on spending habits
Create what-if data scenarios	Using variable values to investigate and sample different outcomes, such as changing the interest rate or payment schedule on a loan

Excel 2007

Getting Started with Excel 2007

Excel 3

Touring the Excel 2007 Window

To start Excel, Microsoft Windows must be running. Similar to starting any program in Office, you can use the Start button on the Windows taskbar, or you may have a shortcut on your desktop you prefer to use. If you need additional assistance, ask your instructor or technical support person. You decide to start Excel and familiarize yourself with the worksheet window.

STEPS

QUICK TIP

For more information on starting a program or opening and saving a file, see the unit "Getting Started with Microsoft Office 2007."

1. **Start Excel, click the Microsoft Office button , then click Open**

2. **In the Open dialog box, navigate to the drive and folder where you store your Data Files, click EX A-1.xlsx, then click Open**

3. **Click , then click Save As**

TROUBLE

If you don't see the extension .xlsx on the filenames in the Open dialog box, don't worry; Windows can be set up to display or not to display the file extensions.

4. **In the Save As dialog box, navigate to the drive and folder where you store your Data Files if necessary, type Tour Guide Payroll Calculator in the File name text box, then click Save**

   Using Figure A-3 as a guide, identify the following items:
   - The **Name box** displays the active cell address. "A1" appears in the Name box.
   - The **formula bar** allows you to enter or edit data in the worksheet. The worksheet window contains a grid of columns and rows. Columns are labeled alphabetically and rows are labeled numerically. The worksheet window can contain a total of 1,048,576 rows and 16,384 columns.
   - The intersection of a column and a row is called a **cell**. Cells can contain text, numbers, formulas, or a combination of all three. Every cell has its own unique location or **cell address**, which is identified by the coordinates of the intersecting column and row.
   - The **cell pointer** is a dark rectangle that outlines the cell in which you are working. This cell is called the **active cell**. In Figure A-3, the cell pointer outlines cell A1, so A1 is the active cell. The column and row headings for the active cell are highlighted, making it easier to locate.
   - **Sheet tabs** below the worksheet grid let you switch from sheet to sheet in a workbook. By default, a workbook file contains three worksheets—but you can use just one, or have as many as 255, in a workbook. The Insert Worksheet button to the right of Sheet 3 allows you to add worksheets to a workbook. **Sheet tab scrolling buttons** let you navigate to additional sheet tabs when available.
   - You can use the **scroll bars** to move around in a document that is too large to fit on the screen at once.
   - The **status bar** is located at the bottom of the Excel window. It provides a brief description of the active command or task in progress. The **mode indicator** in the bottom-left corner of the status bar provides additional information about certain tasks.

5. **Click cell A4**

   Cell A4 becomes the active cell. To activate a different cell, you can click the cell or press the arrow keys on your keyboard to move to it.

6. **Click cell B5, press and hold the mouse button, drag to cell B14, then release the mouse button**

   You selected a group of cells and they are highlighted, as shown in Figure A-4. A selection of two or more cells such as B5:B14 is called a **range**; you select a range when you want to perform an action on a group of cells at once, such as moving them or formatting them. When you select a range, the status bar displays the average, count (or number of items selected), and sum of the selected cells as a quick reference.

FIGURE A-3: Open workbook

Name box and current cell address

Cell pointer indicates active cell

Formula bar

Insert Worksheet button

Sheet tab scrolling buttons

Mode indicator

Add-Ins tab (may not appear on your computer)

Scroll bars

Status bar

Sheet tabs

FIGURE A-4: Selecting a range

Selected cells

Average, Count, and Sum

Understanding Formulas

Excel is a truly powerful program because users at every level of mathematical expertise can make calculations with accuracy. To do so, you use formulas. **Formulas** are equations in a worksheet. You use formulas to make calculations as simple as adding a column of numbers, or as complex as profit-and-loss projections for a global corporation. To tap into the power of Excel, you should understand how formulas work. Managers at QST use the Tour Guide Payroll Calculator workbook to keep track of employee hours prior to submitting them to the Payroll Department. You'll be using this workbook regularly, so you need to understand the formulas it contains and how Excel calculates the results.

STEPS

1. **Click cell E5**

    The active cell contains a formula, which appears on the formula bar. All Excel formulas begin with the equal sign (=). If you wanted a cell to show the result of adding 4 plus 2, the formula in the cell would look like this: =4+2. If you wanted a cell to show the result of multiplying two values in your worksheet, such as the values in cells B5 and D5, the formula would look like this: =B5*D5, as shown in Figure A-5.

2. **Click cell F5**

    While you're entering a formula in a cell, the cell references and arithmetic operators appear on the formula bar. See Table A-2 for a list of common Excel arithmetic operators. When you're finished entering the formula, you can either click the Enter button on the formula bar, or press [Enter]. An example of a more complex formula is the calculation of overtime pay. At QST, overtime pay is calculated at twice the regular hourly rate times the number of overtime hours. The formula used to calculate overtime pay for the employee in row 5 is:

    O/T Hrs times (2 times Hrly Rate)

    In a worksheet cell, you would enter: =C5*(2*D5), as shown in Figure A-6.

    The use of parentheses creates groups within the formula and indicates which calculations to complete first—an important consideration in complex formulas. In this formula, the hourly rate is doubled, and that value is multiplied by the number of overtime hours. Because overtime is calculated at twice the hourly rate, managers are aware that they need to closely watch this expense.

DETAILS

In creating calculations in Excel, it is important to:

*   **Know where the formulas should be**

    Excel formulas are created in the cell where they are viewed. This means that the formula calculating Gross Pay for the employee in row 5 will be entered in cell G5.

*   **Know exactly what cells and arithmetic operations are needed**

    Don't guess; make sure you know exactly what cells are involved before creating a formula.

*   **Create formulas with care**

    Make sure you know exactly what you want a formula to accomplish before it is created. An inaccurate formula may have far-reaching effects if the formula or its results are referenced by other formulas.

*   **Use cell references rather than values**

    The beauty of Excel is that whenever you change a value in a cell, any formula containing a reference to that cell is automatically updated. For this reason, it's important that you use cell references in formulas, rather than actual values whenever possible.

*   **Determine what calculations will be needed**

    Sometimes it's difficult to predict what data will be needed within a worksheet, but you should try to anticipate what statistical information may be required. For example, if there are columns of numbers, chances are good that both column and row totals should be present.

FIGURE A-5: Viewing a formula

Formula appears in formula bar

Result of formula appears in cell

FIGURE A-6: Formula with multiple operators

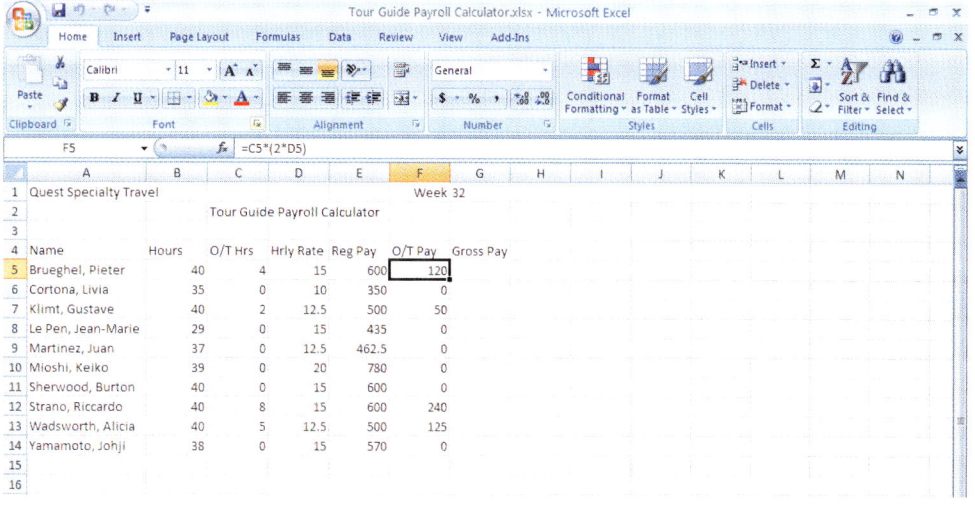

TABLE A-2: Excel arithmetic operators

operator	purpose	example
+	Addition	=A5+A7
-	Subtraction or negation	=A5-10
*	Multiplication	=A5*A7
/	Division	=A5/A7
%	Percent	=35%
^ (caret)	Exponent	=6^2 (same as 6^2)

Entering Labels and Values and Using AutoSum

To enter content in a cell, you can type on the formula bar or directly in the cell itself. When entering content in a worksheet, you should start by entering all the labels first. **Labels** are entries that contain text and numerical information not used in calculations, such as "2009 Sales" or "Travel Expenses." Labels help you identify data in worksheet rows and columns, making your worksheet easier to understand. **Values** are numbers, formulas, and functions that can be used in calculations. To enter a calculation, you type an equal sign (=) plus the formula for the calculation; some examples of an Excel calculation are "=2+2" and "=C5+C6." Functions are Excel's built-in formulas; you learn more about them in the next unit. You want to enter some information in the Tour Guide Payroll Calculator workbook, and use a very simple function to total a range of cells.

STEPS

1. **Click cell A15, then click in the formula bar**

   Notice that the **mode indicator** on the status bar now reads "Edit," indicating you are in Edit mode. You are in Edit mode any time you are entering or changing the contents of a cell.

2. **Type Totals, then click the Enter button ✓ on the formula bar**

   Clicking the Enter button accepts the entry. The new text is left-aligned. Labels are left-aligned by default, and values are right-aligned by default. Excel recognizes an entry as a value if it is a number or it begins with one of these symbols: +, -, =, @, #, or $. When a cell contains both text and numbers, Excel recognizes it as a label.

3. **Click cell B15**

   You want this cell to total the hours worked by all the tour guides. You might think you need to create a formula that looks like this: =B5+B6+B7+B8+B9+B10+B11+B12+B13+B14. However, there's an easier way to achieve this result.

4. **Click the AutoSum button Σ in the Editing group on the Home tab of the Ribbon**

   The SUM function is inserted in your formula, and a suggested range appears in parentheses, as shown in Figure A-7. A **function** is a built-in formula; it includes the **arguments** (the information necessary to calculate an answer), as well as cell references and other unique information. Clicking the AutoSum button sums the adjacent range (that is, the cells next to the active cell) above or to the left, though you can adjust the range if necessary. Using the SUM function is quicker than entering a formula, and using the range B5:B14 is more efficient than entering individual cell references.

5. **Click ✓**

   Excel calculates the total contained in cells B5:B14 and displays the result, 378, in cell B15. The cell actually contains the formula =SUM(B5:B14), and the result is displayed.

6. **Click cell C13, type 6, then press [Enter]**

   The number 6 is right-aligned, the cell pointer moves to cell C14 and the value in cell F13 changes.

7. **Click cell C18, type Average Gross Pay, then press [Enter]**

   The new label is entered in cell C18. The contents appear to spill into the empty cells to the right.

8. **Click and hold cell B15, drag the mouse pointer to cell G15, click the Fill button ⬇ in the Editing group, then click Right in the Fill menu**

   Calculated values appear in the selected range, as shown in Figure A-8. Each filled cell contains a formula that sums the range of cells above. The Fill button fills cells based on the first number sequence in the range.

9. **Save your work**

FIGURE A-7: Creating a formula using the AutoSum button

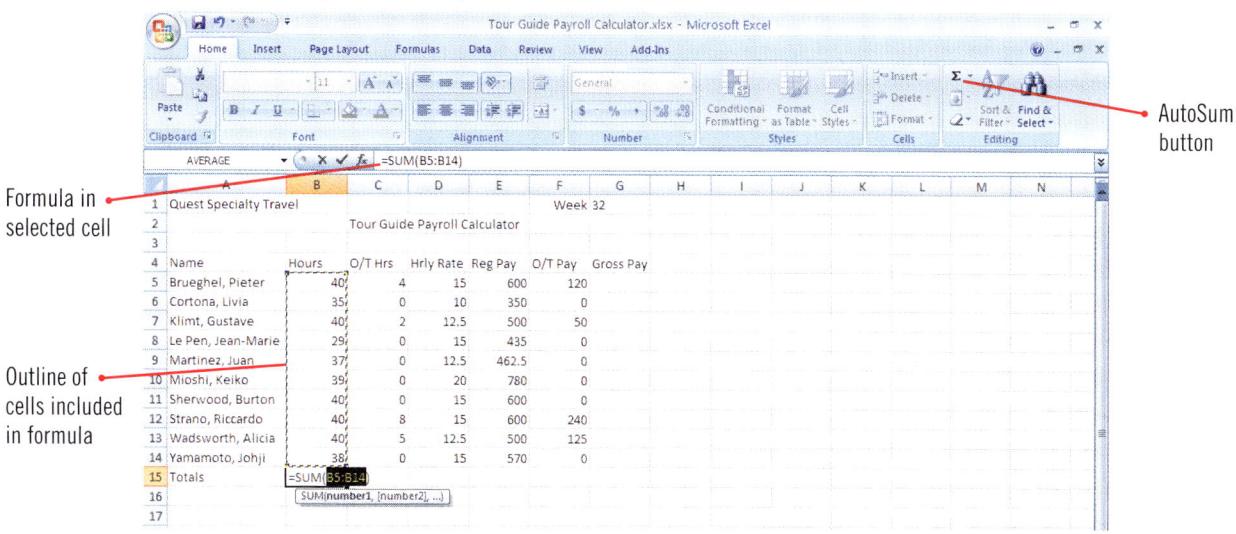

Formula in selected cell

Outline of cells included in formula

AutoSum button

FIGURE A-8: Calculated values

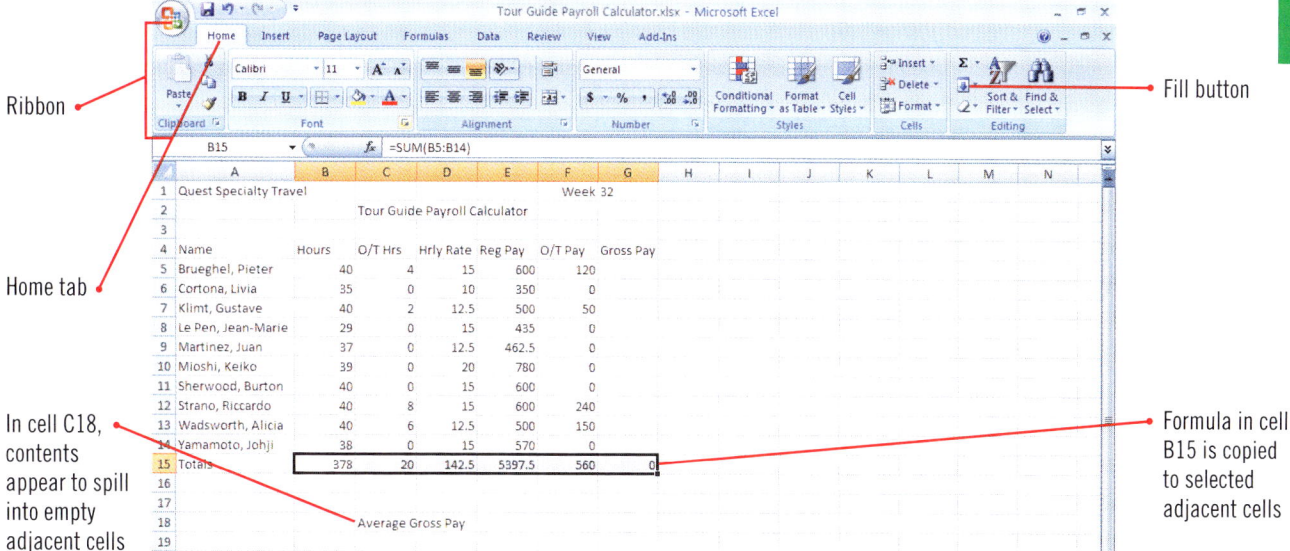

Ribbon

Home tab

In cell C18, contents appear to spill into empty adjacent cells

Fill button

Formula in cell B15 is copied to selected adjacent cells

Navigating a worksheet

With over a million cells available in a worksheet, it is important to know how to move around in, or **navigate**, a worksheet. You can use the arrow keys on the keyboard [↑], [↓], [←], or [→] to move a cell at a time, or press [Page Up] or [Page Down] to move a screen at a time. To move a screen to the left press [Alt][Page Up]; to move a screen to the right press [Alt][Page Down]. You can also use the mouse pointer to click the desired cell. If the desired cell is not visible in the worksheet window, use the scroll bars or the Go To command by clicking the Find & Select button in the Editing group on the Home tab of the Ribbon. To quickly jump to the first cell in a worksheet press [Ctrl][Home]; to jump to the last cell, press [Ctrl][End].

Editing Cell Entries

You can change, or **edit**, the contents of an active cell at any time. To do so, double-click the cell, click in the formula bar, or just start typing. Excel switches to Edit mode when you are making cell entries. Different pointers, shown in Table A-3, guide you through the editing process. 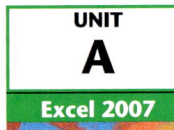 You noticed some errors in the worksheet and want to make corrections. The first error is in cell A5, which contains a misspelled name.

STEPS

QUICK TIP

Pressing [Enter] also accepts the cell entry, but moves the cell pointer down one cell.

1. **Click cell A5, then click to the right of P in the formula bar**

   As soon as you click in the formula bar, a blinking vertical line called the **insertion point** appears on the formula bar at the location where new text will be inserted. See Figure A-9. The mouse pointer changes to I when you point anywhere in the formula bar.

2. **Press [Delete], then click the Enter button ✓ on the formula bar**

   Clicking the Enter button accepts the edit, and the spelling of the employee's first name is corrected. You can also press [Enter] or [Tab] to accept an edit.

QUICK TIP

On some keyboards, you might need to press an "F Lock" key to enable the function keys.

3. **Click cell B6, then press [F2]**

   Excel switches to Edit mode, and the insertion point blinks in the cell. Pressing [F2] activates the cell for editing directly in the cell instead of the formula bar. Some people prefer editing right in the cell instead of using the formula bar, but it's simply a matter of preference; the results in the worksheet are the same.

QUICK TIP

The Undo button allows you to reverse up to 100 previous actions, one at a time.

4. **Press [Backspace], type 8, then press [Enter]**

   The value in the cell changes from 35 to 38, and cell B7 becomes the active cell. Did you notice that the calculations in cells B15 and E15 also changed? That's because those cells contain formulas that include cell B6 in their calculations. If you make a mistake when editing, you can click the Cancel button ✗ on the formula bar *before* pressing [Enter] to confirm the cell entry. The Enter and Cancel buttons appear only when you're in Edit mode. If you notice the mistake *after* you have confirmed the cell entry, click the Undo button ↺ on the Quick Access toolbar.

5. **Click cell A9, press [F2], press and hold [Shift], press [Home], then release [Shift]**

   Pressing and holding [Shift] lets you select text using the keyboard. Pressing [Home] moves the cursor to the beginning of the cell; pressing [End] would move the cursor to the end or the cell.

6. **Type Maez, Javier, then press [Enter]**

   When text is selected, typing deletes it and replaces it with the new text.

7. **Double-click cell C12, press [Delete], type 4, then click ✓**

   Double-clicking a cell activates it for editing directly in the cell. Compare your screen to Figure A-10.

8. **Save your work**

   Your changes to the workbook are saved.

Recovering a lost workbook file

Sometimes while you are using Excel, you may experience a power failure or your computer may "freeze," making it impossible to continue working. If this type of interruption occurs, Excel has a built-in recovery feature that allows you to open and save files that were open at the time of the interruption. When you restart Excel after an interruption, File Recovery mode automatically starts and tries to make any necessary repairs. If you need to use a corrupted workbook, you can try and repair it manually by clicking the Office button, then clicking Open. Select the workbook file you want to repair, click the Open list arrow, then click Open and Repair.

FIGURE A-9: Worksheet in Edit mode

Enter button
Active cell
Insertion point
Mode indicator

FIGURE A-10: Edited worksheet

Edited label
Edited value

TABLE A-3: Common pointers in Excel

name	pointer	use to
Normal	✛	Select a cell or range; indicates Ready mode
Copy	▹⁺	Create a duplicate of the selected cell(s)
Fill handle	✚	Create an alphanumeric series in a range
I-beam	I	Edit contents of formula bar
Move	⁺⁺✛	Change the location of the selected cell(s)

Entering and Editing a Simple Formula

You use formulas in Excel to perform calculations such as adding, multiplying, and averaging. Formulas in an Excel worksheet start with the equal sign (=), also called the **formula prefix**, followed by cell addresses, range names, and values, along with calculation operators. **Calculation operators** indicate what type of calculation you want to perform on the cells, ranges or values. They can include **arithmetic operators**, which perform mathematical calculations such as adding and subtracting, **comparison operators**, which compare values for the purpose of true/false results, **text concatenation operators**, which join strings of text in different cells, and **reference operators**, which enable you to use ranges in calculations. You want to create a formula in the worksheet that calculates gross pay for each employee.

STEPS

1. **Click cell G5**

   This is the first cell where you want to insert the formula. To calculate gross pay, you need to add regular pay and overtime pay. For employee Peter Brueghel, regular pay appears in cell E5 and overtime pay appears in cell F5.

QUICK TIP

You can reference a cell in a formula either by typing the cell reference or clicking the cell in the worksheet; when you click a cell to add a reference, the Mode indicator changes to "Point."

2. **Type =, click cell E5, type +, then click cell F5**

   Compare your formula bar to Figure A-11. The blue and green cell references in cell G5 correspond to the colored cell outlines. When entering a formula, it's a good idea to use cell references instead of values whenever you can. That way, if you later change a value in a cell (if, for example, Peter's regular pay changes to 615), any formula that includes this information reflects accurate, up-to-date results.

3. **Click the Enter button ☑ on the formula bar**

   The results of the formula =E5+F5, 720, appear in cell G5. This same value appears in cell G15 because cell G15 contains a formula that totals the values in cells G5:G14, and there are no other values now.

4. **Click cell F5**

   The formula in this cell calculates overtime pay by multiplying overtime hours (C5) times twice the regular hourly rate (2*D5). You want to edit this formula to reflect a new overtime pay rate.

5. **Click to the right of 2 in the formula bar, then type .5 as shown in Figure A-12**

   The formula that calculates overtime pay has been edited.

6. **Click ☑ on the formula bar**

   Compare your screen to Figure A-13. Notice that the calculated values in cells G5, F15, and G15 have all changed to reflect your edits to cell F5.

7. **Save your work**

Understanding named ranges

It can be difficult to remember the cell locations of critical information in a worksheet, but using cell names can make this task much easier. You can name a single cell or range of contiguous, or touching, cells. For example, you might name a cell that contains data on average gross pay "AVG_GP" instead of trying to remember the cell address C18. A named range must begin with a letter or an underscore. It cannot contain any spaces or be the same as a built-in name, such as a function or another object (such as a different named range) in the workbook. To name a range, select the cell(s) you want to name, click the name box in the formula bar, type the name you want to use, then press [Enter]. You can also name a range by clicking the Formulas tab, clicking the Define Name list arrow in the Defined Names group, then clicking Define Name. Type the new range name in the Name text box of the New Name dialog box, verify the selected range, then click OK. When you use a named range in a formula, the named range appears, rather than the cell address. You can also create a named range using the contents of a cell already in the range. Select the range containing the text you want to use as a name, then click Create from Selection button in the Defined Names group. The Create Names from Selection dialog box opens. Choose the location of the name you want to use, then click OK.

FIGURE A-11: Simple formula in a worksheet

Cell outline color
corresponds to
cell reference

Referenced cells
are inserted in
formula

Mode indicator
changes to Point

FIGURE A-12: Edited formula in a worksheet

Edited value

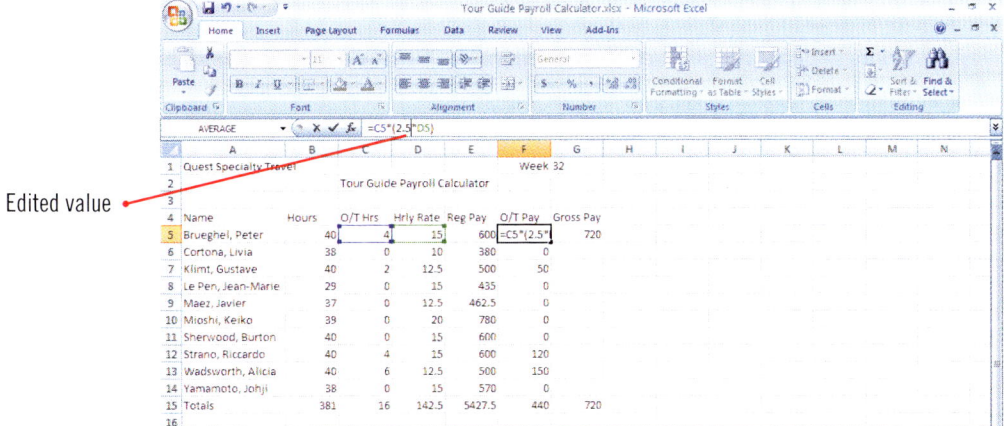

FIGURE A-13: Edited formula with changes

Edited formula
results in
changes to
these other cells

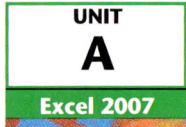

Switching Worksheet Views

You can change your view of the worksheet window at any time, using either the View tab on the Ribbon or the View buttons on the status bar. Changing your view does not affect the contents of a worksheet; it just makes it easier for you to focus on different tasks, such as entering content or preparing a worksheet for printing. The View tab includes a variety of viewing options, such as View buttons, zoom controls, and the ability to show or hide worksheet elements such as gridlines. The status bar offers fewer View options, but can be more convenient to use. You want to make some final adjustments to your worksheet, including adding a header so the document looks more polished.

STEPS

QUICK TIP
Although a worksheet can contain more than a million rows and columns, the current document contains only as many pages as necessary for the current project.

1. **Click the View tab on the Ribbon, then click the Page Layout View button in the Workbook Views group**

   The view switches from the default view, Normal, to Page Layout view. **Normal view** shows the worksheet without including certain details like headers and footers or tools like rulers and a page number indicator; it's great for creating and editing a worksheet, but may not be detailed enough when you want to put the finishing touches on a document. **Page Layout View** provides a more accurate view of how a worksheet will look when printed, as shown in Figure A-14. The margins of the page are displayed, along with a text box for the header. A footer text box appears at the bottom of the page, but your screen may not be large enough to view it without scrolling. Above and to the left of the page are rulers. Part of an additional page appears to the right of this page, but it is dimmed, indicating that it does not contain any data. A page number indicator on the status bar tells you the current page and the total number of pages in this worksheet.

2. **Drag the pointer over the header *without clicking***

   The header is made up of three text boxes: left, center, and right.

QUICK TIP
You can change header and footer information using the Header & Footer Tools Design tab that opens when a header or footer is active. For example, you can insert the date by clicking the Current Date button in the Header & Footer Elements group, or the time by clicking the Current Time button.

3. **Click the left header text box, type Quest Specialty Travel, click the center text box, type Tour Guide Payroll Calculator, click the right header text box, then type Week 32**

   The new text appears in the text boxes, as shown in Figure A-15.

4. **Select the range A1:G2, then press [Delete]**

   The duplicate information you just entered in the header is deleted from cells in the worksheet.

5. **Click the Ruler checkbox in the Show/Hide group on the View tab, then click the Gridlines checkbox**

   The rulers and the gridlines are hidden. By default, gridlines in a worksheet do not print, so hiding them gives you a more accurate image of your final document.

6. **Click the Page Break Preview button on the status bar, then click OK in the Welcome to Page Break Preview dialog box, if necessary**

   Your view changes to **Page Break Preview**, which displays a reduced view of each page of your worksheet, along with page break indicators that you can drag to include more or less information on a page.

7. **Drag the bottom page break indicator to the bottom of row 21**

   See Figure A-16. When you're working on a large worksheet with multiple pages, sometimes you need to adjust where pages break; in this worksheet, however, the information all fits comfortably on one page.

QUICK TIP
Once you view a worksheet in Page Break Preview, the page break indicators appear as dotted lines after you switch back to Normal view.

8. **Click the View tab if necessary, click Page Layout in the Workbook Views group, click the Ruler checkbox in the Show/Hide group in the View tab, then click the Gridlines checkbox**

   The rulers and gridlines are no longer hidden. You can show or hide View tab items in any view.

9. **Save your work**

FIGURE A-14: Page Layout View

Ruler checkbox

Gridlines checkbox

Workbook Views group

Header text box

Vertical ruler

Current page and total number of pages

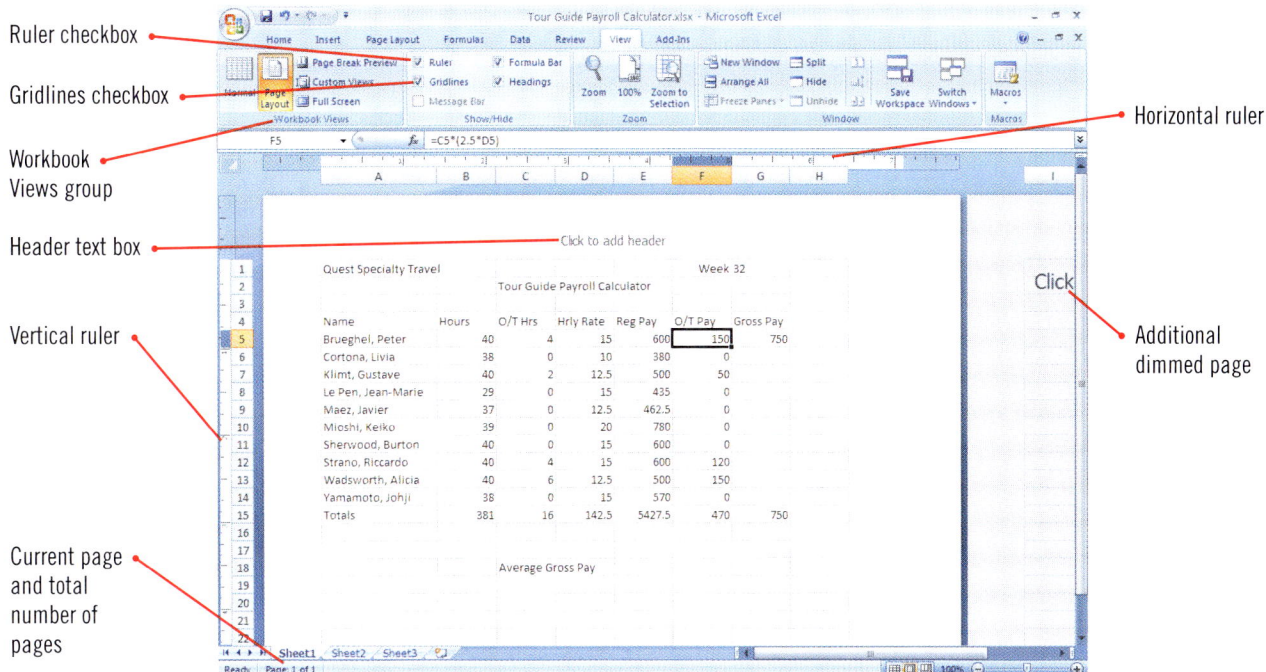

Horizontal ruler

Additional dimmed page

FIGURE A-15: Header boxes

Header areas

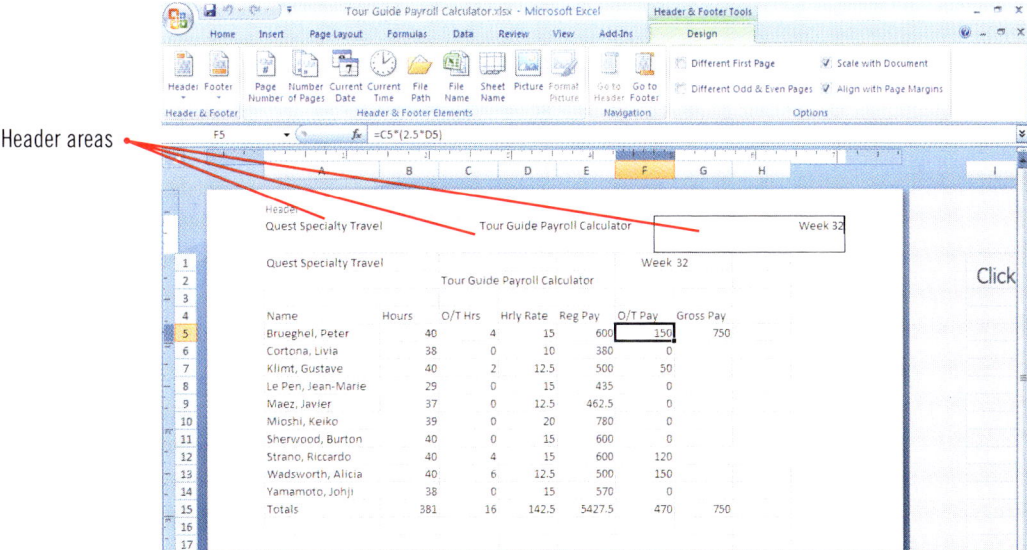

FIGURE A-16: Page Break Preview

Blue outline indicates print area

Bottom page break indicator

Choosing Print Options

Before printing a document, you may want to review it using the Page Layout tab and Print Preview to fine-tune your printed output. You should also review your settings in the Print dialog box, to make sure you are printing the desired number of copies and using the correct printer. Tools on the Page Layout tab include a Page Setup group, where you can adjust print orientation (the direction in which the content prints across the page), paper size, and page breaks. The Scale to Fit group makes it possible to fit a large amount of data on a single page without making changes to individual margins. In the Sheet Options group, you can turn on and off gridlines and column/row headings. Reviewing your final worksheet in Print Preview shows you exactly how the worksheet will look when printed. You are ready to prepare your worksheet for printing.

STEPS

1. Click cell **A21**, type your name, then press **[Enter]**

2. Click the **Page Layout tab** on the Ribbon

   Compare your screen to Figure A-17. The dotted line indicates the **print area**, the area to be printed.

   > **QUICK TIP**
   > You can use the Zoom slider at any time to enlarge your view of specific areas of your worksheet.

3. Click the **Orientation button** in the Page Setup group, then click **Landscape**

   The paper orientation changes to **landscape**, so the contents will print across the length of the page instead of across the width.

4. Click the **Orientation button** in the Page Setup group, then click **Portrait**

   The orientation returns to **portrait**, so the contents will print across the width of the page.

5. Click the **Gridlines View checkbox** in the Sheet Options group on the Page Layout tab, click the **Gridlines Print checkbox** to select it if necessary, then save your work

   Printing gridlines makes the data easier to read, but the gridlines will not print unless the Gridlines Print checkbox is checked.

   > **QUICK TIP**
   > You can print your worksheet using the default settings by clicking the Office button, pointing to Print, then clicking Quick Print.

6. Click the **Office button**, point to **Print**, then click **Print Preview**

   Print Preview shows exactly how your printed copy will look. You can print from this view by clicking the Print button on the Ribbon, or close Print Preview without printing by clicking the Close Print Preview button.

7. Click the **Zoom button** in the Zoom group on the Print Preview tab

   The image of your worksheet is enlarged. Compare your screen to Figure A-18.

   > **QUICK TIP**
   > To change the active printer, click the Name list arrow, then choose a different printer.

8. Click the **Print button** in the Print group, compare your settings to Figure A-19, then click **OK**

   One copy of the worksheet prints.

9. **Exit Excel**

Printing worksheet formulas

Sometimes you need to keep a record of all the formulas in a worksheet. You might want to do this to see exactly how you came up with a complex calculation, so you can explain it to others. You can do this by printing out the formulas in a worksheet rather than the results of those calculations. To do so, open the workbook containing the formulas you want to print. Click the Office button, then click Excel Options. Click Advanced in the left pane, scroll to the Display options for this worksheet section, click the list arrow and select the entire workbook or the sheet in which you want the formulas displayed, click the Show formulas in cells instead of their calculated results checkbox, then click OK.

FIGURE A-17: Worksheet with Portrait orientation

Page Layout tab

Scale field

Dotted line
surrounds
print area

Your name
appears here

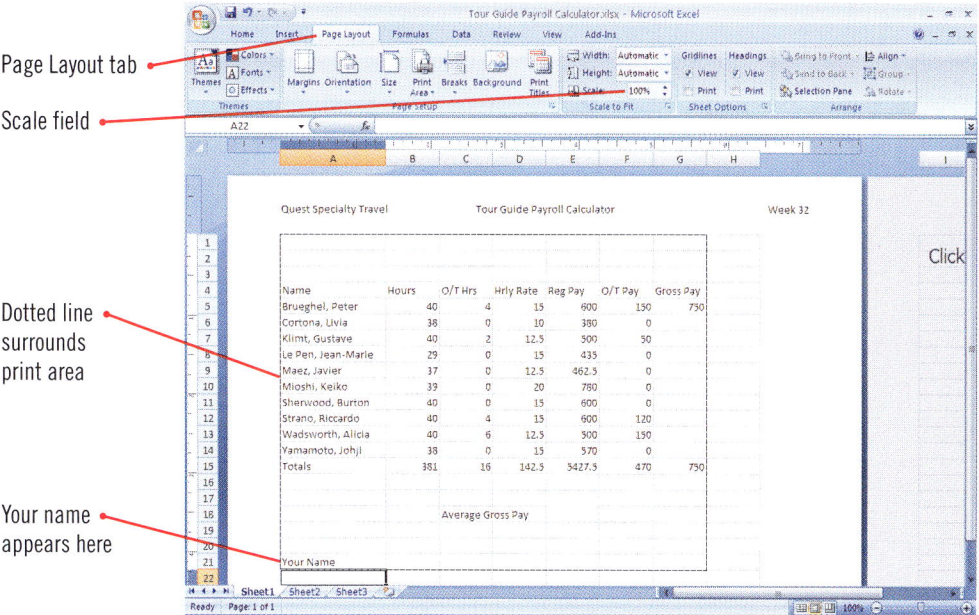

FIGURE A-18: Worksheet in Print Preview

Print button

Zoom button

Close Print
Preview button

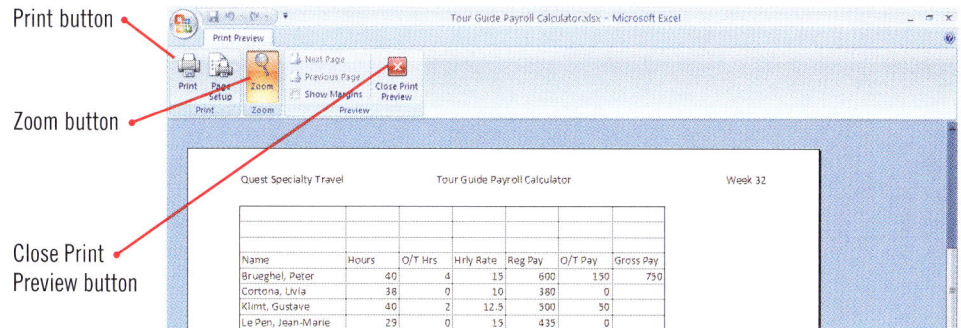

FIGURE A-19: Print dialog box

Active printer: yours
will be different

Choose which
pages to print

Number of
copies field

Scaling to fit

If you have a large amount of data that you want to fit to a single sheet of paper, but you don't want to spend a lot of time trying to adjust the margins and other settings, use the Fit to option in the Page Setup dialog box. Open this dialog box by clicking the launcher in the Scale to Fit group in the Page Layout tab. Make sure the Page tab is selected, then click the Fit to option button. Select the number of pages you want the worksheet to fit on, then click OK. If you're ready to print, click Print and the Print dialog box will open. Select the pages you want to print and the number of copies you want, then click OK.

Practice

▼ CONCEPTS REVIEW

Label the elements of the Excel worksheet window shown in Figure A-20.

FIGURE A-20

(handwritten labels)
1 — normal / pg layout
2 — Tabs
3 — formula bar
4 — horizontal Ruler
5 — insert worksheet button
6 — mode indicator

Match each term with the statement that best describes it.

7. Cell f
8. Normal View D
9. Workbook C
10. Name Box e
11. Formula prefix b
12. Orientation A

a. Direction in which contents of page will print
b. Equal sign preceding a formula
c. File consisting of one or more worksheets
d. Default view in Excel
e. Part of the Excel program window that displays the active cell address
f. Intersection of a column and a row

(handwritten notes)
① wrote normal page instead of normal
④ wrote horizontal Ruler instead of Ruler

Select the best answer from the list of choices.

13. In Excel, order of precedence determines:
- **a.** The order in which worksheets are printed.
- **b.** The colors used to distinguish cell references.
- **c.** The order in which calculations are performed.
- **d.** How values are multiplied.

14. The maximum number of worksheets you can include in a workbook is:
- **a.** 3.
- **b.** 250.
- **c.** 255.
- **d.** Unlimited.

15. A selection of multiple cells is called a:
- **a.** Group.
- **b.** Range.
- **c.** Reference.
- **d.** Package.

16. Using a cell address in a formula is known as:
- **a.** Formularizing.
- **b.** Prefixing.
- **c.** Cell referencing.
- **d.** Cell mathematics.

17. Which worksheet view shows how your worksheet will look when printed?
- **a.** Page Layout
- **b.** Data
- **c.** Review
- **d.** View

18. Which button should you click if you want to print formulas in a worksheet?
- **a.** Save button
- **b.** Fill button
- **c.** Any button on the Quick Access Toolbar
- **d.** Office button

19. Clicking the launcher in the Scale to Fit group on the Page Layout tab opens which dialog box?
- **a.** Print
- **b.** Scale to Fit
- **c.** Width/Height
- **d.** Page Setup

20. In which view can you see the header and footer areas of a worksheet?
- **a.** Normal View
- **b.** Page Layout View
- **c.** Page Break Preview
- **d.** Header/Footer View

21. Which key can you press to switch to Edit mode?
- **a.** [F1]
- **b.** [F2]
- **c.** [F4]
- **d.** [F6]

▼ SKILLS REVIEW

1. Understand spreadsheet software.
- **a.** What is the difference between a workbook and a worksheet?
- **b.** Identify five common business uses for electronic spreadsheets.
- **c.** What is 'what-if' analysis?

2. Tour the Excel 2007 window.
- **a.** Start Excel.
- **b.** Open the file EX A-2.xlsx from the drive and folder where you store your Data Files, then save it as **Weather Statistics**.
- **c.** Locate the formula bar, the Sheet tabs, the mode indicator, and the cell pointer.

3. Understand formulas.
- **a.** What is the average high temperature of the listed cities? (*Hint*: Select the range B5:G5 and use the status bar.)
- **b.** What formula would you create to calculate the difference in altitude between Chicago and Phoenix?

4. Enter labels and values and use AutoSum.
- **a.** Click cell H7, then use the AutoSum button to calculate the total rainfall.
- **b.** Click cell H8, then use the AutoSum button to calculate the total snowfall.
- **c.** Save your changes to the file.

5. Edit cell entries.
- **a.** Use the [F2] key to correct the spelling of Sante Fe in a worksheet cell (the correct spelling is Santa Fe).
- **b.** Click cell A12, then type your name.
- **c.** Save your changes.

6. **Enter and edit a simple formula.**

   a. Change the value 41 in cell B8 to **52**.

   b. Change the value 35 in cell C7 to **35.4**.

   c. Select the range B10:G10, then use the Fill button in the Editing group on the Home tab to fill the formula to the remaining cells in the selection. (*Hint*: If you see a warning icon, click it, then click Ignore Error.)

   d. Save your changes.

7. **Switch worksheet views.**

   a. Click the View tab on the Ribbon, then switch to Page Layout view.

   b. Add the header **Average Annual Weather Statistics** to the center header box.

   c. Add your name to the right header box.

   d. Delete the contents of cell A1.

   e. Delete the contents of cell A12.

   f. Save your changes.

8. **Choose Print options.**

   a. Use the Page Layout tab to change the orientation to Portrait.

   b. Turn off gridlines by deselecting both the Gridlines View and Gridlines Print checkboxes in the Sheet Options group.

   c. View the worksheet in Print Preview, then zoom in to enlarge the preview. Compare your screen to Figure A-21.

   d. Open the Print dialog box, then print one copy of the worksheet.

   e. Save your changes, then close the workbook.

FIGURE A-21

▼ **INDEPENDENT CHALLENGE 1**

A local real estate office has hired you to help them make the transition to using Excel in their office. They would like to list their properties in a worksheet. You've started a worksheet for this project that contains labels but no data.

a. Open the file EX A-3.xlsx from where you store your Data Files, then save it as **Real Estate Listings**.

b. Enter the data shown in Table A-4 in columns A, C, D, and E (the property address information should spill into column B).

TABLE A-4

Property Address	Price	Bedrooms	Bathrooms
1507 Cactus Lane	350000	3	2.5
32 California Lane	325000	3	4
60 Pottery Lane	475500	2	2
902 Fortunata Drive	295000	4	3
Total			

c. Use Page Layout View to create a header with the following components: a title in the center and your name on the right.

d. Create formulas for totals in cells C6:E6.

e. Save your changes, then preview your work and compare it to Figure A-22.

f. Print the worksheet.

g. Close the worksheet and exit Excel.

FIGURE A-22

▼ INDEPENDENT CHALLENGE 2

FIGURE A-23

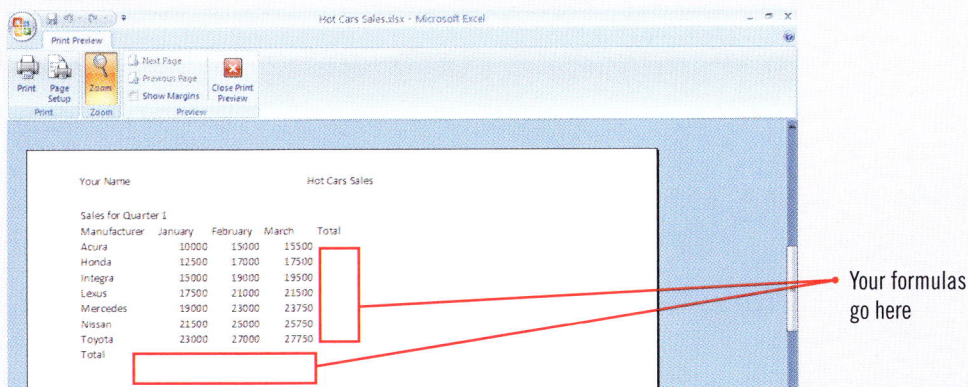

You are the General Manager for Hot Cars, a small auto parts supplier. Although the company is just three years old, it is expanding rapidly, and you are continually looking for ways to save time. You recently began using Excel to manage and maintain data on inventory and sales, which has greatly helped you to track information accurately and efficiently.

a. Start Excel.

b. Save a new workbook as **Hot Cars Sales** in the drive and folder where you store your Data Files.

c. Switch to an appropriate view, then add a header that contains your name in the left header text box and a title in the center header text box.

d. Using Figure A-23 as a guide, create labels for at least seven car manufacturers and sales for three months. Include other labels as appropriate. The car manufacturers should be in column A, and the months in columns B, C, and D. A Total row should be beneath the data, and a Total column should be in column E.

e. Enter values of your choice for the monthly sales for each manufacturer.

f. Add a formula in the Total column to calculate total monthly sales for each manufacturer. Add formulas at the bottom of each column of values to calculate the total for that column. Remember that you can use the SUM function to save time.

g. Save your changes, preview the worksheet, then print it.

Excel 2007

▼ INDEPENDENT CHALLENGE 2 (CONTINUED)

Advanced Challenge Exercise

- Create a label two rows beneath the data in column A that says 15% increase.
- Create a formula in the row containing the 15% increase label that calculates a 15% increase in total monthly sales.
- Save the workbook.
- Display the formulas in the worksheet, then print a copy of the worksheet with formulas displayed.

h. Close the workbook(s) and exit Excel.

▼ INDEPENDENT CHALLENGE 3

FIGURE A-24

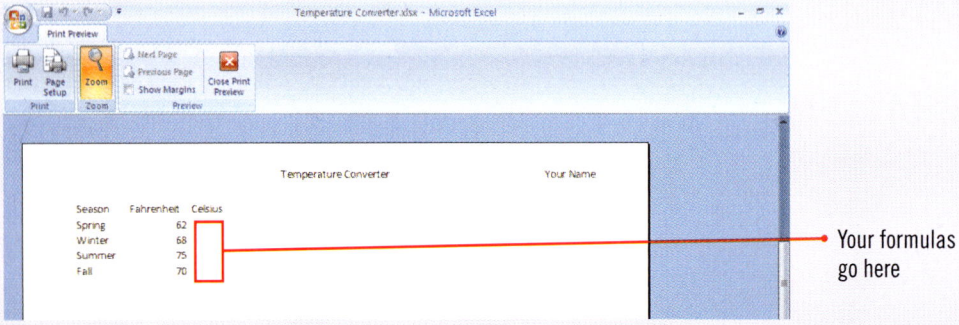

This Independent Challenge requires an Internet connection. Your office is starting a branch in Paris and you think it would be helpful to create a worksheet that can be used to convert Fahrenheit temperatures to Celsius, to help employees who are unfamiliar with this type of temperature measurement.

a. Start Excel, then save a blank workbook as **Temperature Converter** in the drive and folder where you store your Data Files.

b. Create column and row titles using Figure A-24 as a guide.

c. Create labels for each of the seasons.

d. In the appropriate cells, enter what you determine to be an ideal indoor temperature for each season.

e. Use your Web browser to find out the conversion rate for Fahrenheit to Celsius. (*Hint*: Use your favorite search engine to search on a term such as "temperature conversion.")

f. In the appropriate cells, create an equation that calculates the conversion of the Fahrenheit temperature you entered into a Celsius temperature.

g. Preview the worksheet in Page Layout View, adding your name to the header, as well as a meaningful title.

h. Save your work, then print the worksheet.

i. Close the file, then exit Excel.

▼ REAL LIFE INDEPENDENT CHALLENGE

FIGURE A-25

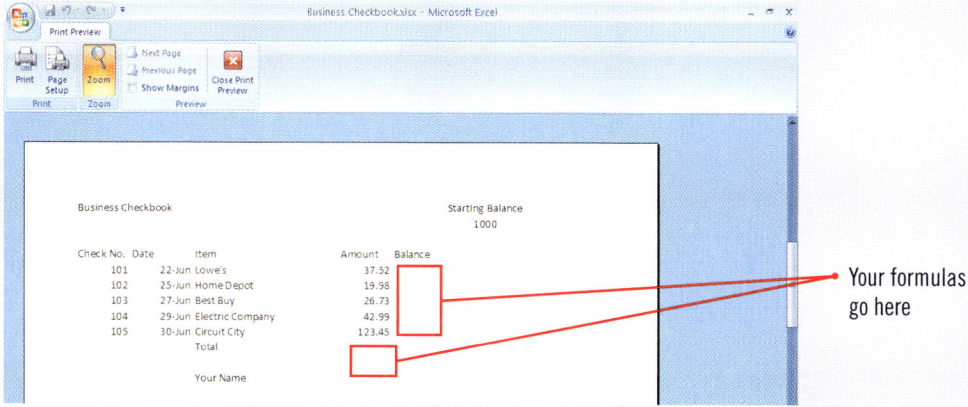

You've decided to quit your day job and turn your favorite hobby into a business. You've set up a small business selling the product or service of your choice. You want to use Excel to keep track of your many start-up costs.

a. Start Excel, open the file EX A-4.xlsx from the drive and folder where you store your Data Files, then save it as **Business Checkbook**.

b. Type check numbers (using your choice of a starting number) in cells A5 through A9.

c. Create sample data for the date, item, and amount in cells B5 through D9.

d. Save your work.

Advanced Challenge Exercise

- Use Help to find out about creating a series of numbers.
- Delete the contents of cells A5:A9.
- Create a series of numbers in cells A5:A9.
- In cell C15, type a brief description of how you created the series.
- Save the workbook.

e. Create formulas in cells E5:E9 that calculate a running balance. (*Hint*: For the first check, the running balance equals the starting balance minus a check; for the following checks, the running balance equals the previous balance value minus each check value.)

f. Create a formula in cell D10 that totals the amount of the checks.

g. Enter your name in cell C12, then compare your screen to Figure A-25.

h. Save your changes to the file, preview and print the worksheet, then exit Excel.

▼ VISUAL WORKSHOP

Open the file EX A-5.xlsx from the drive and folder where you store your Data Files, then save it as **Inventory Items**. Using the skills you learned in this unit, modify your worksheet so it matches Figure A-26. Enter formulas in cells D4 through D13 and in cells B14 and C14. Use the AutoSum button to make entering your formulas easier. Add your name in the left header text box, then print one copy of the worksheet once with the formulas not displayed, and one copy with the formulas displayed.

FIGURE A-26

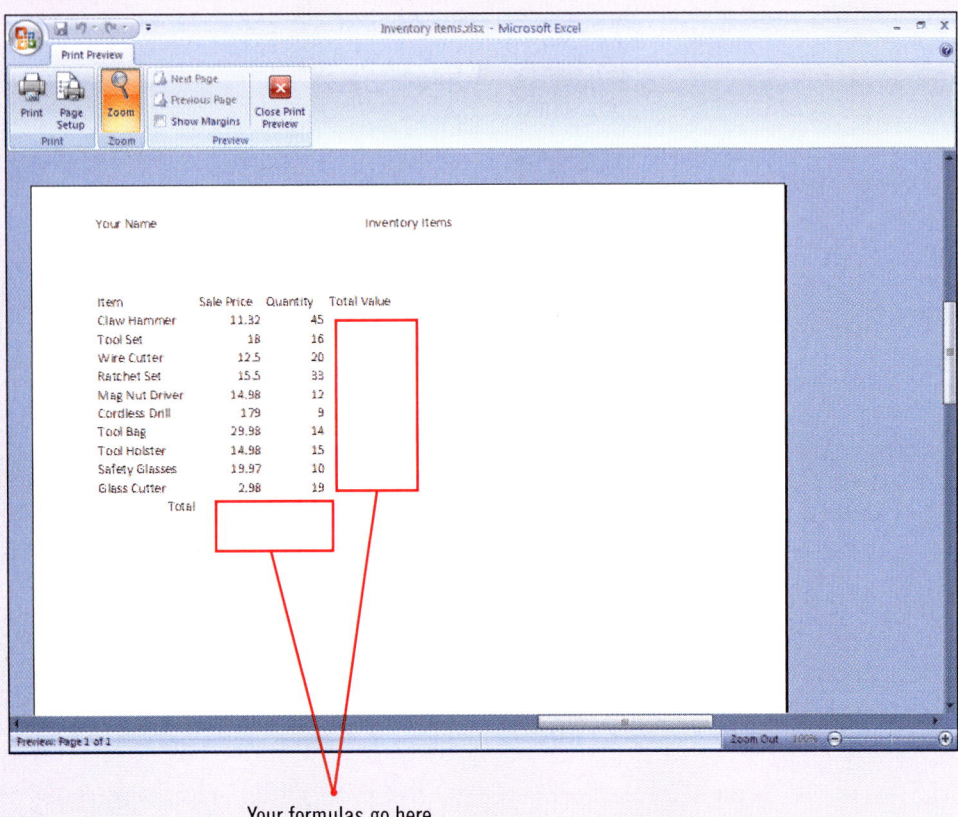

Your formulas go here

Working with Formulas and Functions

Files You Will Need:

EX B-1.xlsx
EX B-2.xlsx
EX B-3.xlsx
EX B-4.xlsx

Using your knowledge of Excel basics, you can expand your worksheets to include more complex formulas and functions. To work more efficiently, you can copy and move existing formulas into other cells instead of manually retyping the same information. When copying or moving, you can also control how cell references are handled, so that your formulas always reference the intended cells. Grace Wong, vice president of finance at Quest Specialty Travel, needs to analyze tour revenue for the current year. She has asked you to prepare a worksheet that summarizes this revenue data and includes some statistical analysis. She would also like you to perform some what-if analysis, to see what quarterly revenues would look like with various projected increases.

OBJECTIVES

Create a complex formula
Insert a function
Type a function
Copy and move cell entries
Understand relative and absolute cell references
Copy formulas with relative cell references
Copy formulas with absolute cell references
Round a value with a function

Creating a Complex Formula

A **complex formula** is one that uses more than one arithmetic operator. You might, for example, need to create a formula that uses addition and multiplication. You can use arithmetic operators to separate tasks within a complex equation. In formulas containing more than one arithmetic operator, Excel uses the standard order of precedence rules to determine which operation to perform first. You can change the order of precedence in a formula by using parentheses around the part you want to calculate first. For example, the formula =4+2*5 equals 14, because the order of precedence dictates that multiplication is performed before addition. However, the formula =(4+2)*5 equals 30, because the parentheses cause 4+2 to be calculated first. You want to create a formula that calculates a 20% increase in tour revenue.

STEPS

1. **Start Excel, open the file EX B-1.xlsx from the drive and folder where you store your Data Files, then save it as** Tour Revenue Analysis

2. **Click cell** B14**, type** =**, click cell** B12**, then type** +
   In this first part of the formula, you are creating references to the total for Quarter 1.

3. **Click cell** B12**, then type** *.2
   The second part of this formula adds a 20% increase (B12*.2) to the original value of the cell. Compare your worksheet to Figure B-1.

4. **Click the** Enter button ☑ **on the formula bar**
   The result, 386122.344, appears in cell B14.

5. **Press [Tab], type** =**, click cell** C12**, type** +**, click cell** C12**, type** *.2**, then click** ☑
   The result, 410969.712, appears in cell C14.

6. **Drag the ✛ pointer from cell** C14 **to cell** E14**, click the** Fill button 🔽 **in the Editing group on the Home tab of the Ribbon, then click** Right
   The calculated values appear in the selected range, as shown in Figure B-2.

7. **Save your work**

Reviewing the order of precedence

When you work with formulas that contain more than one operator, the order of precedence is very important because it affects the final value. For example, you might think the formula 4+2*5 equals 30, but because the order of precedence dictates that multiplication is performed before addition, the actual result is 14. If a formula contains two or more operators, such as 4+.55/4000*25, Excel performs the calculations in a particular sequence based on the following rules: Operations inside parentheses are calculated before any other operations. Reference operators (such as ranges) are calculated first. Exponents are calculated next, then any multiplication and division—progressing from left to right. Finally, addition and subtraction are calculated from left to right. In the example 4+.55/4000*25, Excel performs the arithmetic operations by first dividing 4000 into .55, then multiplying the result by 25, then adding 4. You can change the order of calculations by using parentheses. For example, in the formula (4+.55)/4000*25, Excel would first add 4 and .55, then divide that amount by 4000, then finally multiply by 25.

FIGURE B-1: Formula containing multiple arithmetic operators

Complex formula

Mode indicator

FIGURE B-2: Complex formulas in worksheet

Formula in cell C14 copied to cells D14 and E14

Inserting a Function

Functions are predefined worksheet formulas that enable you to perform complex calculations easily. You can use the Insert Function button on the formula bar to choose a function from a dialog box. In addition to using the AutoSum button on the Ribbon to quickly insert the SUM function, you can click the AutoSum button list arrow to enter other frequently used functions, such as Average. Functions are organized into categories, such as Financial, Date & Time, and Statistical, based on their purpose. You can insert a function on its own, or as part of another formula. For example, you have used the SUM function on its own to add a range of cells. You could also use the SUM function within a formula that adds a range of cells and then multiplies the total by a decimal. If you use a function alone, it always begins with the formula prefix = (the equal sign). 🎨 You need to calculate the average sales for the first quarter of the year, and decide to use a function to do so.

STEPS

1. **Click cell B15**

   This is the cell where you want to enter the calculation that averages revenue for the first quarter. You want to use the Insert Function dialog box to enter this function.

2. **Click the Insert Function button 𝑓𝑥 on the formula bar**

   An equal sign (=) is inserted in the active cell and in the formula bar, and the Insert Function dialog box opens, as shown in Figure B-3. In this dialog box, you specify the function you want to add by clicking it in the Select a function list. The Select a function list initially displays recently used functions. If you don't see the function you want, you can click the Or select a category list arrow to choose the desired category or, if you're not sure what category to choose, you can type the function name or a description in the Search for a function field. The AVERAGE function is a statistical function, but you don't need to open the Statistical category because this function appears in the Most Recently Used list.

3. **Click AVERAGE, if necessary, read the information that appears under the list, then click OK**

   The Function Arguments dialog box opens, where you define the range of cells you want to average.

4. **Click the Collapse button 📠 in the Number1 field of the Function Arguments dialog box, drag the ✛ pointer to select the range B4:B11, release the mouse button, then click the Expand button 📠**

   Clicking the Collapse button minimizes the dialog box so you can select cells in the worksheet. When you click the Expand button, the dialog box is restored, as shown in Figure B-4. You can also begin dragging in the worksheet to automatically minimize the dialog box; after you select the desired range, the dialog box is restored.

5. **Click OK**

   The Function Arguments dialog box closes and the calculated value displays in cell C15. The average revenue per country for Quarter 1 is 40221.0775.

6. **Click cell C15, click the AutoSum button list arrow Σ ▾ in the Editing group on the Home tab, then click Average**

   A ScreenTip beneath cell C15 displays the arguments needed to complete the function. The text number1 is shown in boldface type, telling you that the next step is to supply the first cell in the group you want to average. You want to average a range of cells.

7. **Drag ✛ to select the range C4:C11, then click the Enter button ✓ on the formula bar**

   The average revenue per country for the second quarter appears in cell C15.

8. **Select the range C15:E15, click the Fill button 🔽 in the Editing group, then click Right**

   The formula in cell C15 is copied to the rest of the selected range, as shown in Figure B-5.

9. **Save your work**

FIGURE B-3: Insert Function dialog box

Search for a function field

Your list of recently used functions may differ

Or select a category list arrow

Description of selected function

FIGURE B-4: Expanded Function Arguments dialog box

Function in formula bar

Insert Function button

Argument

Drag title bar of dialog box to move it if necessary

Description and argument format of selected function

FIGURE B-5: Average function in worksheet

Completed function appears in formula bar

Formula in cell C15 copied to cells D15 and E15

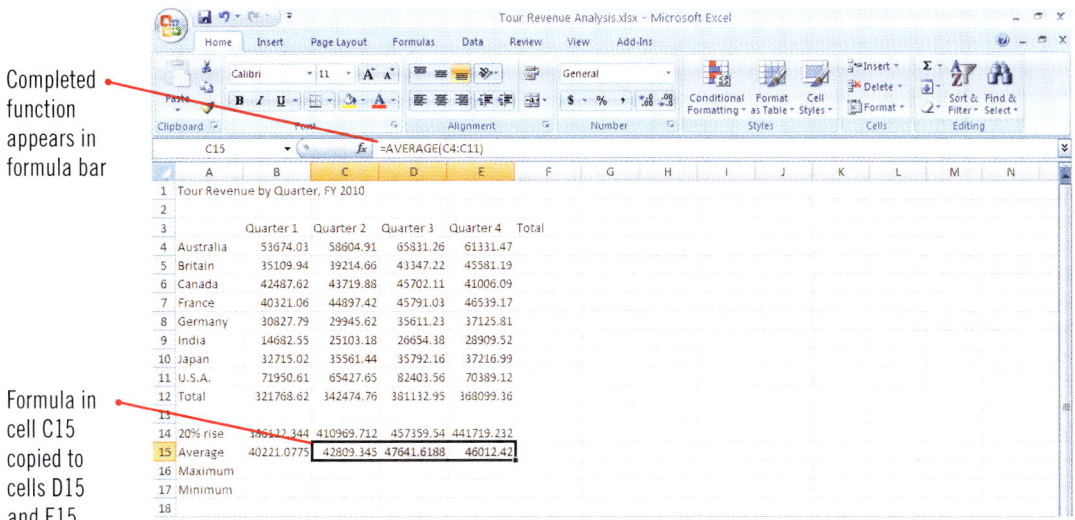

Typing a Function

In addition to entering a function using the Insert Function dialog box or the AutoSum button on the Ribbon, you can manually type the function into a cell and complete the arguments needed. This method requires that you know the name and initial characters of the function, but can be faster than opening several dialog boxes. Experienced Excel users often prefer this method, but it is only an alternative, not better or more correct than any other method. The AutoComplete feature makes it easier to enter function names because it suggests functions depending on the first letters you type. You want to calculate the maximum and minimum quarterly sales in your worksheet, and decide to manually enter these statistical functions.

STEPS

1. **Click cell B16, type =, then type m**

   Since you are manually typing this function, it is necessary to begin with the equal sign (=). The AutoComplete feature displays a list of function names beginning with M. Once you type an equal sign in a cell, each letter you type acts as a trigger to activate the AutoComplete feature. This feature minimizes the amount of typing you need to do to enter a function, and reduces typing and syntax errors.

QUICK TIP

You can single-click any function in the AutoComplete list to open a Screentip describing the selected function.

2. **Click MAX in the list**

   A Screentip appears, describing the function.

3. **Double-click MAX**

   The function is added to the cell and a Screentip appears beneath the cell to help you complete the formula. See Figure B-6.

4. **Select the range B4:B11, as shown in Figure B-7, then click the Enter button ☑ on the formula bar**

   The result, 71950.61, appears in cell B16. When you completed the entry, the closing parenthesis was automatically added to the formula.

5. **Click cell B17, type =, type m, then double-click MIN**

   The argument for the MIN function appears in the cell.

6. **Select the range B4:B11, then press [Enter]**

   The result, 14682.55, appears in cell B17.

7. **Select the range B16:E17, click the Fill button list arrow ▦▾ in the Editing group, then click Right**

   The maximum and minimum values for all of the quarters display in the selected range, as shown in Figure B-8.

8. **Save your work**

Using the COUNT and COUNTA functions

When you select a range, a count of cells in the range that are not blank appears in the status bar. For example, if you select the range A1:A5 and only cells A1 and A2 contain data, the status bar displays "Count: 2." To count nonblank cells more precisely, or to incorporate these calculations in a worksheet, you can use the COUNT and COUNTA functions. COUNT returns the number of cells that contain numeric data, including numbers, dates, and formulas. COUNTA returns the number of cells that contain any data at all, even text or a blank space. For example, the formula =COUNT(A1:A5) returns the number of cells in the range that contain numeric data, and the formula =COUNTA(A1:A5) returns the number of cells in the range that are not blank.

FIGURE B-6: MAX function in progress

13					
14	20% rise	386122.344	410969.712	457359.54	441719.232
15	Average	40221.0775	42809.345	47641.6188	46012.42
16	Maximum	=MAX(			
17	Minimum	MAX(**number1**, [number2], ...)			
18					

FIGURE B-7: Completing the MAX function

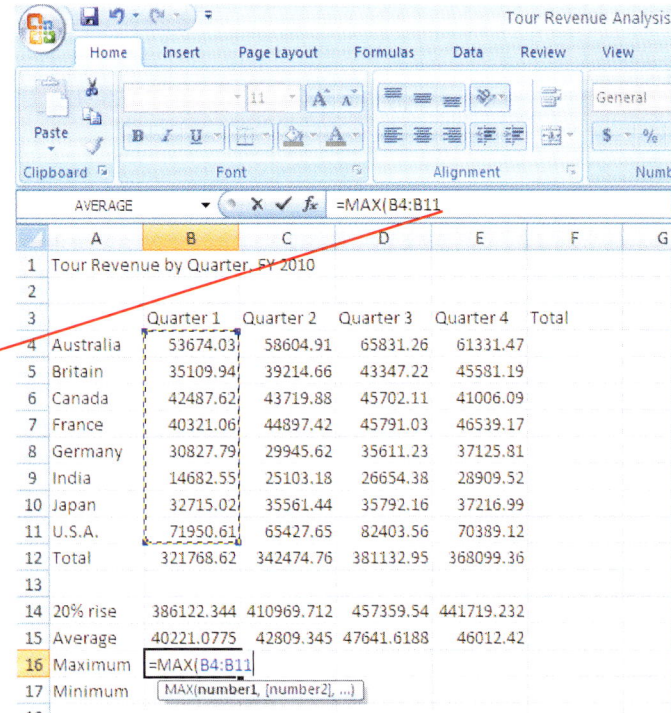

Closing parenthesis will be added automatically when you accept entry

FIGURE B-8: Completed MAX and MIN functions

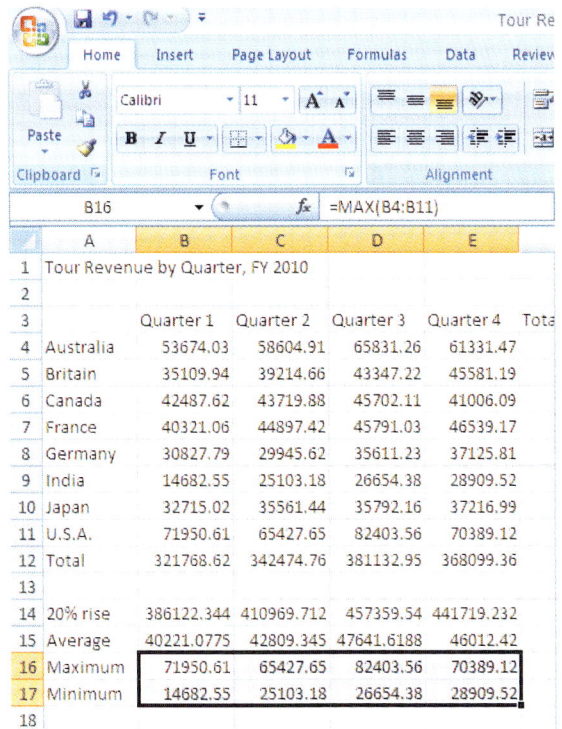

Copying and Moving Cell Entries

You can copy or move cells and ranges (or the contents within them) from one location to another using the Cut, Copy, and Paste buttons; the fill handle in the lower-right corner of the active cell; or the drag-and-drop feature. When you copy cells, the original data remains in the original location; when you cut or move it, the original data is deleted. You can also cut, copy, and paste cells or ranges from one worksheet to another. ▓▓▓▓ In addition to the 20% rise in tour revenue, you also want to show a 30% rise. Rather than retype this information, you copy and move the labels in these cells.

STEPS

QUICK TIP

To cut or copy selected contents within a cell, activate the cell and then select the characters within the cell that you want to cut or copy.

1. **Select the range B3:E3, then click the Copy button 📋 in the Clipboard group**

   The selected range (B3:E3) is copied to the **Office Clipboard**, a temporary storage area that holds the selections you copy or cut. A moving border surrounds the selected range until you press [Esc] or copy an additional item to the Clipboard. Notice that the information you copied remains in the selected range; if you had cut instead of copied, the information would have been deleted once it was pasted.

QUICK TIP

The Clipboard can hold up to 24 items. Once the clipboard is full, the oldest existing item is automatically deleted each time you add an item.

2. **Click the launcher 🔲 in the Clipboard group, click cell B19, then click the Paste button in the Clipboard group**

   The Office Clipboard pane opens, as shown in Figure B-9. Your Clipboard may contain additional items. When pasting an item from the Clipboard into the worksheet, you only need to specify the upper-left cell of the range where you want to paste the selection.

3. **Press [Delete]**

   The selected cells are empty. You have decided to paste the cells in a different row. You can repeatedly paste an item from the Office Clipboard as many times as you like, as long as the item remains in the Clipboard.

QUICK TIP

You can also close the Clipboard pane by clicking the launcher in the Clipboard group.

4. **Click cell B20 , click the first item in the Office Clipboard, then click the Close button on the Clipboard pane**

   Cells B20:E20 contain the copied labels.

5. **Click cell A14 , press and hold [Ctrl], point to any edge of the cell until the pointer changes to ⤧, drag ⤧ to cell A21, then release [Ctrl]**

   As you drag, the pointer changes to ⤧, as shown in Figure B-10.

6. **Click to the right of 2 in the formula bar, press [Backspace] , type 3, then press [Enter]**

7. **Click cell B21, type =, click cell B12 , type *1.3, then click ✓ on the formula bar**

   This new formula calculates a 30% increase of the revenue for Quarter 1, though using a different method from what you used previously. Anything you multiply by 1.3 returns an amount that's 130% of the original amount, or a 30% increase. Compare your screen to Figure B-11.

8. **Save your work**

Working with Formulas and Functions

FIGURE B-9: Copied data in Clipboard

Paste button

Copy button

Clipboard launcher

Item in Clipboard

FIGURE B-10: Copying cell contents with drag-and-drop

Cell contents being copied

Plus (+) indicates copying in progress

Indicates new location of copy

FIGURE B-11: Formula to calculate 30% increase

Formula calculates 30% increase

Inserting and deleting selected cells

As you add formulas to your workbook, you may need to insert or delete cells. When you do this, Excel automatically adjusts cell references to reflect their new locations. To insert cells, click the Insert button list arrow in the Cells group on the Home tab, then click Insert Cells. The Insert dialog box opens, asking if you want to insert a cell and move the selected cell down or to the right of the new one. To delete one or more selected cells, click the Delete button list arrow in the Cells group, click Delete Cells, and in the Delete dialog box, indicate which way you want to move the adjacent cells. When using this option, be careful not to disturb row or column alignment that may be necessary to maintain the accuracy of cell references in the worksheet. Click the Insert or Delete button to add/delete a single cell.

Understanding Relative and Absolute Cell References

As you work in Excel, you may want to reuse formulas in different parts of a worksheet to reduce the amount of data you have to retype. For example, you might want to include a what-if analysis in one part of a worksheet showing a set of sales projections if sales increase by 10%, and another analysis in another part of the worksheet showing projections if sales increase by 50%; you can copy the formulas from one section to another and just change the "1" to a "5". But when you copy formulas, it is important to make sure that they refer to the correct cells. To do this, you need to understand the difference between relative and absolute cell references. ▓▓▓▓ You plan to reuse formulas in different parts of your worksheets, so you want to understand relative and absolute cell references.

- ### Use relative references when you want to preserve the relationship to the formula location

  When you create a formula that references other cells, Excel normally does not "record" the exact cell address. Instead, it looks at the relationship that cell has to the cell containing the formula. For example, in Figure B-12, cell F5 contains the formula: =SUM(B5:E5). When Excel retrieves values to calculate the formula in cell F5, it actually looks for "the cell four columns to the left of the formula," which in this case is cell B5. This way, if you copy the cell to a new location, such as cell F6, the results will reflect the new formula location, and will automatically retrieve the values in cells B6, C6, D6, and E6. These are **relative cell references**, because Excel is recording the input cells *in relation to* or *relative to* the formula cell.

  In most cases, you want to use relative cell references when copying or moving, so this is the Excel default. In Figure B-12, the formulas in F5:F12 and in B13:F13 contain relative cell references. They total the "four cells to the left of" or the "eight cells above" the formulas.

- ### Use absolute cell references when you want to preserve the exact cell address in a formula

  There are times when you want Excel to retrieve formula information from a specific cell, and you don't want the cell address in the formula to change when you copy it to a new location. For example, you might have a price in a specific cell that you want to use in all formulas, regardless of their location. If you used relative cell referencing, the formula results would be incorrect, because Excel would use a different cell every time you copied the formula. Therefore you need to use an **absolute cell reference** , a reference that does not change when you copy the formula.

  You create an absolute cell reference by placing a $ (dollar sign) in front of both the column letter and the row number of the cell address. You can either type the dollar sign when typing the cell address in a formula (for example, "=C12*B16"), or you can select a cell address on the formula bar and then press [F4] and the dollar signs are added automatically. Figure B-13 show formulas containing both absolute and relative references. The formulas in cells B19 to E26 use absolute cell references to refer to a potential sales increase of 50%, shown in cell B16.

FIGURE B-12: Formulas containing relative references

Formula containing relative references

Copied formulas adjust to preserve relationship of formula to referenced cells

FIGURE B-13: Formulas containing absolute and relative references

Cell referenced in absolute formulas

Relative references in copied formulas adjust

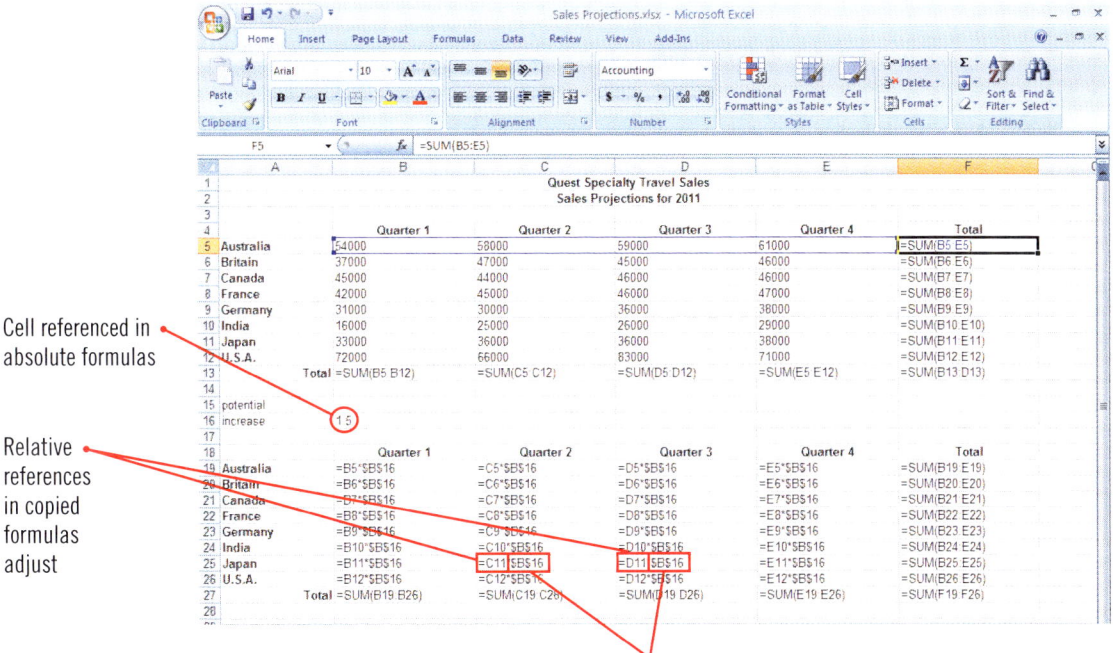

Absolute references in copied formulas do not adjust

Using a mixed reference

Sometimes when you copy a formula, you want to change the row reference, but keep the column reference the same. This type of cell referencing combines elements of both absolute and relative referencing and is called a **mixed reference**. For example, when copied, a formula containing the mixed reference C$14 would change the column letter relative to its new location, but not the row number.

In the mixed reference $C14, the column letter would not change, but the row number would be updated relative to its location. Like the absolute reference, a mixed reference can be created using the [F4] function key. With each press of the [F4] key, you cycle through all the possible combinations of relative, absolute, and mixed references (C14, C$14, $C14, C14).

Copying Formulas with Relative Cell References

Copying and moving a cell allows you to reuse a formula you've already created. Copying cells is usually faster than retyping the formulas in them, and helps to prevent typing errors. You can use the Copy and Paste commands or the fill handle to copy formulas. The Fill button list arrow can also be used to fill cells containing formulas going left, right, up, down, and in series. If the cells you are copying contain relative cell references and you want to maintain the relative referencing, you don't need to make any changes to the cells before copying them. ▧▨▩ You want to copy the formula in cell B21, which calculates the 30% increase in quarterly sales for quarter 1, to cells C21 through E21. You also want to create formulas to calculate total sales for each tour country.

STEPS

1. **Click cell B21, if necessary, then click the Copy button ▣ in the Clipboard group**

   The formula for calculating the 30% sales increase during Quarter 1 is copied to the Clipboard. Notice that the formula =B12*1.3 appears in the formula bar and a moving border surrounds the active cell.

QUICK TIP

To specify components of the copied cell or range prior to pasting, click the Paste button list arrow in the Clipboard group, then click Paste Special. You can selectively copy formulas, values, or other choices.

2. **Click cell C21, then click the Paste button in the Clipboard group**

   The formula from cell B21 is copied into cell C21, where the new result of 445217.188 appears. Notice in the formula bar that the cell references have changed, so that cell C12 is referenced in the formula. This formula contains a relative cell reference, which tells Excel to substitute new cell references within the copied formulas as necessary. This maintains the same relationship between the new cells containing the formula and the cells within the formula. In this case, Excel adjusted the formula so that cell C12—the cell reference nine rows above C21—replaced cell B12, the cell reference nine rows above B21. You can drag the fill handle in a cell to copy cells or to continue a series of data (such as Quarter 1, Quarter 2, etc.) based on previous cells. This option is called **Auto Fill**.

3. **Point to the fill handle in cell C21 until the pointer changes to ✛, press and hold the left mouse button, drag ✛ to select the range C21:E21, then release the mouse button**

   See Figure B-14. A formula similar to the one in cell C21 now appears in the range D21:E21. After you release the mouse button, the **Auto Fill Options button** appears, so you can fill the cells with only specific elements of the copied cell if you wish.

4. **Click cell F4, click the AutoSum button Σ in the Editing group, then click the Enter button ✓ on the formula bar**

QUICK TIP

You can use the Paste button in the Clipboard group of the Home tab to paste specific elements of a selection; click the Paste button arrow, then click an option in the list, such as Transpose (to paste column data as rows and row data as columns), No Borders (to remove any borders around pasted cells), or Paste Special (to open the Paste Special dialog box, where the complete set of paste options is available).

5. **Click ▣ in the Clipboard group, select the range F5:F6, then click Paste**

   See Figure B-15. After you release the mouse button, the **Paste Options button** appears, so you can paste only specific elements of the copied selection if you wish. The formula for calculating quarterly revenue for tours in Britain appears in the formula bar. You would like totals to appear in cells F7:F11. The Fill command in the Editing group can be used to copy the formula into the remaining cells.

6. **Select the range F6:F11**

7. **Click the Fill button list arrow ▣▾ in the Editing group, then click Down**

   The formulas are copied to each cell. Compare your worksheet to Figure B-16.

8. **Save your work**

FIGURE B-14: Copying a formula with the fill handle

Paste button
list arrow

Auto Fill
Options
button

Fill handle

FIGURE B-15: The results of using the Paste button

Paste
Options
button

FIGURE B-16: Copying cells using Fill Down

Fill button
list arrow

Filled cells

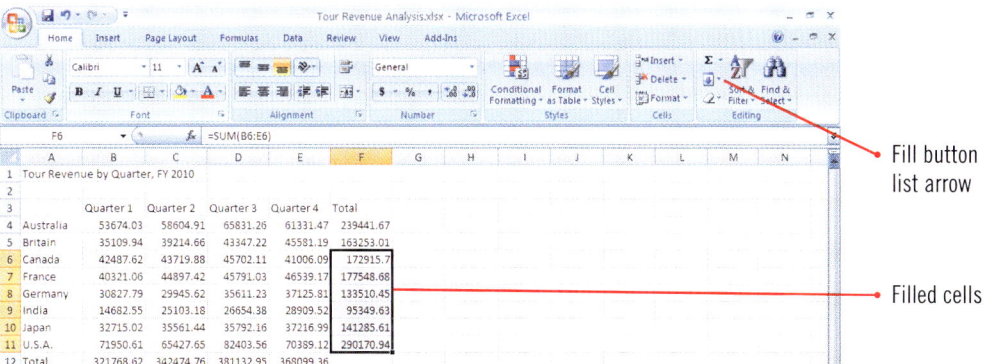

Using Auto Fill options

When you use the fill handle to copy cells, the Auto Fill Options button appears. Auto Fill options differ depending on what you are copying. If you had selected cells containing a series (such as "Monday" and "Tuesday") and then used the fill handle, you would see options for continuing the series (such as "Wednesday" and "Thursday") or for simply pasting the copied cells. Clicking the Auto Fill Options button opens a list that lets you choose from the following options: Copy Cells, Fill Series (if applicable), Fill Formatting Only, or Fill Without Formatting. Choosing Copy Cells means that the cell and its formatting will be copied. The Fill Formatting Only option copies only the formatting attributes, but not the formula and its cell references. The Fill Without Formatting option copies the formula and its cell references, but no formatting attributes. Copy Cells is the default option when using the fill handle to copy a formula, so if you want to copy the cell, its references and formatting, you can ignore this button.

Copying Formulas with Absolute Cell References

When copying formulas, you might want one or more cell references in the formula to remain unchanged in relation to the formula. In such an instance, you need to apply an absolute cell reference before copying the formula, to preserve the specific cell address when the formula is copied. You create an absolute reference by placing a dollar sign ($) before the row letter and column number of the address (for example A1). You need to do some what-if analysis to see how various sales percentage increases might affect total revenues. You decide to add a column that calculates a possible increase in the total tour revenue, and then change the percentage to see various potential results.

STEPS

1. Click cell **H1**, type **Change**, then press [→]

2. Type **1.1**, then press [Enter]

   You store the increase factor that will be used in the what-if analysis in this cell. The value 1.1 can be used to calculate a 10% increase; anything you multiply by 1.1 returns an amount that's 110% of the original amount, or a 10% increase.

3. Click cell **H3**, type **What if?**, then press [Enter]

4. In cell **H4**, type =, click **F4**, type *, click cell **I1**, then click the **Enter button** ✓ on the formula bar

   The result, 263385.8, appears in cell H4. This value represents the total annual revenue for Australia if there is a 10% increase. You want to perform a what-if analysis for all the tour countries.

QUICK TIP
Before you copy or move a formula, check to see if you need to use an absolute cell reference.

5. Drag the **fill handle** of cell **H4** to extend the selection to cell **H11**

   The resulting values in the range H5:H11 are all zeros, which is not the result you wanted. See Figure B-17. Because you used relative cell addressing in cell H4, the copied formula adjusted so that the formula in cell H5 is =F5*I2. Because there is no value in cell I2, the result is 0, an error. You need to use an absolute reference in the formula to keep the formula from adjusting itself. That way, it will always reference cell I1.

6. Click cell **H4**, press [F2] to change to Edit mode, then press [F4]

   When you press [F2], the range finder outlines the arguments of the equation in blue and green. When you press [F4], dollar signs are inserted in the cell address, changing the I1 cell reference to an absolute reference.

7. Click ✓, then drag ✚ to extend the selection to range **H4:H11**

   The formula correctly contains an absolute cell reference, and the value of H4 remains unchanged. The correct values for a 10% increase appear in cells H4:H11. You now want to see a 20% increase in sales.

8. Click cell **I1**, type **1.2**, then click ✓

   The values in the range H4:H11 change to reflect the 20% increase. Compare your worksheet to Figure B-18.

9. Save your work

FIGURE B-17: Creating an absolute reference in formula

Absolute cell reference in formula

Incorrect values from relative referencing in copied formulas

FIGURE B-18: What-if analysis with modified change factor

Modified value

Using the fill handle for sequential text or values

Often, you need to fill cells with sequential text: months of the year, days of the week, years, or text plus a number (Quarter 1, Quarter 2,...). For example, you might want to create a worksheet that calculates data for every month of the year. Using the fill handle, you can quickly and easily create labels for the months of the year just by typing January in a cell. Drag the fill handle from the cell containing January until you have all the monthly labels you need. You can easily fill cells using sequences by dragging the fill handle. As you drag the fill handle, Excel automatically extends the existing sequence. (The content of the last filled cell appears in the ScreenTip.) Use the Fill button list arrow in the Editing group, then click Series to examine all the fill series options for the current selection.

Rounding a Value with a Function

The more you explore features and tools in Excel, the more ways you'll find to simplify your work and convey information more efficiently. For example, cells containing financial data are often easier to read if they contain fewer decimals than those that appear by default. You can achieve this result by using the ROUND function, to round down your results. In your worksheet, you'd like to round the cells showing the 20% rise in sales to show fewer digits; after all, it's not important to show cents in the projections, only whole dollars. You want Excel to round the calculated value to the nearest integer. You decide to edit cell B14 so it includes the ROUND function, and then copy the edited formula into the other formulas in this row.

1. **Click cell B14, then click to the right of = on the formula bar**

   You want to position the function at the beginning of the formula, before any values or arguments.

QUICK TIP

In the Insert Function dialog box the ROUND function is in the Math & Trig category.

2. **Type RO**

   AutoComplete displays a list of functions beginning with RO.

3. **Double-click ROUND in the AutoComplete list**

   The new function and an opening parenthesis are added to the formula, as shown in Figure B-19. A few additional modifications are needed to complete your edit of the formula. You need to indicate the number of digits to which the function should round numbers down, and you also need to add a closing parenthesis around the set of arguments that come after the ROUND function.

TROUBLE

If you have too many or too few parentheses, the extraneous parenthesis displays in green, or a warning dialog box opens with a suggested solution to the error.

4. **Press [END], type ,0), then click the Enter button ☑ on the formula bar**

   The comma separates the arguments within the formula, and 0 indicates that you don't want any decimals to appear in the calculated value. When you complete the edit, the parenthesis at either end of the formula briefly become bold, indicating that the formula has the correct number of open and closed parentheses and is balanced.

5. **Click the fill handle of cell B14, then drag the ✚ pointer to cell E14**

   When you release the mouse button, the formula in cell B14 is copied to the selected range. All the values are rounded to display no decimals. Compare your worksheet to Figure B-20.

6. **Click cell A25, type your name, then click ☑ on the formula bar**

7. **Save your work, preview and print the worksheet, then exit Excel**

FIGURE B-19: Adding a function to an existing formula

ROUND function and opening parenthesis inserted in formula

ScreenTip indicates what information is needed

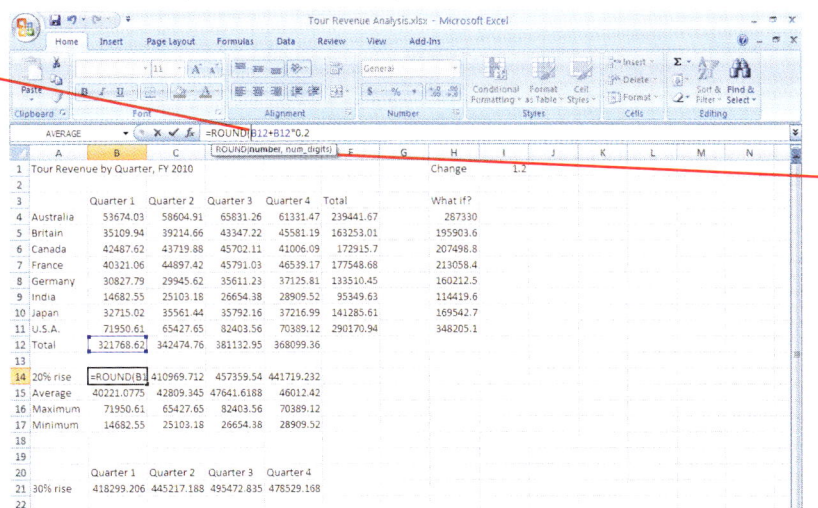

FIGURE B-20: Function added to formula

Function surrounds existing formula

Calculated values with no decimals

Creating a new workbook using a template

Excel **templates** are predesigned workbook files intended to save time when you create common documents such as balance sheets, expense statements, loan amortizations, sales invoices, or timecards. They contain labels, values, formulas, and formatting, so when you use a template all you have to do is customize it with your own information. Excel comes with many templates, and you can also create your own or find additional templates on the Web. Unlike a typical workbook, which has the file extension .xlsx, a template has the extension .xltx. To create a workbook using a template, click the Office button, then click New. The New Workbook dialog box opens. The Blank Workbook template is selected by default, because this is the template used to create a blank workbook with no content or special formatting. The left pane lists templates installed on your computer as well as many categories of templates available through Microsoft Office Online. Click a category, find the template you want, as shown in Figure B-21, click Download, then click Continue. A new workbook is created based on the template, so when you save the new file in the default format, it will have the

regular .xlsx extension. To save a workbook of your own as a template, open the Save As dialog box, then click the Save as type list arrow and change the file type to Excel Template.

FIGURE B-21: New Workbook dialog box

Practice

▼ CONCEPTS REVIEW

Label each element of the Excel worksheet window shown in Figure B-22.

FIGURE B-22

1. *paste*
2. *copy*
3. *insert function*
4. *auto-fill options button*
5. *fill handle*
6. *fill*
7. *Autosum*

Tour Revenue Analysis.xlsx - Microsoft Excel

C21   =C12*1.3

	A	B	C	D	E	F	G
1	Tour Revenue by Quarter, FY 2010						
2							
3		Quarter 1	Quarter 2	Quarter 3	Quarter 4	Total	
4	Australia	53674.03	58604.91	65831.26	61331.47		
5	Britain	35109.94	39214.66	43347.22	45581.19		
6	Canada	42487.62	43719.88	45702.11	41006.09		
7	France	40321.06	44897.42	45791.03	46539.17		
8	Germany	30827.79	29945.62	35611.23	37125.81		
9	India	14682.55	25103.18	26654.38	28909.52		
10	Japan	32715.02	35561.44	35792.16	37216.99		
11	U.S.A.	71950.61	65427.65	82403.56	70389.12		
12	Total	321768.62	342474.76	381132.95	368099.36		
13							
14	20% rise	386122.344	410969.712	457359.54	441719.232		
15	Average	40221.0775	42809.345	47641.6188	46012.42		
16	Maximum	71950.61	65427.65	82403.56	70389.12		
17	Minimum	14682.55	25103.18	26654.38	28909.52		
18							
19							
20		Quarter 1	Quarter 2	Quarter 3	Quarter 4		
21	30% rise	418299.206	445217.188	495472.835	478529.168		
22							
23							
24							
25							
26							
27							

Match each term or button with the statement that best describes it.

8. Launcher *b*
9. Formula AutoComplete *d*
10. Drag-and-drop *c*
11. Fill handle *e*
12. [Delete] *a*

a. Clears the contents of selected cells

b. Item on the Ribbon that opens a dialog box or task pane

c. Lets you move data from one cell to another without using the Clipboard

d. Displays an alphabetical list of functions from which you can choose

e. Lets you copy cell contents or continue a series of data into a range of selected cells

Select the best answer from the list of choices.

13. **What type of cell reference changes when it is copied?**
    a. Circular
    b. Absolute
    c. Relative
    d. Specified

14. **What type of cell reference is C$19?**
    a. Relative
    b. Absolute
    c. Mixed
    d. Certain

15. **Which key do you press to convert a relative cell reference to an absolute cell reference?**
    a. [F2]
    b. [F4]
    c. [F5]
    d. [F6]

16. **You can use any of the following features to enter a function *except*:**
    a. Insert Function button.
    b. Formula AutoComplete.
    c. AutoSum button list arrow.
    d. Clipboard.

17. **Which key do you press to copy while dragging-and-dropping selected cells?**
    a. [Alt]
    b. [Ctrl]
    c. [F2]
    d. [Tab]

▼ SKILLS REVIEW

1. **Create a complex formula.**
   a. Open the file EX B-2.xlsx from the drive and folder where you store your Data Files, then save it as **Candy Supply Company Inventory**.
   b. In cell B11, create a complex formula that calculates a 30% decrease in the total number of cases of Snickers bars.
   c. Use the Fill button to copy this formula into cell C11 through cell E11, as shown in Figure B-23.
   d. Save your work.

FIGURE B-23

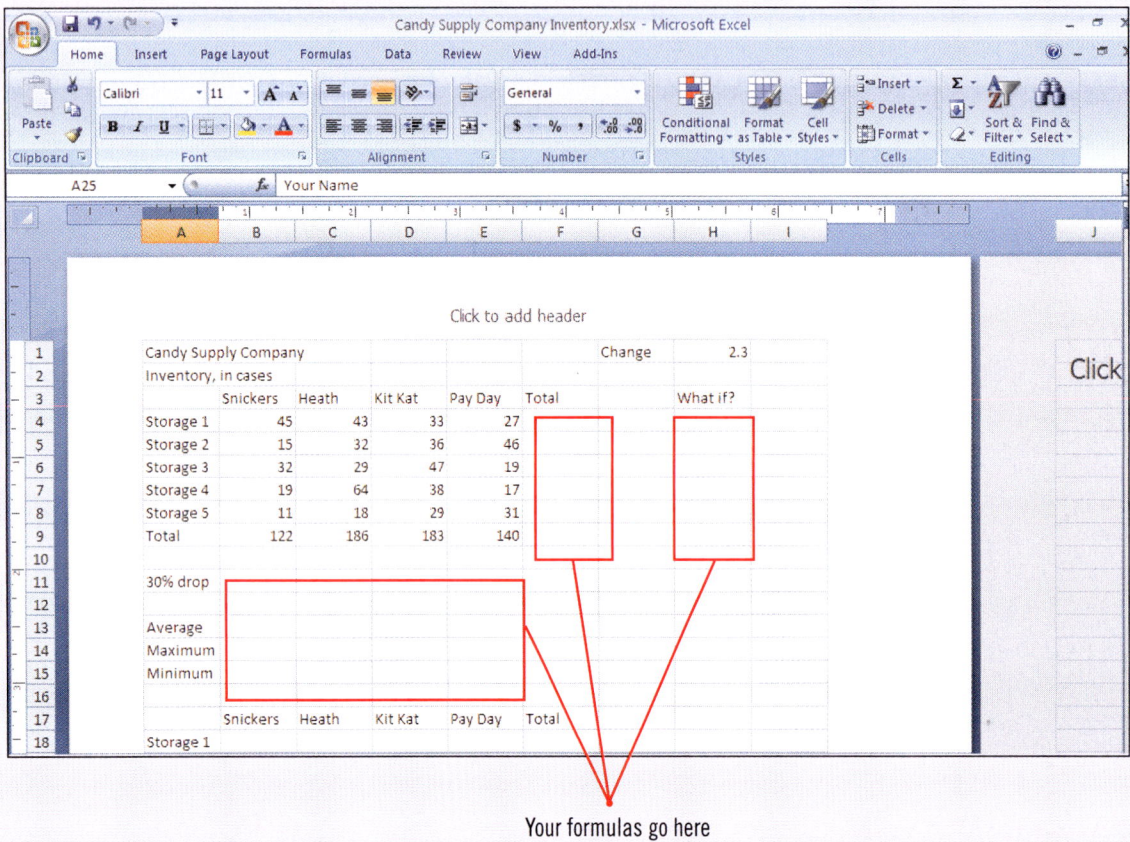

Your formulas go here

2. **Insert a function.**
   a. Use the AutoSum button to create a formula in cell B13 that averages the number of cases of Snickers bars in each storage area. (*Hint*: Click the AutoSum button list arrow to open a list of available functions.)
   b. Use the Insert Function button to create a formula in cell B14 that calculates the most cases of Snickers bars in a storage area.
   c. Use the AutoSum button to create a formula in cell B15 that calculates the minimum number of cases of Snickers bars in a storage area.
   d. Save your work.

3. **Type a function.**
   a. In cell C13, type a formula that includes a function to average the number of cases of Heath bars. (*Hint*: Use AutoComplete to enter the function.)
   b. In cell C14, type a formula that includes a function to calculate the maximum number of cases of Heath bars in a storage area.
   c. In cell C15, type a formula that includes a function to calculate the minimum number of cases of Heath bars in a storage area.
   d. Save your work.

4. Copy and move cell entries.

   a. Select the range B3:F3.

   b. Copy the selection into the Clipboard.

   c. Open the Clipboard task pane, then paste the selection into cell B17.

   d. Select the range A4:A9.

   e. Use the drag-and-drop method to copy the selection to cell A18. (*Hint*: The results should fill the range A18:A23.)

   f. Select the range H1:I1.

   g. Move the selection using the drag-and-drop method to cell G1.

   h. Save your work.

5. Understand relative and absolute cell referencess.

   a. Write a brief description of the difference between relative and absolute references.

   b. List at least three situations in which you think a business might use an absolute reference in its calculations. Examples can include calculations for different types of worksheets, such as timecards, invoices, and budgets.

6. Copy formulas with relative cell references.

   a. Select the range C13:C15.

   b. Use the fill handle to copy these cells to the range D13:E15.

   c. Calculate the total in cell F4.

   d. Use the Fill button to copy the formula in cell F4 down to cells F5:F9.

   e. Use the fill handle to copy the formula in cell E11 to cell F11.

   f. Save your work.

7. Copy formulas with absolute cell references.

   a. In cell H1, enter the value **1.575**.

   b. In cell H4, create a formula that multiplies F4 and an absolute reference to cell H1.

   c. Use the fill handle to copy the formula in cell H4 to cells H5 and H6.

   d. Use the Copy and Paste buttons to copy the formula in cell H4 to cells H7 and H8.

   e. Change the amount in cell H1 to **2.3**.

   f. Save your work.

8. Round a value with a function.

   a. Click cell H4.

   b. Edit this formula to include the ROUND function showing one digit.

   c. Use the fill handle to copy the formula in cell H4 to the range H5:H8.

   d. Enter your name in cell A25, then compare your work to Figure B-23.

   e. Save, preview, print, and close the workbook, then exit Excel.

▼ INDEPENDENT CHALLENGE 1

You are thinking of starting a small breakfast and lunch diner. Before you begin, you need to evaluate what you think your monthly expenses will be. You've started a workbook, but need to complete the entries and add formulas.

a. Open the file EX B-3.xlsx from the drive and folder where you store your Data Files, then save it as **Estimated Diner Expenses**.

b. Make up your own expense data and enter it in cells B4:B10. (Monthly sales are included in the worksheet.)

c. Create a formula in cell C4 that calculates the annual rent.

d. Copy the formula in cell C4 to the range C5:C10.

e. Move the label in cell A15 to cell A14.

f. Create a formula in cells B11 and C11 that totals the expenses.

g. Create a formula in cell C13 that calculates annual sales.

h. Create a formula in cell B14 that determines whether you will make a profit or loss, then copy the formula into cell C14.

i. Copy the labels in cells B3:C3 to cells E3:F3.

j. Type **Projection increase** in cell G1, then type **.2** in cell I1.

k. Create a formula in cell E4 that calculates an increase in the monthly rent by the amount in cell I1. You will be copying this formula to other cells, so you'll need to use an absolute reference.

l. Create a formula in cell F4 that calculates an annual increase based on the calculation in cell E4.

m. Create formulas in cells E13 and E14 and cells F13 and F14 that calculates monthly and annual sales and profit/loss based on the increase in cell E4.

n. Copy the formulas in cells E4:F4 in the remaining monthly and annual expenses.

o. Change the projection increase to **.15**, then compare your work to the sample in Figure B-24.

p. Enter your name in a cell in the worksheet.

q. Save your work, preview and print the worksheets, then close the workbook and exit Excel.

FIGURE B-24

▼ INDEPENDENT CHALLENGE 2

The Pamper Yourself Salon & Day Spa is a small, growing spa that has hired you to organize its accounting records using Excel. The owners want you to track the company's expenses. Before you were hired, one of the bookkeepers began entering last year's expenses in a workbook, but the analysis was never completed.

a. Start Excel, open the file EX B-4.xlsx from the drive and folder where you store your Data Files, then save it as **Pamper Yourself Finances**. The worksheet includes labels for functions such as the Average, Maximum, and Minimum amounts of each of the expenses in the worksheet.

b. Think about what information would be important for the bookkeeping staff to know.

c. Create formulas in the Total column and row using the Sum function.

d. Create formulas in the Average, Maximum, and Minimum columns and rows using the method of your choice.

e. Save your work, then compare your worksheet to the sample shown in Figure B-25.

Advanced Challenge Exercise

- Create the label **Expense categories** in cell B19.
- In cell A19, create a formula using the COUNT function that determines the total number of expense categories listed per quarter.
- Save the workbook.

f. Enter your name in cell A25.

g. Preview the worksheet, then print it.

h. Save your work, then close the workbook and exit Excel.

FIGURE B-25

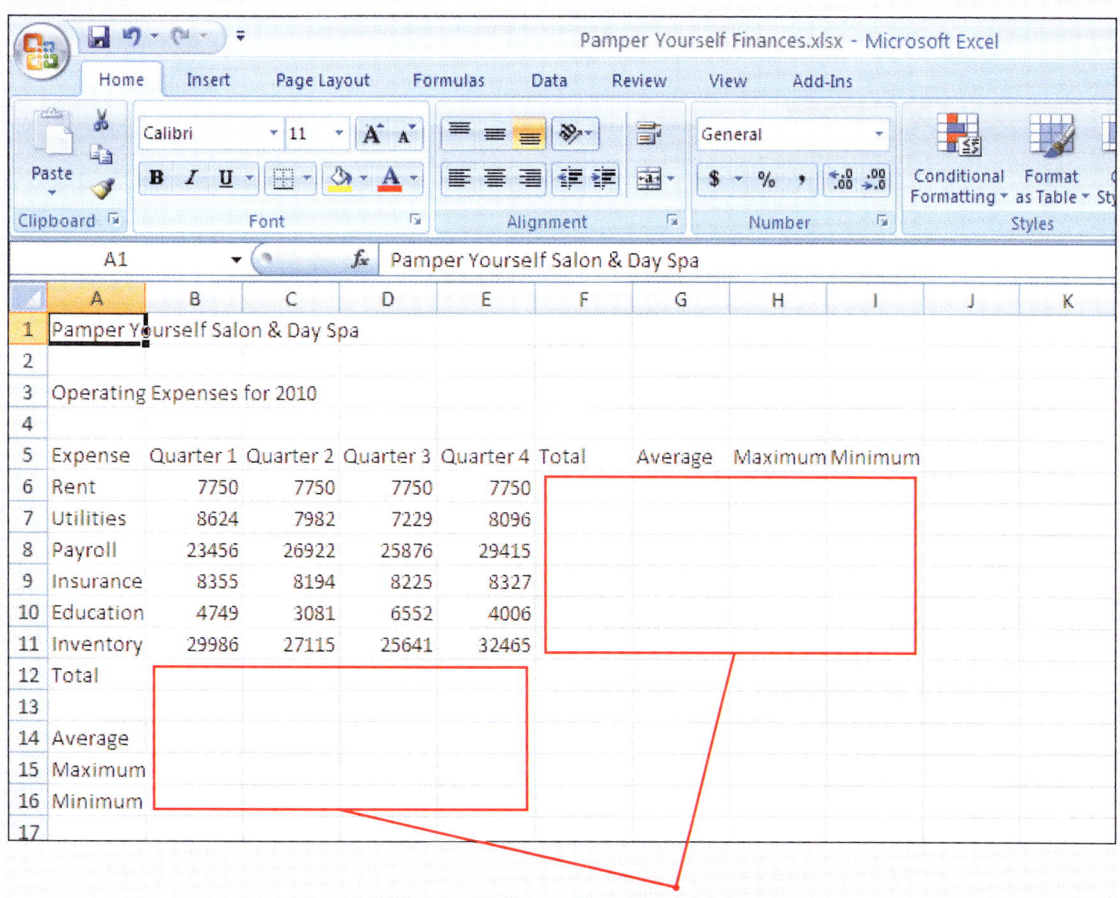

Your formulas go here

▼ INDEPENDENT CHALLENGE 3

As the accounting manager of a locally-owned clothing store, it is your responsibility to calculate and submit accrued sales tax payments on a monthly basis to the state government. You've decided to use an Excel workbook to make these calculations.

a. Start Excel, then save a new, blank workbook to the drive and folder where you store your Data Files as **Sales Tax Calculations**.

b. Decide on the layout for all columns and rows. The worksheet will contain data for four stores, which you can name by store number, neighborhood, or another method of your choice. For each store, you will calculate total sales tax based on the local sales tax rate. You'll also calculate total tax owed for all four stores.

c. Make up sales data for at least four stores.

d. Enter the rate to be used to calculate the sales tax, using your own local rate.

e. Create formulas to calculate the sales tax owed for each store. If you don't know the local tax rate, use **6.5%**.

f. Create a formula to total all the owed sales tax, then compare your work to the sample shown in Figure B-26.

Advanced Challenge Exercise

- Use the ROUND function to eliminate any decimals in the sales tax figures for each store and the total due.
- Save the workbook.

g. Add your name to the header.

h. Save your work, preview and print each worksheet, then close the workbook and exit Excel.

FIGURE B-26

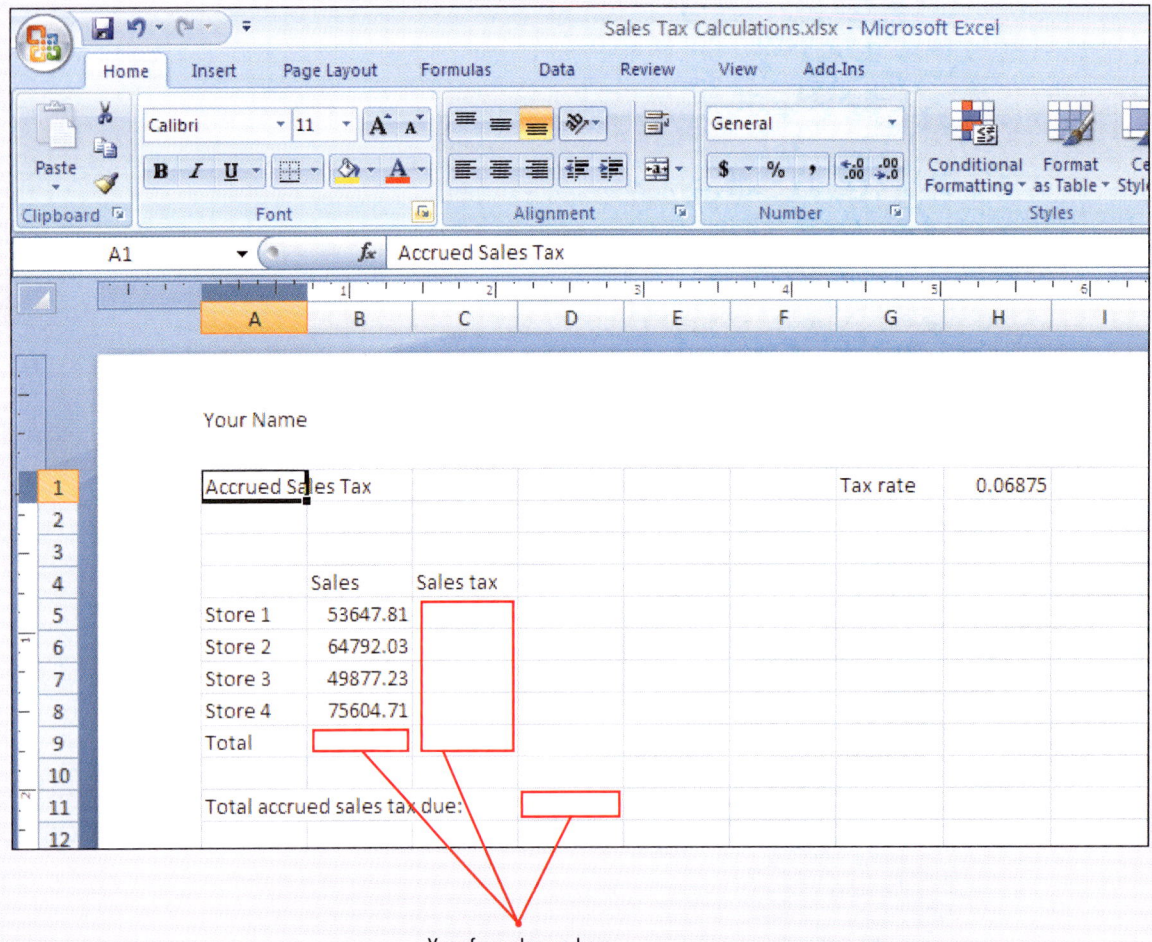

Your formulas go here

▼ REAL LIFE INDEPENDENT CHALLENGE

Many of your friends are purchasing homes, and you are thinking about taking the plunge yourself. As you begin the round of open houses and realtors' listings, you notice that there are many fees associated with buying a home. Some fees are based on a percentage of the purchase price and others are a flat fee; overall, they seem to represent a substantial amount above the purchase prices you see listed. You've seen three houses so far that interest you; one is moderately priced, one is more expensive, and the third is still more expensive. You decide to create an Excel workbook to figure out the real cost of buying each one.

a. Find out the typical cost or percentage rate of at least three fees that are usually charged when buying a home and taking out a mortgage. (*Hint*: If you have access to the Internet you can research the topic of home-buying on the Web, or you can ask friends about standard rates or percentages for items such as title insurance, credit reports, and inspection fees.)

b. Start Excel, then save a new, blank workbook to the drive and folder where you store your Data Files as **Home Purchase Fees**.

c. Create labels and enter data for three homes. If you enter this information across the columns in your worksheet, you should have one column for each house, with the purchase price in the cell below each label. Be sure to enter a different purchase price for each house.

FIGURE B-27

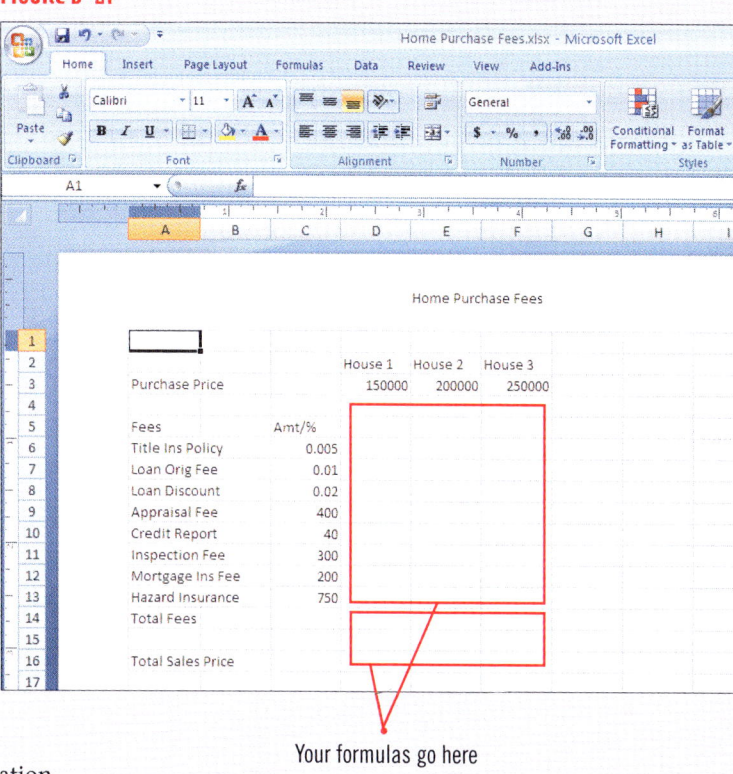

Your formulas go here

d. Create labels for the Fees column and for an Amount or Rate column. Enter the information on the three fees you have researched.

e. In each house column, enter formulas that calculate the fee for each item. The formulas (and use of absolute or relative referencing) will vary depending on whether the charges are a flat fee or based on a percentage of the purchase price.

f. Total the fees for each house, create formulas that add the total fees to the purchase price, then compare your work to the sample in Figure B-27.

g. Enter a title for the worksheet in the header.

h. Enter your name in the header, preview the worksheet, then print it.

i. Save your work, then close the file and exit Excel.

▼ VISUAL WORKSHOP

Create the worksheet shown in Figure B-28 using the skills you learned in this unit. Save the workbook as **Sales Analysis** to the drive and folder where you store your Data Files. Enter your name in the header as shown, then preview and print one copy of the worksheet. Print a second copy of the worksheet with the formulas showing.

FIGURE B-28

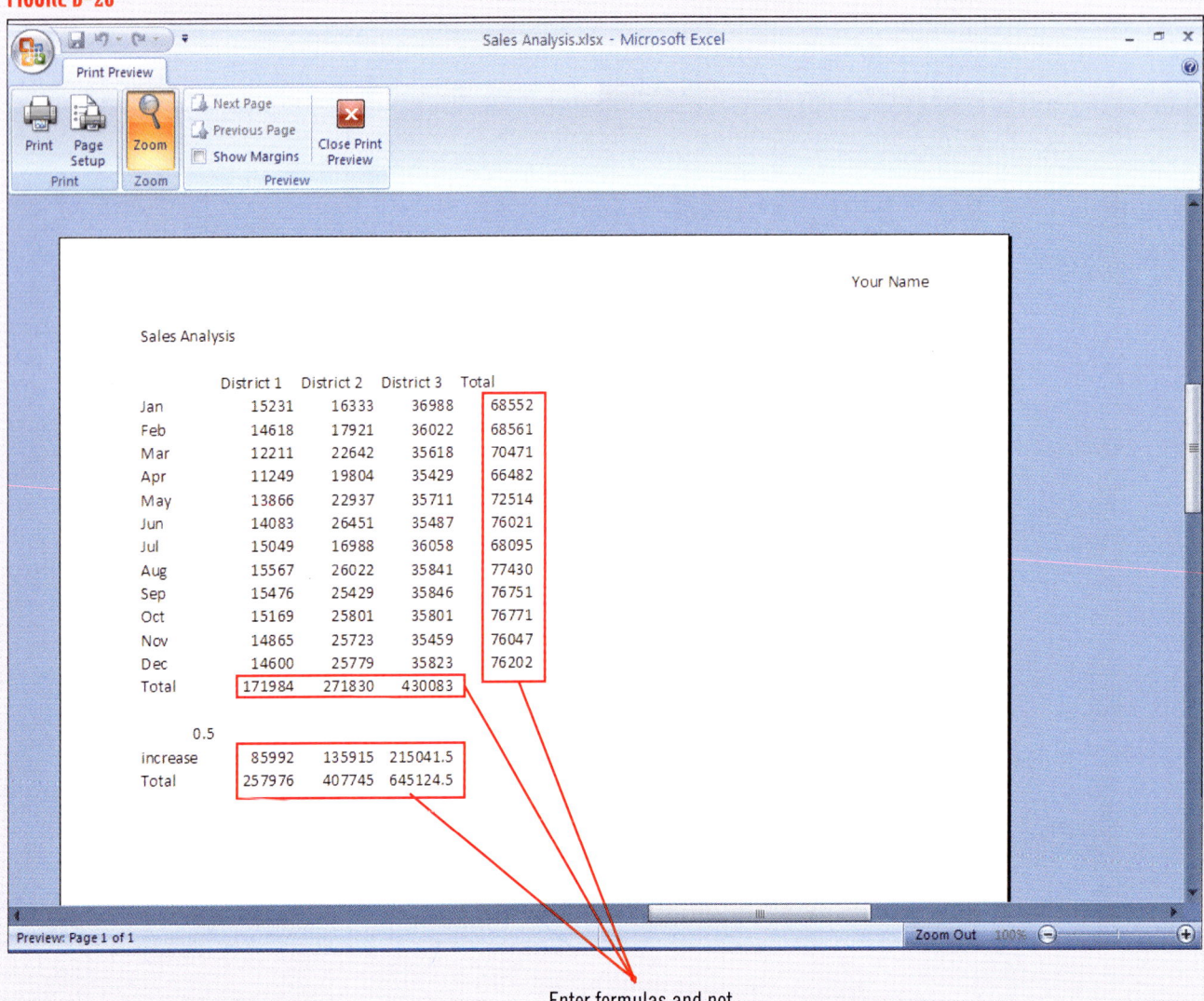

Enter formulas and not
values in these cells

Formatting a Worksheet

Files You Will Need:

EX C-1.xlsx
EX C-2.xlsx
EX C-3.xlsx
EX C-4.xlsx
EX C-5.xlsx

You can use formatting features to make a worksheet more attractive or easier to read, and to emphasize key data. You can apply different formatting attributes such as colors, font styles, and font sizes to the cell contents, you can adjust column width and row height, and you can insert or delete columns and rows. You can also apply conditional formatting so that cells meeting certain criteria are formatted differently. This makes it easy to emphasize selected information, such as sales that exceed or fall below a certain threshold. The marketing managers at QST have requested information on advertising expenses for all QST locations during the past four quarters. Grace Wong has created a worksheet listing this information. She asks you to format the worksheet to make it easier to read and to call attention to important data.

OBJECTIVES

Format values

Change font and font size

Change attributes and alignment

Adjust column width

Insert and delete rows and columns

Apply colors, patterns, and borders

Apply conditional formatting

Name and move a sheet

Check spelling

Formatting Ualues

The **format** of a cell determines how the labels and values look—for example, whether the contents appear boldfaced, italicized, or with dollar signs and commas. Formatting changes only the appearance of a value or label; it does not alter the actual data in any way. To format a cell or range, first you select it, then you apply the formatting using the Ribbon or a keyboard shortcut. You can apply formatting before or after you enter data in a cell or range. Grace has provided you with a worksheet that lists individual advertising expenses, and you're ready to improve its appearance and readability. You decide to start by formatting some of the values so they display as currency, percentages, and dates.

STEPS

1. **Start Excel, open the file EX C-1.xlsx from the drive and folder where you store your Data Files, save it as QST Advertising Expenses, click the View tab on the Ribbon, then click the Page Layout button**

   This worksheet is difficult to interpret because all the information looks the same. In some columns, the contents appear cut off because there is too much data to fit given the current column width. You decide not to widen the columns yet, because the other changes you plan to make might affect column width and row height. The first thing you want to do is format the data showing the cost of each ad.

2. **Select the range E4:E32, then click the Accounting Number Format button $ in the Number group on the Home tab**

   The default Accounting Number format adds dollar signs and two decimal places to the data, as shown in Figure C-1. Formatting this data in accounting format makes it easier to recognize. Excel automatically resizes the column to display the new formatting. The Accounting and Currency formats are both used for monetary values, but the Accounting format aligns currency symbols and decimal points of numbers in a column.

3. **Select the range G4:I32, then click the Comma Style button ⁹ in the Number group**

   The values in columns G, H, and I display the Comma Style format, which does not include a dollar sign but can be useful for some types of accounting data.

4. **Select the range J4:J32, click the Number Format list arrow, click Percentage, then click the Increase Decimal button in the Number group**

   The data in the % of Total column is now formatted with a percent sign (%) and three decimal places. The Format list arrow lets you choose from popular number formats and shows an example of what the selected cell or cells would look like in each format (when multiple cells are selected, the example is based on the first cell in the range). Each time you click the Increase Decimal button, you add one decimal place; clicking the button twice would add two decimal places.

5. **Click the Decrease Decimal button in the Number group twice**

   Two decimal places are removed.

6. **Select the range B4:B31, click the launcher in the Number group**

   The Format Cells dialog box opens with the Date category already selected on the Number tab.

7. **Select the first 14-Mar-01 format in the Type list box as shown in Figure C-2, then click OK**

   The dates in column B appear in the 14-Mar-01 format. The second 14-Mar-01 format in the list displays all days in two digits (it adds a leading zero if the day is only a single-digit number), while the one you chose displays single-digit days without a leading zero. You can also open the Format Cells dialog box by right-clicking a selected range.

8. **Select the range C4:C31, right-click the range, click Format Cells on the shortcut menu, click 14-Mar in the Type list box in the Format Cells dialog box, then click OK**

   Compare your worksheet to Figure C-3.

9. **Press [Ctrl][Home], then save your work**

Formatting a Worksheet

FIGURE C-1: Advertising expense worksheet

Number Format list arrow

Accounting Number Format button

Commands in Number group change the appearance of numbers

Format as Table button

Decrease Decimal button

Increase Decimal button

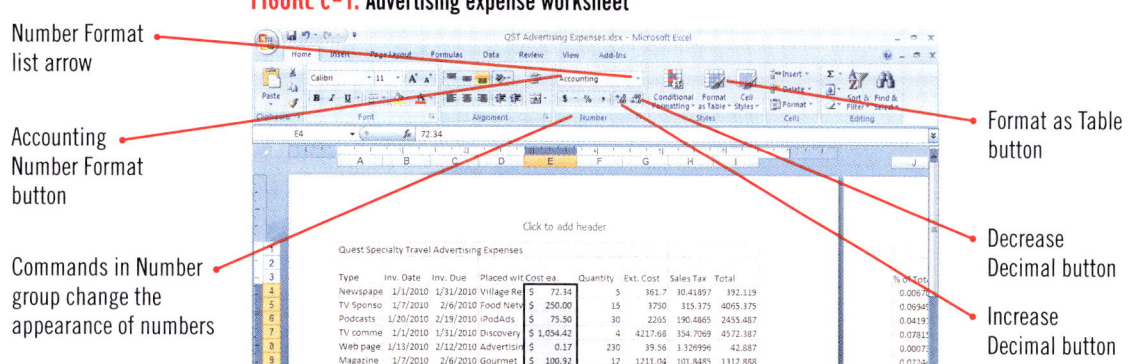

FIGURE C-2: Format Cells dialog box

Number format categories

Date formats

Sample of selected type

This format looks similar to the one below it but displays single digit days without a leading zero

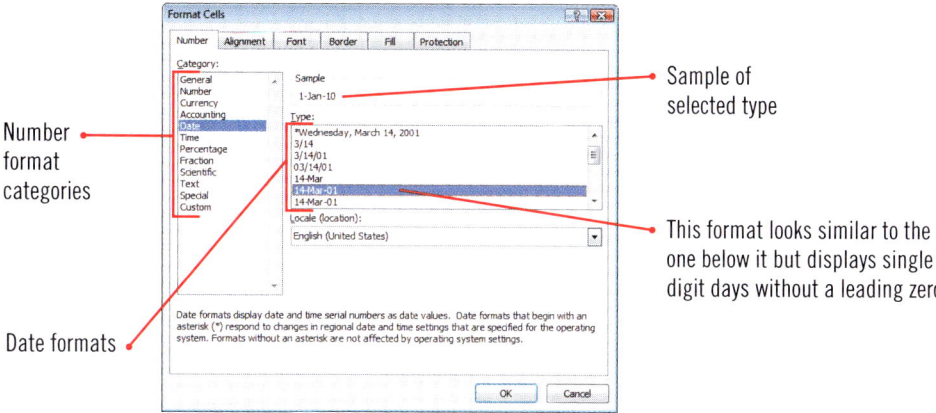

FIGURE C-3: Worksheet with formatted values

New format displays in the format box

Date formats appear without year

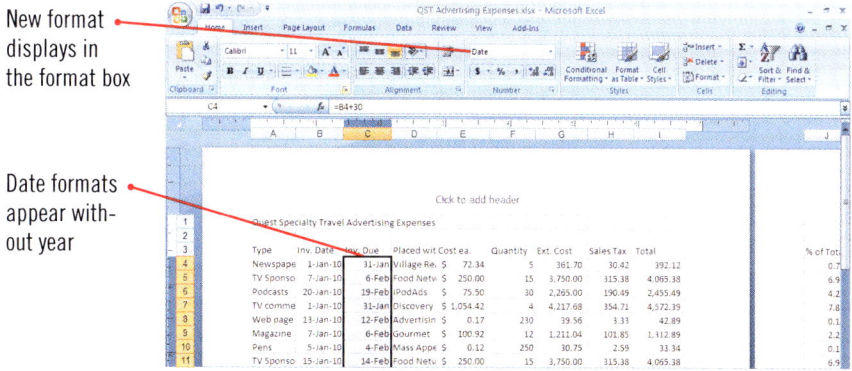

Formatting as a table

Excel includes 60 predefined table styles to make it easy to format selected worksheet cells as a table. You can apply table styles to any range of cells that you want to format quickly, or even to an entire worksheet, but they're especially useful for those ranges with labels in the left column and top rows, and totals in the bottom row or right column. To apply a table style, select the data to be formatted or click anywhere within the intended range (Excel can automatically detect a range of cells), click the Format as Table button in the Styles group on the Home tab, then click a style in the gallery, as shown in Figure C-4. Table styles are organized in three categories (Light, Medium, and Dark). Once you click a style, Excel confirms the range selection, then applies the style. Once you have formatted a range as a table, you can use Live Preview to preview with different choices by pointing to any style in the Table Styles gallery.

FIGURE C-4: Table Styles gallery

Changing Font and Font Size

A **font** is the name for a collection of characters (letters, numerals, symbols, and punctuation marks) with a similar, specific design. The **font size** is the physical size of the text, measured in units called points. A **point** is equal to 1/72 of an inch. The default font in Excel is 11-point Calibri. Table C-1 shows several fonts in different sizes. You can change the font and font size of any cell or range using the Ribbon, the Format Cells dialog box, or the Mini toolbar. You can open the Format Cells dialog box by clicking the launcher in the Font, Alignment, or Number group on the Home tab, or by right-clicking a selection, then clicking Format Cells in the shortcut menu. The Mini toolbar opens when you right-click a cell or range. You want to change the font and size of the labels and the worksheet title so that they stand out more from the data.

STEPS

1. **Right-click cell A1, click Format Cells on the shortcut menu, then click the Font tab in the Format Cells dialog box if necessary**
   See Figure C-5.

2. **Scroll down in the Font list to see an alphabetical listing of the fonts available on your computer, click Times New Roman in the Font list box, click 20 in the Size list box, preview the results in the Preview area, then click OK**
   The title appears in 20-point Times New Roman, and the Font group on the Home tab displays the new font and size information.

3. **Click the Increase Font Size button 𝐀 in the Font group twice**
   The size of the title increases to 24-point.

4. **Select the range A3:J3, right-click, then click the Font list arrow on the Mini toolbar**
   The Mini toolbar includes the most commonly used formatting tools, so it's great for making quick formatting changes. Notice that the font names on this font list are displayed in the font they represent.

5. **Click Times New Roman, click the Font Size list arrow, then click 14**
   The Mini toolbar closes when you move the pointer away from the selection. Compare your worksheet to Figure C-6. Notice that some of the column headings are now too wide to appear fully in the column. Excel does not automatically adjust column widths to accommodate cell formatting; you have to adjust column widths manually. You'll learn to do this in a later lesson.

6. **Save your work**

TABLE C-1: Examples of fonts and font sizes

font	12 point	24 point
Calibri	Excel	Excel
Playbill	Excel	Excel
Comic Sans MS	Excel	Excel
Times New Roman	Excel	Excel

FIGURE C-5: Font tab in the Format Cells dialog box

Currently selected font

Available fonts might differ on your computer

Effects options

Type a custom font size or select from the list

Font style options

Preview area shows sample of selected formatting

FIGURE C-6: Worksheet with formatted title and labels

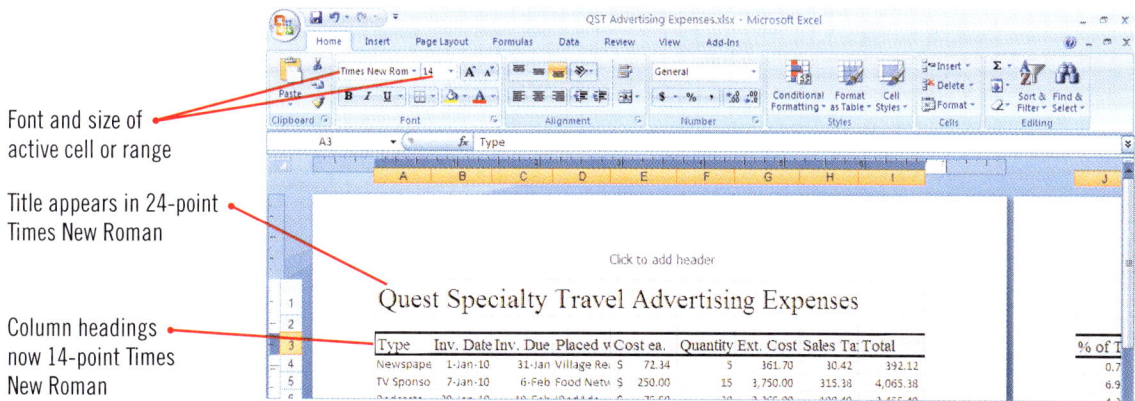

Font and size of active cell or range

Title appears in 24-point Times New Roman

Column headings now 14-point Times New Roman

Inserting and adjusting clip art and other images

You can illustrate your worksheets using clip art and other images. A **clip** is an individual media file, such as art, sound, animation, or a movie. **Clip art** refers to images such as a corporate logo, a picture, or a photo. Microsoft Office comes with many clips available for your use. To add a clip to a worksheet, click Clip Art in the Illustrations group on the Insert tab. The Clip Art task pane opens. Here you can search for clips by typing one or more keywords (words related to your subject) in the Search for text box, then click Go. Clips that relate to your keywords appear in the Clip Art task pane, as shown in Figure C-7. (If you have a standard Office installation and an active Internet connection, you will see many clips available through Microsoft Office Online in addition to those on your computer.) Click the image you want, and it is inserted at the location of the active cell. You can also add your own images to a worksheet by clicking the Insert tab on the Ribbon, then clicking the Picture button. Navigate to the file you want, then click Insert Picture from File. To resize an image, drag any corner sizing handle. To move an image, point inside the clip until the pointer changes to ⬚, then drag it to a new location.

FIGURE C-7: Results of Clip Art search

Type keyword(s) here

Click to begin search

Changing Attributes and Alignment

Attributes are styling formats such as bold, italic, and underlining that you can apply to affect the way text and numbers look in a worksheet. You can "paint" or copy a cell's format into other cells by using the Format Painter button in the Clipboard group on the Home tab of the Ribbon. This is similar to using copy and paste, but instead of copying cell contents, it copies only the cell's formatting. You can also change the **alignment** of labels and values in cells to be left, right, or center. You can apply attributes and alignment options using the Home tab, the Format Cells dialog box, or the Mini toolbar. See Table C-2 for a description of common attribute and alignment buttons that are available on the Home tab of the Ribbon and the Mini toolbar. You want to further enhance the worksheet's appearance by adding bold and underline formatting and centering some of the labels.

STEPS

1. **Press [Ctrl][Home], then click the Bold button B in the Font group**

   The title in cell A1 appears in bold.

2. **Click cell A3, then click the Underline button U in the Font group**

   The column heading is now underlined, though this may be difficult to see with the cell selected.

3. **Click the Italic button I in the Font group, then click B**

   The heading now appears in boldface, underlined, italic type. Notice that the Bold, Italic, and Underline buttons in the Font group are all selected.

4. **Click I**

   The italic attribute is removed from cell A3, but the bold and underline attributes remain.

5. **Click the Format Painter button ✔ in the Clipboard group, then select the range B3:J3**

   The formatting in cell A3 is copied to the rest of the labels in the column headings. You can turn off the Format Painter by pressing [Esc] or by clicking ✔. You decide the title would look better if it were centered over the data columns.

6. **Select the range A1:J1, then click the Merge & Center button ⊞ in the Alignment group**

   The Merge & Center button creates one cell out of the 10 cells across the row, then centers the text in that newly created large cell. The title "Quest Specialty Travel Advertising Expenses" is centered across the 10 columns you selected. You can change the alignment within individual cells using buttons on the Home tab; you can split merged cells into their original components by selecting the merged cells, then clicking the Merge & Center button.

7. **Select the range A3:J3, right-click, then click the Center button ☰ on the Mini toolbar**

   Compare your screen to Figure C-8. Although they may be difficult to read, notice that all the headings are centered within their cells.

8. **Save your work**

FIGURE C-8: Worksheet with formatting attributes applied

Formatting buttons selected

Title centered across columns

Merge & Center button

Center button

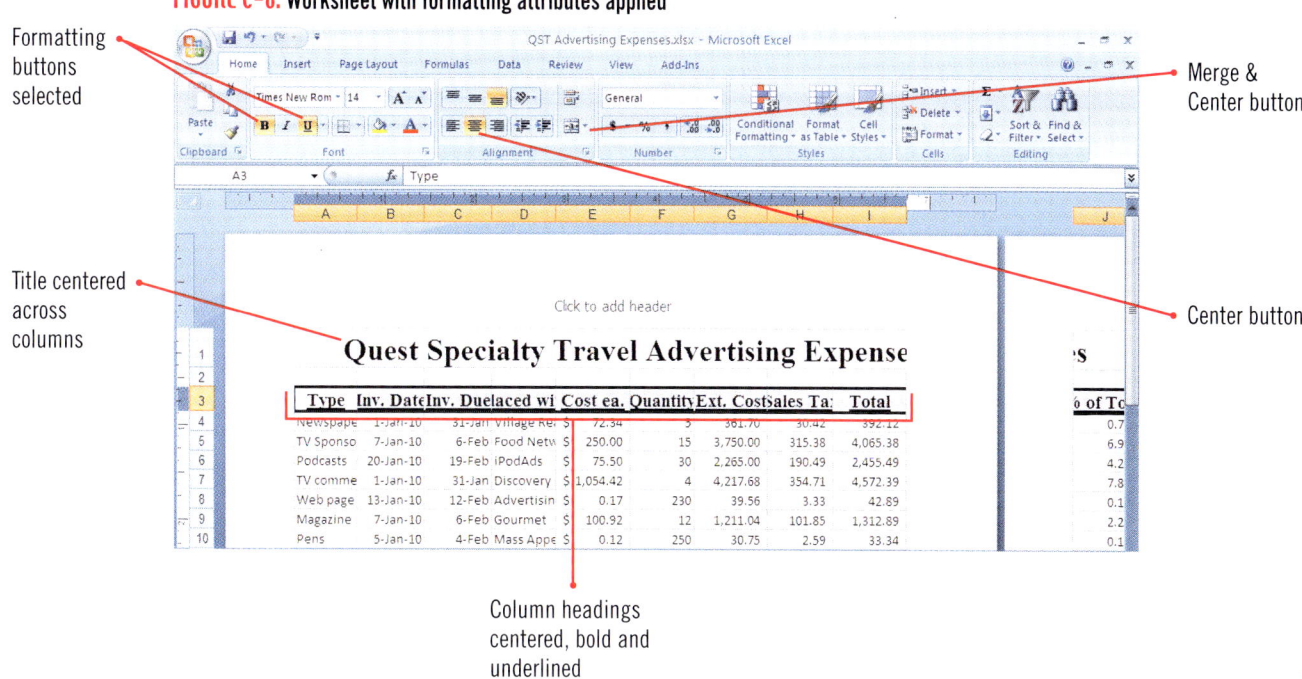

Column headings centered, bold and underlined

Rotating and indenting cell entries

In addition to applying fonts and formatting attributes, you can rotate or indent data within a cell to further change its appearance. You can rotate text within a cell by altering its alignment. To change alignment, select the cells you want to modify, then click the launcher ⌐ in the Alignment group to open the Alignment tab of the Format Cells dialog box. Click a position in the Orientation box or type a number in the Degrees text box to change from the default horizontal alignment, then click OK. You can indent cell contents using the Increase Indent button ⌐ on the Alignment group on the Home tab on the Ribbon, which moves cell contents to the right one space, or the Decrease Indent button ⌐, which moves cell contents to the left one space.

TABLE C-2: Common attribute and alignment buttons

button	description	button	description
B	Bolds text	▤	Aligns text at the left edge of the cell
I	Italicizes text	▤	Centers text horizontally within the cell
U	Underlines text	▤	Aligns text at the right edge of the cell
▦	Adds lines or borders	▦	Centers text across columns, and combines two or more selected, adjacent cells into one cell

Adjusting Column Width

As you format a worksheet, you might need to adjust the width of one or more columns to accommodate text or larger font size or style. The default column width is 8.43 characters wide, a little less than one inch. With Excel, you can adjust the width of one or more columns by using the mouse, the Ribbon, or the shortcut menu. Using the mouse, you can drag or double-click the right edge of a column heading. The Ribbon and shortcut menu include commands for making more detailed width adjustments. Table C-3 describes common column adjustment commands. You notice that some of the labels in column A don't fit in the cells. You want to adjust the widths of the columns so that the labels appear in their entirety.

STEPS

1. **Position the mouse pointer on the line between the column A and column B headings until it changes to ⊹**

   See Figure C-9. The **column heading** is the box at the top of each column containing a letter. Before you can adjust column width using the mouse, you need to position the pointer on the right edge of the column you want to adjust. The entries for TV commercials are the widest in the column.

2. **Click and drag the ⊹ to the right until the column displays the TV commercials entries fully**

3. **Position the pointer on the column line between columns B and C until it changes to ⊹, then double-click**

   Column B automatically widens to fit the widest entry, in this case, the column label. Double-clicking activates the **AutoFit** feature, which automatically resizes a column so it accommodates the widest entry in a cell.

4. **Use AutoFit to resize columns C, D, and J**

5. **Select the range F5:I5**

   You can change the width of multiple columns at once, by first selecting either the column headings or at least one cell in each column.

6. **Click the Format button in the Cells group, then click Column Width**

   The Column Width dialog box opens. Column width measurement is based on the number of characters that will fit in the column when formatted in the Normal font and font size (in this case, 11 pt Calibri).

7. **Drag the dialog box by its title bar if its placement obscures your view of the worksheet, type 11 in the Column width text box, then click OK**

   The widths of columns F, G, H, and I change to reflect the new setting. See Figure C-10.

8. **Save your work**

Changing row height

Changing row height is as easy as changing column width. Row height is calculated in points, the same units of measure used for fonts. The row height must exceed the size of the font you are using. Normally, you don't need to adjust row heights manually, because row height adjusts automatically to accommodate other formatting changes. If you format something in a row to be a larger point size, Excel adjusts the row to fit the largest point size in the row. However, you have just as many options for changing row height as you do column width. Using the mouse, you can place the ⊹ pointer on the line dividing the row heading from the heading below, and dragging to the desired height; double-clicking the line autofits the row height where necessary. You can also select one or more rows, then use the Row Height command on the shortcut menu, or the Row Height or AutoFit Row Height command on the Format button in the Cells group on the Home tab.

FIGURE C-9: Preparing to change the column width

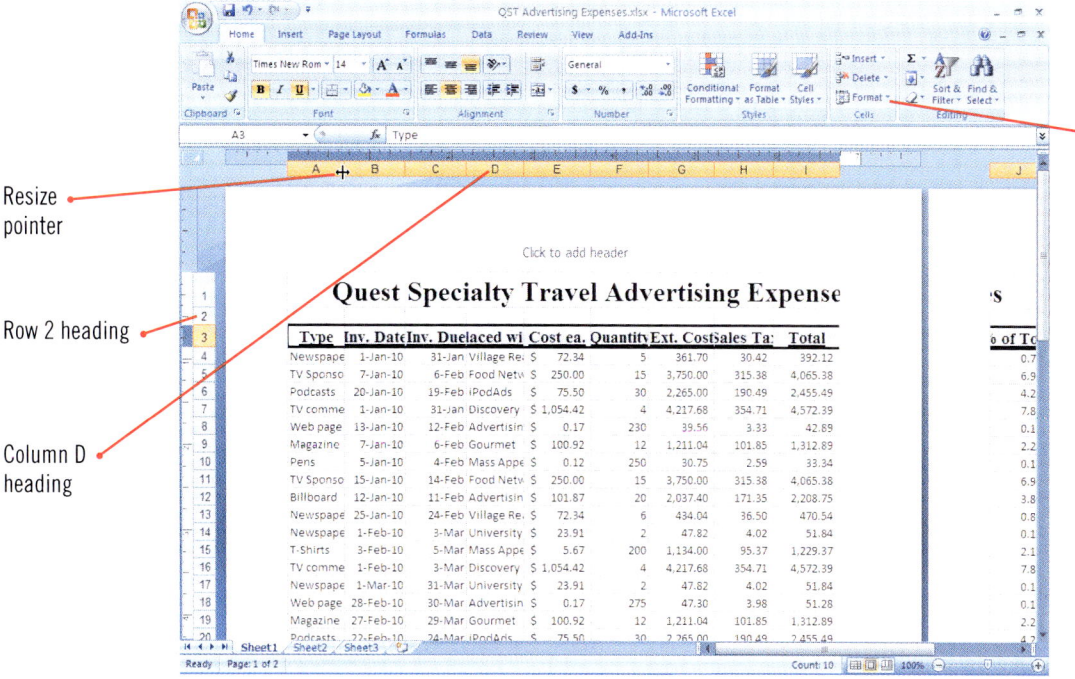

Resize pointer

Row 2 heading

Column D heading

Click to change column or row formatting

FIGURE C-10: Worksheet with column widths adjusted

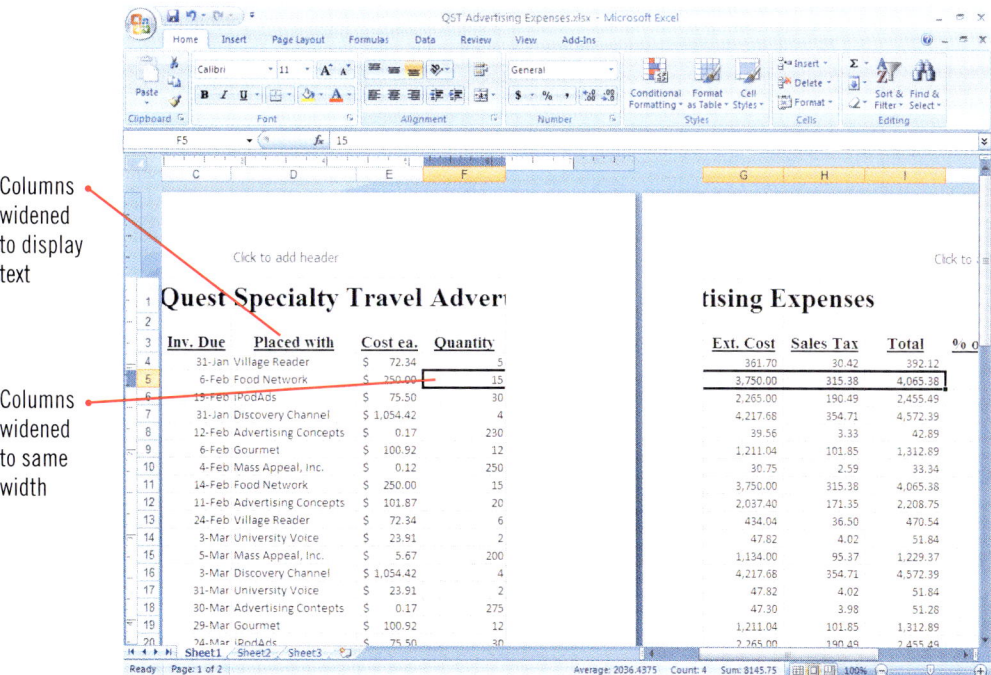

Columns widened to display text

Columns widened to same width

TABLE C-3: Common column formatting commands

command	description	available using
Column Width	Sets the width to a specific number of characters	Format button, shortcut menu
AutoFit Column Width	Fits to the widest entry in a column	Format button, mouse
Hide & Unhide	Hides or displays hidden column(s)	Format button, shortcut menu
Default Width	Changes the default column width for current worksheet	Format button

Inserting and Deleting Rows and Columns

As you modify a worksheet, you might find it necessary to insert or delete rows and columns to keep your worksheet current. For example, you might need to insert rows to accommodate new inventory products or remove a column of yearly totals that are no longer necessary. When you insert a new row, the contents of the worksheet shift down from the newly inserted row. When you insert a new column, the contents of the worksheet shift to the right from the point of the new column. Excel inserts rows above the cell pointer and inserts columns to the left of the cell pointer. To insert multiple rows, drag across row headings to select the same number of rows as you want to insert. You want to improve the overall appearance of the worksheet by inserting a row between the last row of data and the totals. Also, you have learned that row 27 and column J need to be deleted from the worksheet.

STEPS

1. **Right-click cell A32, then click Insert on the shortcut menu**

   The Insert dialog box opens. See Figure C-11. You can choose to insert a column or a row, or you can shift the data in the cells in the active column right or in the active row down. An additional row between the last row of data and the totals will visually separate the totals.

   > **QUICK TIP**
   >
   > To insert a single row or column, you can also right-click the row heading immediately below where you want the new row or the column heading to the right of where you want the new column, then click Insert in the shortcut menu.

2. **Click the Entire row option button, then click OK**

   A blank row appears between the Billboard data and the totals, and the formula result in cell E33 has not changed. The Insert Options button ⊘ appears beside cell A33. Pointing to the button displays a list arrow, which you can click and then choose from the following options: Format Same As Above, Format Same As Below, or Clear Formatting. You want the default formatting, Same as Above.

3. **Click the row 27 heading**

   All of row 27 is selected, as shown in Figure C-12.

   > **QUICK TIP**
   >
   > If you inadvertently click the Delete list arrow instead of the button itself, click Delete Sheet Rows in the menu that opens.

4. **Click the Delete button in the Cells group; *do not click the button arrow***

   Excel deletes row 27, and all rows below this shift up one row. You must use the Delete button or the Delete command on the shortcut menu to delete a row or column; pressing [Delete] on the keyboard removes only the *contents* of a selected row or column.

5. **Click the column J heading**

   The percentage information is calculated elsewhere and is no longer necessary in this worksheet.

   > **QUICK TIP**
   >
   > After inserting or deleting rows or columns in a worksheet, be sure to proof formulas that contain relative cell references.

6. **Click the Delete button in the Cells group**

   Excel deletes column J. The remaining columns to the right shift left one column.

7. **Save your work**

Hiding and unhiding columns and rows

When you don't want data in a column or row to be visible, but you don't want to delete it, you can hide the column or row. To hide a selected column, click the Format button in the Cells group, point to Hide & Unhide, then click Hide Columns. A hidden column is indicated by a dark black vertical line in its original position. This black line disappears when you click elsewhere in the worksheet. You can display a hidden column by selecting the columns on either side of the hidden column, clicking the Format button in the Cells group, pointing to Hide & Unhide, and then clicking Unhide Columns. (To hide or unhide one or more rows, substitute Hide Rows and Unhide Rows for the Hide Columns and Unhide Columns commands.)

FIGURE C-11: Insert dialog box

Entire row option button

FIGURE C-12: Worksheet with row 27 selected

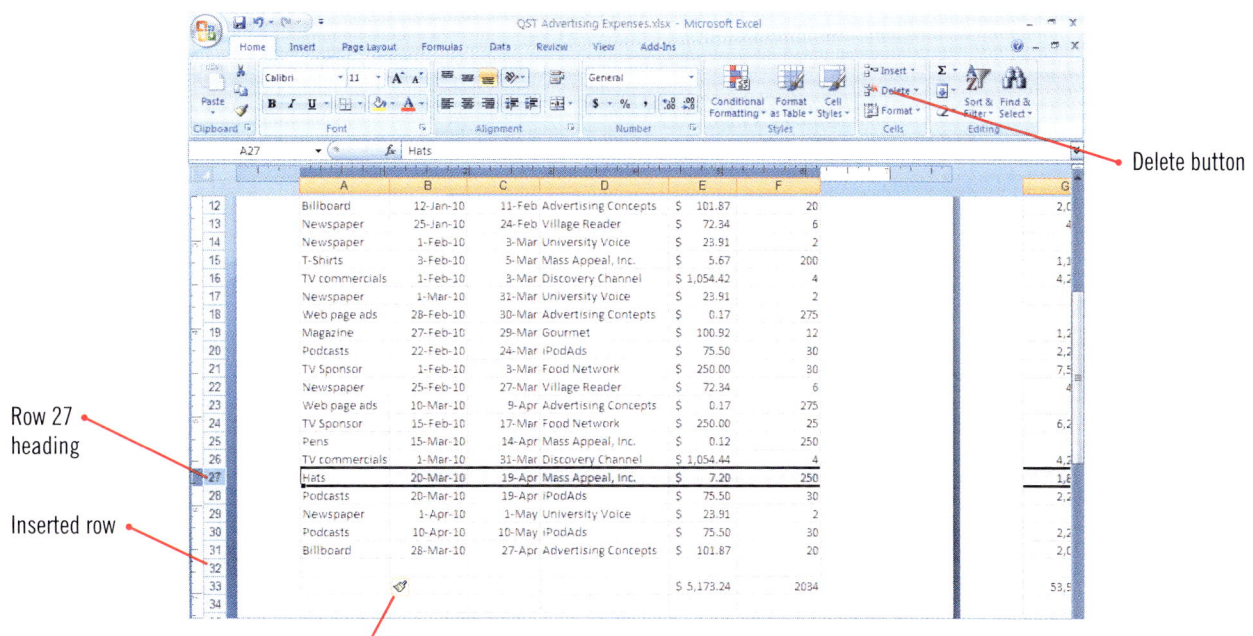

Delete button

Row 27 heading

Inserted row

On your screen, the Insert Options button might appear in a different location

Adding and editing comments

Much of your work in Excel may be in collaboration with teammates with whom you share worksheets. You can share ideas with other worksheet users by adding comments within selected cells. To include a comment in a worksheet, click the cell where you want to place the comment, click the Review tab on the Ribbon, then click the New Comment button in the Comments group. A resizable text box containing the computer user's name opens in which you can type your comments. A small, red triangle appears in the upper-right corner of a cell containing a comment. If comments are not already displayed in a workbook, other users can point to the triangle to display the comment. To see all worksheet comments, as shown in Figure C-13, click the Show All Comments button in the Comments group. To edit a comment, click the cell containing the comment, then click the Edit Comment button in the Comments group. To delete a comment, click the cell containing the comment, then click the Delete button in the Comments group.

FIGURE C-13: Comments in worksheet

18	Web page abs	28-Feb-10	30-Mar Advertising Concepts	$	0.17
19	Magazine	27-Feb-10	29-Mar Gourmet	$	100.92
20	Podcasts	22-Feb-10	24-Mar iPodAds	$	75.50
21	TV Sponsor	1-Feb-10	3-Mar Food Network		
22	Newspaper	25-Feb-10	27-Mar Village Read		
23	Web page ads	10-Mar-10	9-Apr Advertising C		
24	TV Sponsor	15-Feb-10	17-Mar Food Networ		
25	Pens	15-Mar-10	14-Apr Mass Appeal, Inc.	$	0.12
26	TV commercials	1-Mar-10	31-Mar Discovery Channel		
27	Podcasts	20-Mar-10	19-Apr iPodAds		
28	Newspaper	1-Apr-10	1-May University Vo		
29	Podcasts	10-Apr-10	10-May iPodAds		
30	Billboard	28-Mar-10	27-Apr Advertising Concepts	$	101.87
31					
32				$5,166.04	

Grace Wong: Should we continue with this market, or expand to other publications?

Grace Wong: I think this will turn out to be a very good decision.

Applying Colors, Patterns, and Borders

You can use colors, patterns, and borders to enhance the overall appearance of a worksheet and to make it easier to read. You can add these enhancements by using the Border and Fill Color buttons in the Font group on the Home tab of the Ribbon and on the Mini toolbar, or by using the Fill tab and the Border tab in the Format Cells dialog box. You can apply a color to the background of a cell or a range, or to cell contents, and you can apply a pattern to a cell or range. You can apply borders to all the cells in a worksheet or only to selected cells to call attention to selected information. To save time, you can also apply **cell styles**, predesigned combinations of formatting attributes. You want to add a pattern, a border, and color to the title of the worksheet to give the worksheet a more professional appearance.

STEPS

1. **Select cell A1, click the Fill Color list arrow button 🎨 in the Font group, then hover the pointer over the Turquoise, Accent 2 color (first row, sixth column from the left)**
   See Figure C-14. Live Preview shows you how the color will look *before* you apply it.

> **QUICK TIP**
> When you change fill or font color, the color on the Fill Color and Font Color buttons changes to the last color you selected.

2. **Click the Turquoise, Accent 2 color (first row, sixth column from the left)**
   The color is applied to the background or fill of this cell. (Remember that cell A1 spans columns A through I because the Merge and Center command was applied.)

3. **Right-click cell A1, then click Format Cells on the shortcut menu**
   The Format Cells dialog box opens. Adding a pattern to cells can add to the visual interest of your worksheet. To format an entire row or column at once, click the row heading or column heading button.

> **QUICK TIP**
> Use fill colors and patterns sparingly. Too many colors can be distracting or make it hard to see which information is important.

4. **Click the Fill tab, click the Pattern Style list arrow, click the 6.25% Gray style (first row, sixth column from the left), then click OK**

5. **Click the Borders list arrow 🔲 in the Font group, then click Thick Bottom Border**
   Unlike underlining, which is a text-formatting tool, borders extend to the width of the cell, and can appear at the bottom of the cell, at the top, or on either side. It can be difficult to see a border when the cell is selected.

> **QUICK TIP**
> You can also create custom cell borders. Click the Borders list arrow in the Font group, click More Borders, then click the individual border buttons to create borders or boxes.

6. **Select the range A3:I3, click the Font Color list arrow 🅰 in the Font group, then click the Blue, Accent 1 color (first Theme color row, fifth column from the left) on the palette**
   The new color is applied to the selected range.

7. **Select the range J1:K1, click the Cell Styles button in the Styles group, then click the Neutral button (first row, fourth column from the left) on the palette**
   The font and color change in the range, as shown in Figure C-15.

8. **Save your work**

FIGURE C-14: Viewing fill color using LivePreview

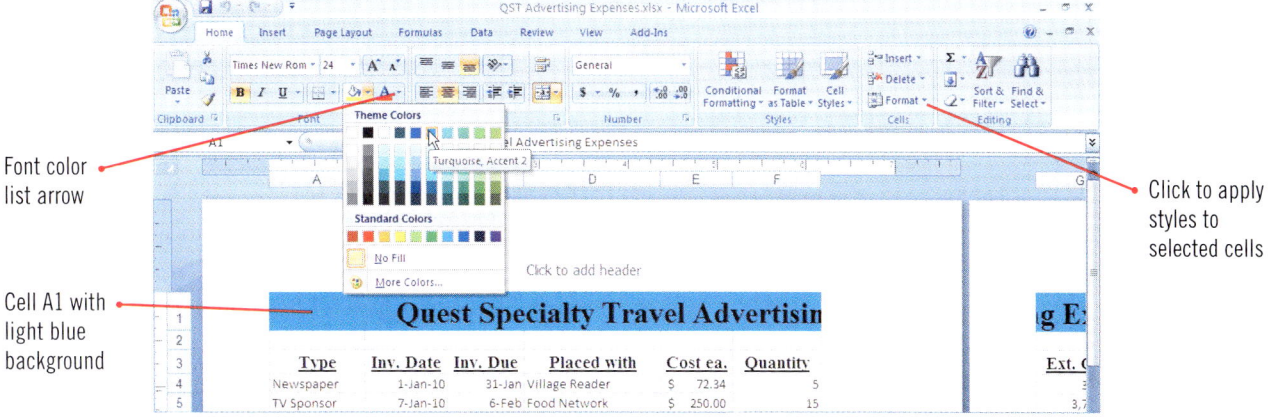

Font color list arrow

Cell A1 with light blue background

Click to apply styles to selected cells

FIGURE C-15: Worksheet with color, patterns, border, and style applied

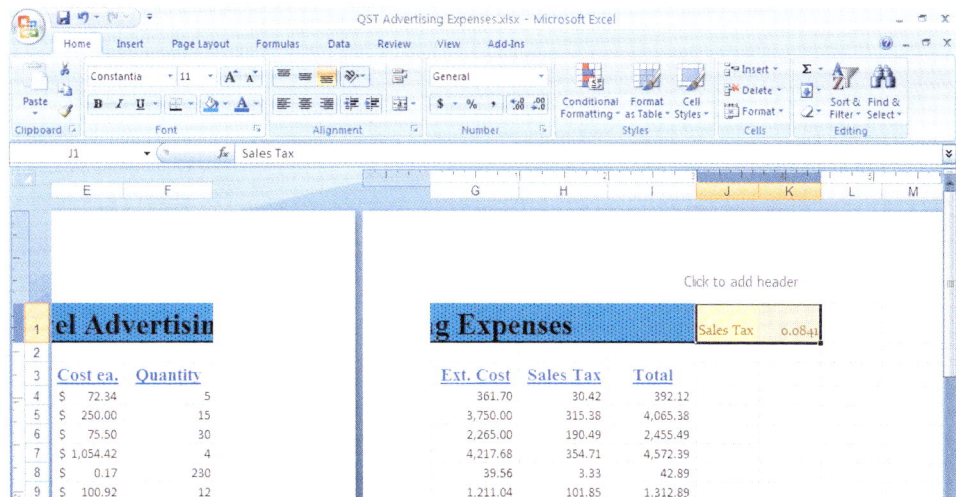

Saving time with themes and cell styles

You can save yourself time by formatting with themes and cell styles. A **theme** is a predefined set of attributes that gives your Excel worksheet a professional look. Formatting choices included in a theme are colors, fonts, and line and fill effects. A theme can be applied using the Themes button in the Themes group on the Page Layout tab on the Ribbon, as shown in Figure C-16. **Cell styles** are sets of attributes based on themes, so they are automatically updated if you change a theme. For example, if you apply the 20% - Accent1 cell style to cell A1 in a worksheet that has no theme applied, the fill color changes to light blue and the font changes to Constantia. If you change the theme of the worksheet to Metro, cell A1's fill color changes to light green and the font changes to Corbel, because these are the attributes that coordinate with the selected theme. Using themes and cell styles makes it easier to ensure that your worksheets are consistent and saves you from a lot of reformatting every time you make a change.

FIGURE C-16: Themes gallery

Applying Conditional Formatting

So far, you've used formatting to change the appearance of different types of data, such as dates, dollar amounts, worksheet titles, and column labels. But you can also use formatting to highlight important aspects of the data itself. For example, you can apply formatting that automatically changes the font color to red for any cells where ad costs exceed $100 and to green where ad costs are below $50. This type of formatting is called **conditional formatting** because Excel automatically applies different formats depending on conditions you specify. If the data meets your conditions, Excel applies the formats you specify. The formatting is updated if you change data in the worksheet. Data bars are a type of conditional formatting that visually illustrate differences among values. Grace is concerned about advertising costs exceeding yearly budget. You decide to use conditional formatting to highlight certain trends and patterns in the data, so it's easy to spot the most expensive expenditures.

STEPS

1. **Select the range I4:I30, click the Conditional Formatting button in the Styles group, point to Data Bars, then point to the Light Blue Data Bar (second row, second from left)**

   Live Preview shows how this formatting will appear in the worksheet, as shown in Figure C-17. Notice that the length of the bar in each cell reflects its value relative to other cells in the selection.

2. **Preview the Green Data Bar (first row, second from left), then click it**

3. **Select the range G4:G30, click the Conditional Formatting button in the Styles group, then point to Highlight Cells Rules**

   The Conditional Formatting menu displays choices for creating different types of formatting rules. For example, you can create a rule for values that are greater than a certain amount, less than a certain amount, or between two amounts.

   > **QUICK TIP**
   >
   > You can apply an Icon Set to a selected range by clicking the Conditional Formatting button in the Styles group, then pointing to Icon Sets; icons appear within the cells to illustrate differences in values.

4. **Click Between**

   The Between dialog box opens. Depending on the choice you made in the Highlight Cells Rules menu (such as "Greater Than" or "Less Than"), this dialog box displays different input boxes. You can define multiple different conditions and then assign formatting attributes to each one. You define the condition first. The default setting for the first condition is "Cell Value Is" "between." The value can be a constant, formula, cell reference, or date. The formatting default format is exactly what you want: Light Red Fill with Dark Red Text.

   > **QUICK TIP**
   >
   > You can copy conditional formats the same way you copy other formats.

5. **Type 2000 in the first text box, type 4000 in the second text box, compare your settings to Figure C-18, then click OK**

   All cells with values between 2000 and 4000 in column G appear with a light red fill and dark red text.

6. **Click cell G7, type 3975.55, then press [Enter]**

   When the value in cell G7 changes, the formatting also changes, because the new value meets the condition to apply the format. Compare your results to Figure C-19.

7. **Press [Ctrl][Home] to select cell A1, then save your work**

Managing conditional formatting rules

If you create a conditional formatting rule and then want to change the conditions to reflect a different value or format, you don't need to create a new rule; instead, you can modify the rule using the Rule Manager. Select the cell(s) containing conditional formatting, click the Conditional Formatting button in the Styles group, then click Manage Rules. The Conditional Formatting Rules Manager dialog box opens. Select the rules you want to edit or delete, click Edit Rule, modify the settings in the Edit the Rule Description area, click OK, then click OK again to close the dialog box. The rule is modified, and the new conditions are applied to the selected cells.

FIGURE C-17: Previewing a Data Bar

Data bars displayed
in sheet

FIGURE C-18: Setting conditions in Between dialog box

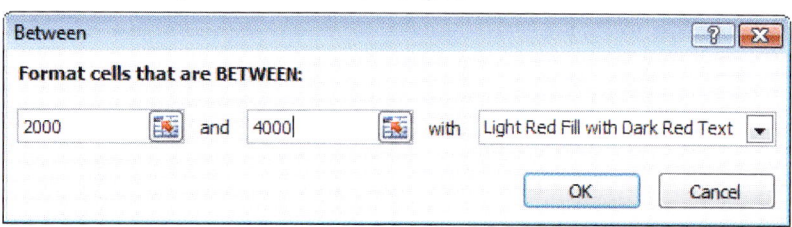

FIGURE C-19: Results of Conditional Formatting

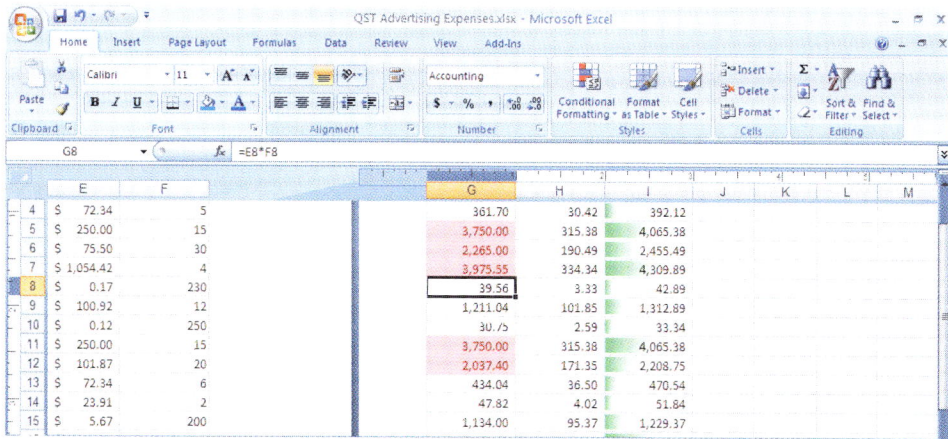

Naming and Moving a Sheet

By default, an Excel workbook initially contains three worksheets, named Sheet1, Sheet2, and Sheet3. The sheet name appears on the sheet tab at the bottom of the worksheet. When you open a workbook, the first worksheet is the active sheet. To move from sheet to sheet, you can click any sheet tab at the bottom of the worksheet window. The sheet tab scrolling buttons, located to the left of the sheet tabs, are useful when a workbook contains too many sheet tabs to display at once. To make it easier to identify the sheets in a workbook, you can rename each sheet and add color to the tabs. You can also organize them in a logical way. For instance, to better track performance goals, you could name each workbook sheet for an individual salesperson, and you could move the sheets so they appeared in alphabetical order. In the current worksheet, Sheet1 contains information on advertising expenses. Sheet2 contains an advertising budget, and Sheet3 contains no data. You want to name the two sheets in the workbook to reflect their contents, add color to a sheet tab to easily distinguish one from the other, and change their order.

STEPS

1. **Click the Sheet2 tab**
    Sheet2 becomes active, appearing in front of the Sheet1 tab; this is the worksheet that contains the budgeted expenses. See Figure C-20.

2. **Click the Sheet1 tab**
    Sheet1, which contains the actual expenses, becomes active again.

QUICK TIP

You can also rename a sheet by right-clicking the tab, clicking Rename on the shortcut menu, typing the new name, then pressing [Enter].

3. **Double-click the Sheet2 tab, type Budget, then press [Enter]**
    The new name for Sheet2 automatically replaces the default name on the tab. Worksheet names can have up to 31 characters, including spaces and punctuation.

QUICK TIP

To delete a worksheet, select the worksheet you want to delete, click the Delete button list arrow in the Cells group, then click Delete Sheet. To insert a worksheet, click the Insert Worksheet button to the right of the sheet tabs.

4. **Right-click the Budget tab, point to Tab Color on the shortcut menu, then click the Bright Green, Accent 4, Lighter 80% color (second row, third column from the right) as shown in Figure C-21**
    The tab color changes to a bright green gradient.

5. **Double-click the Sheet1 tab, type Actual, then press [Enter]**
    Notice that the color of the Budget tab changes depending on whether it is the active tab; when the Actual tab is active, the color of the Budget tab changes to solid bright green. You decide to rearrange the order of the sheets, so that the Budget tab is to the left of the Actual tab.

6. **Click the Budget sheet tab, hold down the mouse button, drag it to the left of the Actual sheet tab, as shown in Figure C-22, then release the mouse button**
    As you drag, the pointer changes to , the sheet relocation pointer, and a small, black triangle shows its position. The first sheet in the workbook is now the Budget sheet. See Figure C-23. To see hidden sheets, click the far left tab scrolling button to display the first sheet tab; click the far right navigation button to display the last sheet tab. The left and right buttons move one sheet in their respective directions.

7. **Click the Actual sheet tab, then enter your name in the left-side header box**

8. **Click the Page Layout tab on the Ribbon, click the Orientation button in the Page Setup group, then click Landscape**

9. **Press [Ctrl][Home], then save your work**

FIGURE C-20: Sheet tabs in workbook

Sheet1 tab   Sheet2 tab

FIGURE C-21: Tab Color palette

Available colors

FIGURE C-22: Sheet during move

Sheet   Sheet1   Indicates
relocation   renamed   tab color
pointer

FIGURE C-23: Reordered sheets

Budget sheet comes
before Actual sheet

Excel 2007

Copying worksheets

There are times when you may want to copy a worksheet. For example, a workbook might contain a sheet with Quarter 1 expenses, and you want to use that sheet as the basis for a sheet containing Quarter 2 expenses. To copy a sheet within the same workbook, press and hold [Ctrl], drag the sheet tab to the desired tab location, release the mouse button, then release [Ctrl]. A duplicate sheet appears with the same name as the copied sheet followed by "(2)" indicating it is a copy. You can then rename the sheet to a more meaningful name. To copy a sheet to a different workbook, both the source and destination workbooks must be open. Select the sheet to copy or move, right-click the sheet tab, then click Move or Copy in the shortcut menu. Complete the information in the Move or Copy dialog box. Be sure to click the Create a copy check box if you are copying rather than moving the worksheet. Carefully check your calculation results whenever you move or copy a worksheet.

Checking Spelling

Excel includes a spelling checker to help you ensure that the words in your worksheet are spelled correctly. The spelling checker scans your worksheet, displays words it doesn't find in its built-in dictionary, and suggests replacements when they are available. To check other sheets in a multiple-sheet workbook, you need to display each sheet and run the spelling checker again. Because the built-in dictionary cannot possibly include all the words that anyone needs, you can add words to the dictionary, such as your company name, an acronym, or an unusual technical term. Once you add a word or term, the spelling checker will no longer consider that word misspelled. Any words you've added to the dictionary using Word, Access, or PowerPoint are also available in Excel. Another feature, AutoCorrect, automatically corrects some spelling errors as you type. Before you distribute this workbook to Grace and the marketing managers, you check its spelling.

STEPS

QUICK TIP

The Spelling dialog box lists the name of the language currently being used in its title bar.

1. **Click the Review tab on the Ribbon, then click the Spelling button in the Proofing group**

   The Spelling: English (U.S.) dialog box opens, as shown in Figure C-24, with "iPodAds" selected as the first misspelled word in the worksheet. For any word, you have the option to Ignore this case of the flagged word, Ignore All cases of the flagged word, or Add the word to the dictionary.

2. **Click Ignore All**

   Next, the spelling checker finds the word "Contepts" and suggests "Concepts" as an alternative.

QUICK TIP

To customize AutoCorrect to add or remove automatic corrections, click the Office button, click Excel Options, click Proofing, click AutoCorrect Options, choose options in the AutoCorrect dialog box for how you want this feature to work, then click OK.

3. **Verify that the word Concepts is selected in the Suggestions list, then click Change**

   When no more incorrect words are found, Excel displays a message indicating that all the words on the worksheet have been checked.

4. **Click OK**

5. **Click the Home tab, click Find & Select in the Editing group, then click Replace**

   The Find and Replace dialog box opens. You can use this dialog box to replace a word or phrase. It might be a misspelling that the Spelling Checker didn't recognize as wrong, such as a word that wasn't corrected with the spelling checker, or simply something you want to change. Grace has just told you that each instance of 'Billboard' in the worksheet should be changed to 'Sign'.

6. **Type Billboard in the Find what text box, press [Tab], then type Sign in the Replace with text box**

   Compare your dialog box to Figure C-25.

7. **Click Replace All, click OK to close the warning box, then click Close to close the Find and Replace dialog box**

   Excel has made two replacements.

QUICK TIP

The Fit to option button is on the Page tab of the Page Setup dialog box.

8. **Save your work, view the Actual sheet in Print Preview, click the Page Setup button on the Ribbon, fit the worksheet to one page, then return to Print Preview**

   Compare your worksheet to Figure C-26.

9. **Print one copy of the worksheet, close it, then exit Excel**

E-mailing a workbook

You can send an entire workbook from within Excel using your installed email program, such as Microsoft Office Outlook or Outlook Express. To send a workbook as an e-mail message attachment, open the workbook, click the Office button, point to Send, then click E-mail. An email message opens with the workbook automatically attached; the filename appears in the Attached field. Complete the To and optional Cc fields, include a message if you wish, then click Send.

FIGURE C-24: Spelling: English dialog box

Misspelled word

Suggested replacements for misspelled word

Click to ignore all occurrences of misspelled word

Click to add word to dictionary

FIGURE C-25: Find and Replace dialog box

FIGURE C-26: Viewing worksheet in Print Preview

Practice

▼ CONCEPTS REVIEW

Label each element of the Excel worksheet window shown in Figure C-27.

FIGURE C-27

Match each command or button with the statement that best describes it.

8. **Spelling & Grammar button** d
9. ⬜ e
10. ⬜ f
11. **[Ctrl][Home]** c
12. **Conditional Formatting** b
13. **[Delete]** a

a. Erases the contents of a cell
b. Changes formatting of a cell based on cell contents
c. Moves cell pointer to cell A1
d. Checks for apparent misspellings in a worksheet
e. Displays options for erasing the contents of a cell
f. Centers cell contents over multiple cells

Select the best answer from the list of choices.

14. **Which of the following is an example of an accounting number format?**
    a. 5555
    c. 55.55%
    b. $5,555.55
    d. 5,555.55

15. **What feature is used to delete a conditional formatting rule?**
    a. Rule Reminder
    c. Rule Manager
    b. Conditional Rule Manager
    d. Format Manager

16. **Which button removes boldface formatting from selected cells?**
    a. *I*
    c. [.00 icon]
    b. **B**
    d. **B** [highlighted]

17. **Which button opens the Format Cells dialog box?**
    a. [dialog launcher icon]
    c. **B**
    b. [format painter icon]
    d. [undo icon]

18. **What is the name of the feature used to resize a column to accommodate its widest entry?**
    a. AutoFormat
    c. AutoResize
    b. AutoFit
    d. AutoRefit

19. **Which button increases the number of decimal places in selected cells?**
    a. [indent icon]
    c. [.00 icon]
    b. [.00 decrease icon]
    d. [indent icon]

20. **Which button applies multiple formatting styles to selected cells?**
    a. [undo icon]
    c. [cell styles icon]
    b. [format painter icon]
    d. [paste icon]

▼ SKILLS REVIEW

1. **Format values.**
   a. Start Excel, open the file EX C-2.xlsx from the drive and folder where you store your Data Files, then save it as **Health Insurance Premiums**.
   b. Enter a formula in cell B10 that totals the number of employees.
   c. Create a formula in cell C5 that calculates the monthly insurance premium for the accounting department. (*Hint:* Make sure you use the correct type of cell reference in the formula. To calculate the monthly premium, multiply the number of employees by the monthly premium.)
   d. Copy the formula in cell C5 to the range C6:C10.
   e. Format the range C5:C10 using the Accounting Number Format.
   f. Change the format of the range C6:C9 to the Comma Style.
   g. Reduce the number of decimals to 0 in cell B14, using a button in the Number group.
   h. Save your work.

2. **Change fonts and font sizes.**
   a. Select the range of cells containing the column labels (in row 4).
   b. Change the font of the selection to Times New Roman.
   c. Increase the font size of the selection to 12 points.
   d. Increase the font size of the label in cell A1 to 14 points.
   e. Save your changes.

3. **Change attributes and alignment.**
   a. Apply the bold and italic attributes to the worksheet title **QST Corporate Office**.
   b. Use the Merge & Center button to center the Health Insurance Premiums label over columns A through C.
   c. Apply the italic attribute to the Health Insurance Premiums label.
   d. Add the bold attribute to the labels in row 4.
   e. Use the Format Painter to copy the format in cell A4 to the range A5:A10.
   f. Apply the format in cell C10 to cell B14.

   g. Change the alignment of cell A10 to Align Right.

   h. Select the range of cells containing the column titles, then center them.

   i. Remove the italic attribute from the Health Insurance Premiums label, then increase the font size to 14.

   j. Move the Health Insurance Premiums label to cell A3, then add the bold and underline attributes.

   k. Add a bottom double border to the last cell in the Employees column, above the total number of employees.

   l. Save your changes.

4. Adjust column width.

   a. Resize column C to a width of 10.71.

   b. Use the AutoFit feature to resize columns A and B.

   c. Clear the contents of cell A13 (do not delete the cell).

   d. Change the text in cell A14 to **Monthly Insurance Premium**, then change the width of the column to **25**.

   e. Resize any remaining columns as needed to view all the data.

   f. Save your changes.

5. Insert and delete rows and columns.

   a. Insert a new row between rows 5 and 6.

   b. Add a new department—**Humanitarian Aid**—in the newly inserted row. Enter **5** for the Employees.

   c. Copy the formula in cell C5 to C6.

   d. Add the following comment to cell A6: **New department**. Display the comment, then drag to move it out of the way, if necessary.

   e. Add a new column between the Department and Employees columns with the title **Family Coverage**, then resize the column using AutoFit.

   f. Delete the Legal row.

   g. Move the comment out of the way, if necessary.

   h. Save your changes.

6. Apply colors, patterns, and borders.

   a. Add an outside border around the range A4:D10.

   b. Apply the Aqua, Accent 5, Lighter 80% fill color to the labels in the Department column (do not include the Total label).

   c. Apply the Orange, Accent 6, Lighter 60% fill color to the range A4:D4.

   d. Change the color of the font in the range A4:D4 to Red, Accent 2, Darker 25%.

   e. Add a 12.5% Gray pattern style to cell A1.

   f. Format the range A14:B14 with a pattern style of Thin Diagonal Stripes, a pattern color of White, Background 1, and a background color of Dark Blue, Text 2, Lighter 40%. Apply the bold attribute.

   g. Save your changes.

7. Apply conditional formatting.

   a. Select the range D5:D9, then create a conditional format that changes cell contents to green fill with dark green text if the value is between 4000 and 7000.

   b. Select the range C5:C9, then create a conditional format that changes cell contents to red text if the number of employees exceeds 10.

   c. Select the range C5:C9, then create a blue data bar.

   d. Use the Rule Manager to modify the conditional format in cell C5 to display the cell contents in bold red text.

   e. Copy the format in cell C5 to the range in C6:C9.

   f. Merge and center the title over columns A-D.

8. Name and move a sheet.

   a. Name the Sheet 1 tab **Insurance Data**.

   b. Name the Sheet 3 tab **Employee Data**.

   c. Change the Insurance Data tab color to Red, Accent 2, Lighter 40%.

   d. Change the Employee Data tab color to Aqua, Accent 5, Lighter 40%.

▼ SKILLS REVIEW (CONTINUED)

e. Move the Employee Data sheet so it comes after (to the right of) the Insurance Data sheet.

f. Make the Insurance Data sheet active, enter your name in cell A20, then save your work.

9. Check spelling.

a. Move the cell pointer to cell A1.

b. Use the Find & Select feature to replace the Accounting label in cell A5 with Accounting/Legal.

c. Check the spelling in the worksheet using the spelling checker, and correct any spelling errors.

d. Save your changes.

e. Preview and print the Insurance Data sheet, compare your work to Figure C-28, then close the workbook and exit Excel.

FIGURE C-28

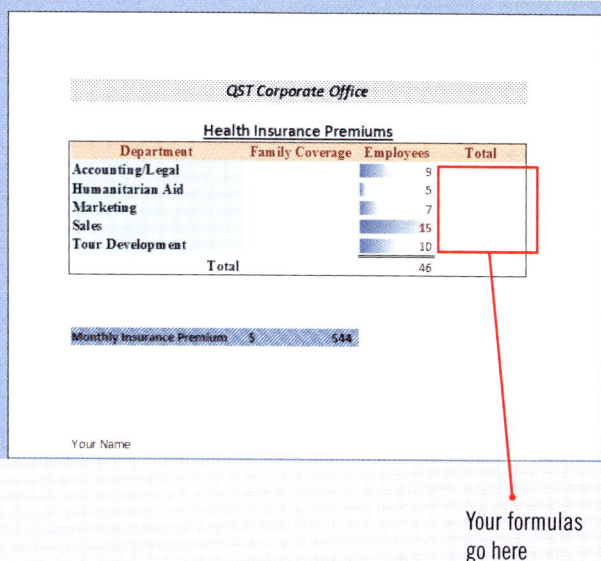

Your formulas go here

▼ INDEPENDENT CHALLENGE 1

You run a freelance accounting business, and one of your newest clients is Lovely Locks, a small beauty salon. Now that you've converted the salon's accounting records to Excel, the manager would like you to work on an analysis of the inventory. Although more items will be added later, the worksheet has enough items for you to begin your modifications.

a. Start Excel, open the file EX C-3.xlsx from the drive and folder where you store your Data Files, then save it as **Lovely Locks Inventory**.

b. Create a formula in cell E4 that calculates the value of the on-hand inventory, based on the price paid for the item, in cell B4. Format the cell in the Comma Style.

c. Use an absolute reference to calculate the sale price of the item in cell F4, using the markup value shown in cell I1.

d. Copy the formulas created above into the range E5:F14; first convert any necessary cell references to absolute so that the formulas work correctly.

e. Add the bold attribute to the column headings, and italicize the items in column A.

f. Make sure all columns are wide enough to display the data and headings.

g. Format the Sale Price column so it displays the Accounting Number Format with two decimal places.

h. Change the Price Paid column so it displays the Comma style with two decimal places.

i. Add a row under #2 Curlers for **Nail files**, price paid **$0.31**, sold individually **(each)**, with **56** on hand.

j. Verify that all the formulas in the worksheet are correct. Adjust any items as needed, and check the spelling.

k. Use conditional formatting to call attention to items with a quantity of less than 20 on hand. Use yellow fill with dark yellow text.

l. Create an icon set for the range D4:D15 using the symbols of your choosing.

m. Add an outside border around the data in the Item column.

n. Delete the row containing the Pins item.

o. Enter your name in an empty cell below the data, then save the file.

p. Preview and print the worksheet, compare your work to the sample of page 1 shown in Figure C-29, close the workbook, then exit Excel.

FIGURE C-29

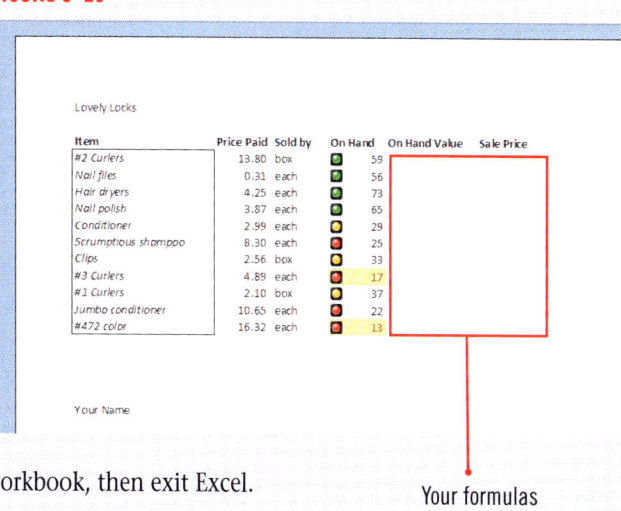

Your formulas go here

Excel 2007

▼ INDEPENDENT CHALLENGE 2

You volunteer several hours each week with the Assistance League of South Bend, and are in charge of maintaining the membership list. You're currently planning a mailing campaign to members in certain regions of the city. You also want to create renewal letters for members whose membership expires soon. You decide to format the list to enhance the appearance of the worksheet and make your upcoming tasks easier to plan.

a. Start Excel, open the file EX C-4.xlsx from the drive and folder where you store your Data Files, then save it as **South Bend Assistance League**.

b. Remove any blank columns.

c. Create a conditional format in the Zip Code column so that entries greater than 46649 appear in light red fill with dark red text.

d. Make all columns wide enough to fit their data and headings.

e. Use formatting enhancements, such as fonts, font sizes, and text attributes, to make the worksheet more attractive.

f. Center-align the column labels.

g. Use conditional formatting so that entries for Year of Membership Expiration that are between 2011 and 2013 appear in a bold, contrasting color.

h. Adjust any items as necessary, then check the spelling.

i. Change the name of the Sheet 1 tab to one that reflects the sheet's contents, then add a tab color of your choice.

j. Enter your name in an empty cell, then save your work.

k. Before printing, preview the worksheet, make any final changes you think necessary, then print a copy. Compare your work to the sample shown in Figure C-30.

l. Close the workbook, then exit Excel.

FIGURE C-30

▼ INDEPENDENT CHALLENGE 3

Fine Line Writing Instruments is a Chicago-based company that manufactures high-quality pens and markers. As the finance manager, one of your responsibilities is to analyze the monthly reports from your five district sales offices. Your boss, Joanne Bennington, has just asked you to prepare a quarterly sales report for an upcoming meeting. Because several top executives will be attending this meeting, Joanne reminds you that the report must look professional. In particular, she asks you to emphasize the company's surge in profits during the last month and to highlight the fact that the Northeastern district continues to outpace the other districts.

a. Plan a worksheet that shows the company's sales during the first quarter. Assume that all pens are the same price. Make sure you plan to include:

- The number of pens sold (units sold) and the associated revenues (total sales) for each of the five district sales offices. The five sales districts are: Northeastern, Midwestern, Southeastern, Southern, and Western.
- Calculations that show month-by-month totals for January, February, and March, and a three-month cumulative total.
- Calculations that show each district's share of sales (percent of Total Sales).
- Labels that reflect the month-by-month data as well as the cumulative data.
- Formatting enhancements and data bars that emphasize the recent month's sales surge and the Northeastern district's sales leadership.

b. Ask yourself the following questions about the organization and formatting of the worksheet: What worksheet title and labels do you need, and where should they appear? How can you calculate the totals? What formulas can you copy to save time and keystrokes? Do any of these formulas need to use an absolute reference? How do you show dollar amounts? What information should be shown in bold? Do you need to use more than one font? Should you use more than one point size?

c. Start Excel, then save a new, blank workbook as **Fine Line Writing Instruments** to the drive and folder where you store your Data Files.

d. Build the worksheet with your own price and sales data. Enter the titles and labels first, then enter the numbers and formulas. You can use the information in Table C-4 to get started.

e. Adjust the column widths as necessary.

f. Change the height of row 1 to 33 points.

g. Format labels and values, and change the attributes and alignment if necessary.

h. Resize columns and adjust the formatting as necessary.

i. Add data bars for the monthly Units Sold columns.

j. Add a column that calculates a 25% increase in sales dollars. Use an absolute cell reference in this calculation. (*Hint*: Make sure the current formatting is applied to the new information.)

TABLE C-4

Fine Line Writing Instruments										
1st Quarter Sales Report										
		January		February		March		Total		
Office	Price	Units Sold	Sales	Units Sold	Sales	Units Sold	Sales	Units Sold	Sales	
Northeastern										
Midwestern										
Southeastern										
Southern										
Western										

▼ INDEPENDENT CHALLENGE 3 (CONTINUED)

Advanced Challenge Exercise

- Use the Format as Table feature to add a table style of your choice to the data.
- Insert a clip art image related to pens in an appropriate location, adjusting its size and position as necessary.
- Save your work.

l. Enter your name in an empty cell.

m. Check the spelling in the workbook, then save your work.

n. Preview, compare your work to Figure C-31, then print the worksheet in landscape orientation.

o. Close the workbook file, then exit Excel.

FIGURE C-31

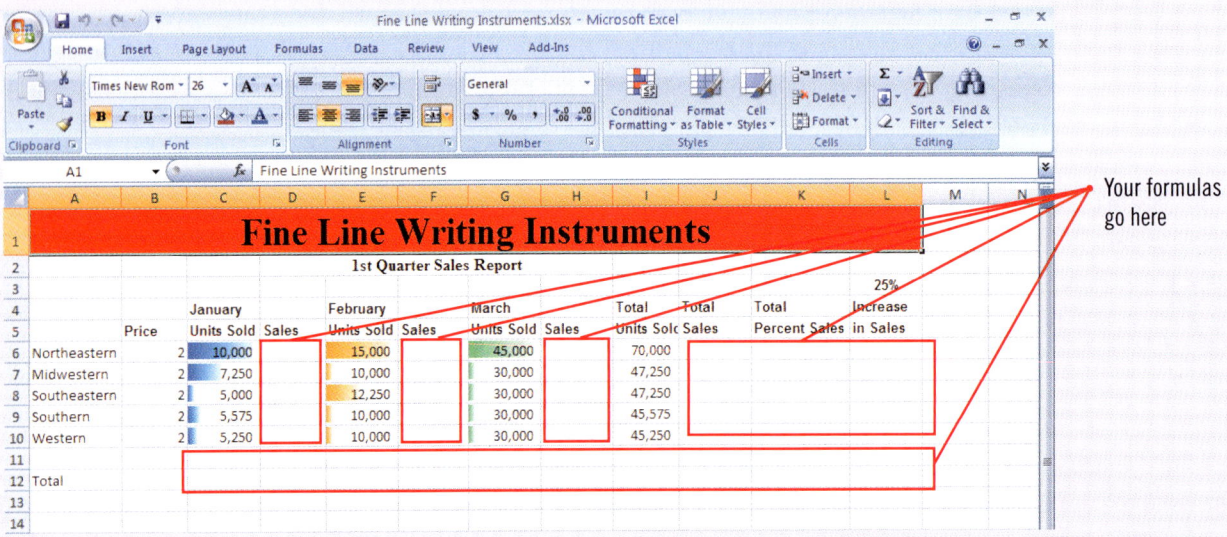

▼ REAL LIFE INDEPENDENT CHALLENGE

Note: **This project requires an Internet connection.**

You are saving up to take an international trip you have always dreamed about. You plan to visit seven different countries over the course of two months, and budgeting an identical spending allowance in each country. To help work toward your goal, you want to create a worksheet that calculates the amount of native currency you will have in each country. You want the workbook to reflect the currency information for each country.

a. Start Excel, then save a new, blank workbook as **World Tour Budget** to the drive and folder where you store your Data Files.

b. Think of seven countries you would like to visit, then enter column and row labels for your worksheet. (*Hint*: You may wish to include row labels for each country, plus column labels for the country, the $1 equivalent in native currency, the total amount of native currency you'll have in each country, and the name of each country's monetary unit.)

c. Decide how much money you want to bring to each country (for example, $1000), and enter that in the worksheet.

d. Use your favorite search engine to find your own information sources on currency conversions for the countries you plan to visit.

e. Enter the cash equivalent to **$1** in U.S. dollars for each country in your list. Also include the name of the currency used in each country.

f. Create an equation that calculates the amount of native currency you will have in each country, using an absolute cell reference in the formula.

▼ REAL LIFE INDEPENDENT CHALLENGE (CONTINUED)

g. Format the entries in column B with three decimal places and in column C with two decimal places, using the correct currency unit for each country. (*Hint*: Use the Number tab in the Format cells dialog box; choose the appropriate currency format from the Symbol list, using two decimal places.)

h. Create a conditional format that changes the font attributes of the calculated amount in the "$1,000 US" column to bold and red if the amount exceeds **500 units** of the local currency.

i. Merge and center the title over the column headings.

j. Add any formatting attributes to the column headings, and resize the columns as necessary.

k. Add a background color to the title.

Advanced Challenge Exercise

■ Modify the conditional format in the "$1,000 US" column so that entries between 1500 and 3999 display in red, boldface type, and entries above 4000 appear in blue, boldface type.

■ Delete all the unused sheets in the workbook.

■ Save your work as **World Tour Budget ACE** where you store your Data Files.

■ If you have access to an e-mail account, e-mail this workbook to your instructor as an attachment.

l. Enter your name in the header of the worksheet.

m. Spell check, save, preview and compare your work to Figure C-32, then print the worksheet.

n. Close the workbook and exit Excel.

FIGURE C-32

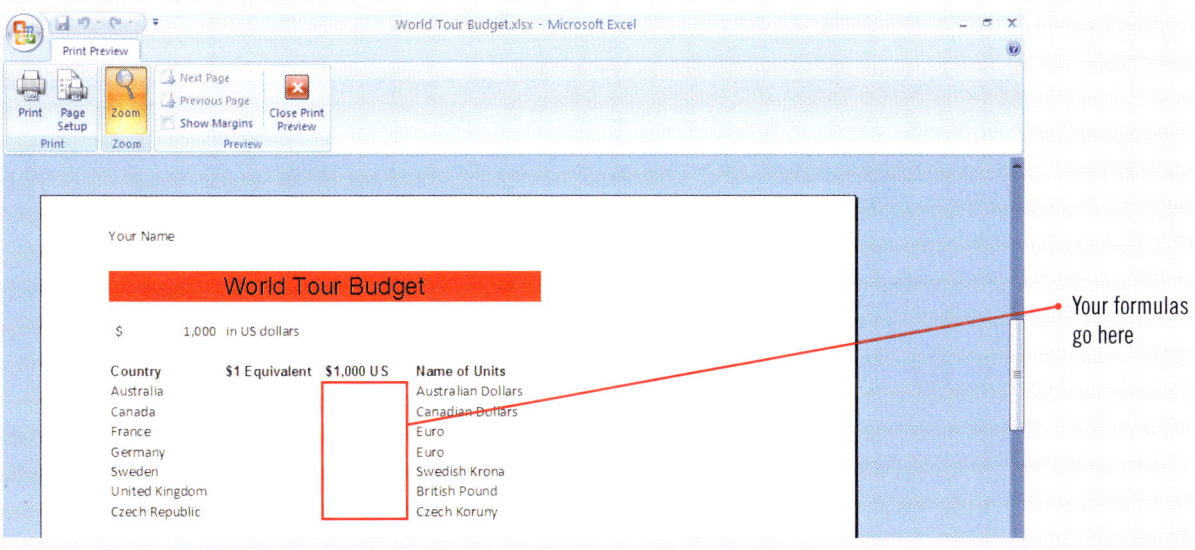

Your formulas go here

▼ VISUAL WORKSHOP

Open the file EX C-5.xlsx from the drive and folder where you store your Data Files, then save it as **Top Notch Personnel**. Use the skills you learned in this unit to format the worksheet so it looks like the one shown in Figure C-33. Create a conditional format in the Level column so that entries greater than 3 appear in red text. Create an additional conditional format in the Review Cycle column so that any value equal to 4 appears in green bold text. Replace the Accounting department label with Legal. (*Hint*: The only additional font used in this exercise is 16-point Times New Roman in row 1.) Enter your name in cell A25, check the spelling in the worksheet, then save and print your work.

FIGURE C-33

Employee Name	Hire Date	Department	Level	Review Cycle
Anderson, Frank	05/18/92	Legal	4	2
Carlson, Marie	12/16/03	Information Technology	3	4
DiCarlo, Yvonne	03/07/81	Administration	6	1
Farnsworth, William	07/14/96	Administration	4	2
Garrott, Josh	10/03/98	Administration	3	4
Gemsen, Seth	08/12/01	Legal	2	3
Jamison, Jennifer	09/28/81	Marketing	6	3
Kirshner, Violet	01/16/04	Legal	1	1
Martinez, Arturo	04/24/01	Marketing	2	2
Mattingly, Emily	06/20/94	Information Technology	5	2
Stevensburg, Stewart	09/01/04	Information Technology	2	3
Tewksbury, Edith	11/19/96	Marketing	4	4
VanGinhoven, Margaret	04/22/99	Marketing	3	2
Watson, Emily	10/05/89	Information Technology	6	3
Williams, Earl	09/26/00	Marketing	3	3

Working with Charts

Files You Will Need:

EX D-1.xlsx
EX D-2.xlsx
EX D-3.xlsx
EX D-4.xlsx
EX D-5.xlsx
EX D-6.xlsx

Worksheets provide an effective layout for calculating and organizing data, but the grid layout is not always the best format for presenting your work to others. To display information so it's easier to interpret, you can create a chart. **Charts**, often called graphs, present information in a pictorial format, making it easier to see patterns, trends, and relationships. In this unit, you learn how to create a chart, how to edit the chart and change the chart type, how to add text annotations and arrows, and how to preview and print the chart. At the upcoming annual meeting, Grace Wong wants to emphasize a growth trend at Quest Specialty Travel. She asks you to create a chart showing the increase in company revenues over the past four quarters.

OBJECTIVES

Plan a chart
Create a chart
Move and resize a chart
Change the chart design
Change the chart layout
Format a chart
Annotate and draw on a chart
Create a pie chart

Planning a Chart

Before creating a chart, you need to plan the information you want your chart to show and how you want it to look. Planning ahead helps you to decide what type of chart to create and how to organize the data. Understanding the parts of a chart makes it easier to format it and change specific elements so that the chart best illustrates your data. In preparation for creating the chart for Grace's presentation, you identify your goals for the chart and plan it.

DETAILS

Use the following guidelines to plan the chart:

- **Determine the purpose of the chart and identify the data relationships you want to communicate graphically**

  You want to create a chart that shows quarterly revenues throughout Quest Specialty Travel. This worksheet data is shown in Figure D-1. In the first quarter, the Marketing department launched an international advertising campaign. The campaign resulted in greatly increased sales starting in the second quarter. You want to create a chart for the annual meeting that illustrates the increase and compares sales across the quarters for each location.

- **Determine the results you want to see, and decide which chart type is most appropriate**

  Different chart types display data in distinctive ways. For example, a pie chart compares parts to the whole, so it's useful for showing what proportion of a budget amount was spent on print ads relative to what was spent on direct mail or radio commercials. A line chart, in contrast, is best for showing trends over time. To choose the best chart type for your data, you should first decide how you want your data displayed and interpreted. Table D-1 describes several different types of charts you can create in Excel and their corresponding buttons on the Insert tab of the Ribbon. Because you want to compare QST revenues in multiple locations over a period of four quarters, you decide to use a column chart.

- **Identify the worksheet data you want the chart to illustrate**

  Sometimes you use all the data in a worksheet to create a chart, while at other times you may need to select a range within the sheet. The worksheet from which you are creating your chart contains revenue data for the past year. You will need to use all the quarterly data contained in the worksheet.

- **Understand the elements of a chart**

  The chart shown in Figure D-2 contains basic elements of a chart. In the figure, QST locations are on the horizontal axis (also called the **x-axis**) and monthly sales are on the vertical axis (also called the **y-axis**). The horizontal axis is also called the **category axis** because it often contains the names of data groups, such as locations, months, or years. The vertical axis is also called the **value axis** because it often contains numerical values that help you interpret the size of chart elements. (3-D charts also contain a **z-axis**, for comparing data across both categories and values.) The area inside the horizontal and vertical axes is the **plot area**. The **tick marks** at the left edge of the vertical axis and **gridlines** (extending across the plot area) create a scale of measure for each value. Each value in a cell you select for your chart is a **data point**. In any chart, a **data marker** visually represents each data point, which in this case is a column. A collection of related data points is a **data series**. In this chart, there are four data series (Quarter 1, Quarter 2, Quarter 3, and Quarter 4), so you include a **legend** to make it easy to identify them.

FIGURE D-1: Worksheet containing revenue data

FIGURE D-2: Chart elements

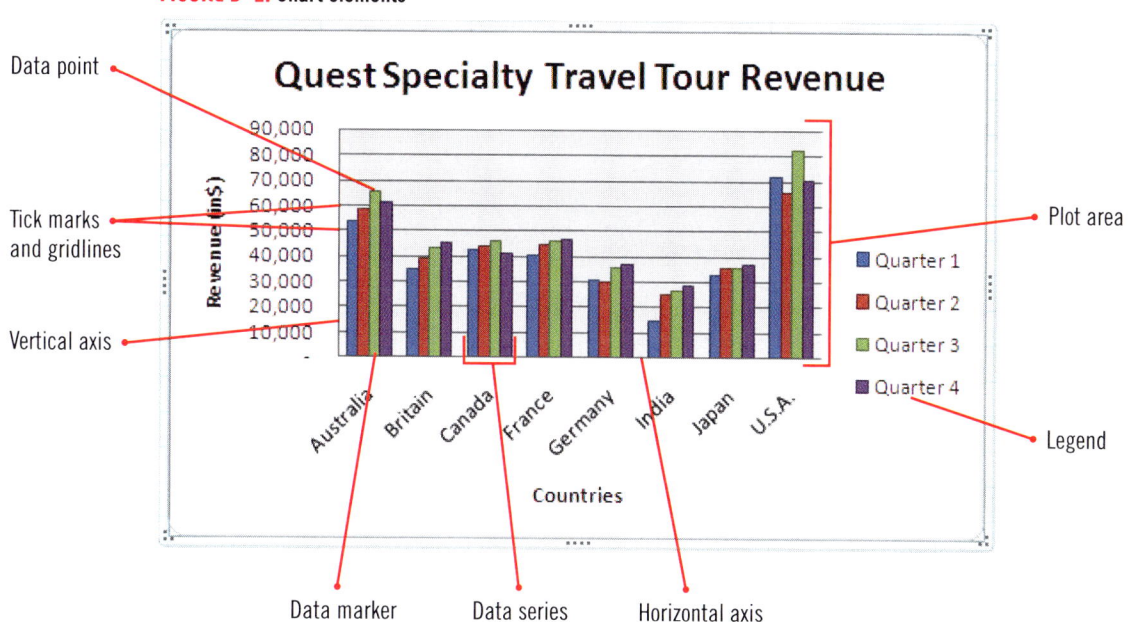

TABLE D-1: Common chart types

type	button	description
Column		Compares distinct object levels using a vertical format; the Excel default; sometimes referred to as a bar chart in other spreadsheet programs
Line		Compares trends over even time intervals; looks similar to an area chart, but does not emphasize total
Pie		Compares sizes of pieces as part of a whole; used for a single series of numbers
Bar		Compares distinct object levels using a horizontal format; sometimes referred to as a horizontal bar chart in other spreadsheet programs
Area		Shows how individual volume changes over time in relation to total volume
Scatter		Compares trends over uneven time or measurement intervals; used in scientific and engineering disciplines for trend spotting and extrapolation

Creating a Chart

To create a chart in Excel, you first select the range in a worksheet containing the data you want to chart. Once you've selected a range, you can use buttons on the Insert tab of the Ribbon to create and modify a chart. Using the worksheet containing the quarterly revenue data, you create a chart that shows the growth trend that occurred.

STEPS

QUICK TIP

When charting data for a particular time period, make sure all series are for the same time period.

1. **Start Excel, open the file EX D-1.xlsx from the drive and folder where you store your Data Files, then save it as** Quarterly Tour Revenue

   You want the chart to include the quarterly tour revenue figures, as well as quarter and country labels. You don't include the Total column and row because the quarterly figures make up the totals, and these figures would skew the chart.

QUICK TIP

To select nonadjacent cells, press and hold [Ctrl] while selecting each range.

2. **Select the range** A4:E12, **then click the** Insert tab **on the Ribbon**

   The Insert tab contains groups for inserting various types of objects, including charts. The Charts group includes buttons for each major chart type, plus an Other Charts button for additional chart types, such as stock charts for charting stock market data.

3. **Click the** Column chart button, **then click the** Clustered Column button **on the Column palette, as shown in Figure D-3**

   The chart is inserted in the center of the worksheet, and three contextual Chart Tools tabs open on the Ribbon: Design, Layout, and Format. On the Design tab, which is currently in front, you can quickly change the chart type, chart layout, and chart format and you can swap the data between the columns and rows. Currently, the countries are charted along the horizontal axis, with the quarterly revenues charted along the y-axis. This lets you easily compare quarterly revenues for each country.

4. **Click the** Switch Row/Column button **in the Data group on the Chart Tools Design tab**

   Clicking this button switches the data in the columns and rows, as shown in Figure D-4, so that the quarterly revenues are charted along the horizontal axis and the countries are plotted as the data points.

5. **Click the** Undo button 🔄 **on the Quick Access toolbar**

   The chart returns to its original configuration.

6. **Click the** Chart Tools Layout tab, **click the** Chart Title button **in the Labels group, then click** Above Chart **on the palette**

   A title placeholder appears above the chart.

QUICK TIP

You can also triple-click to select a line of text.

7. **Click anywhere in the** Chart Title text box, **press [Ctrl][A] to select the text, type** Quarterly Tour Revenue, **then click anywhere in the chart to deselect the title**

   Adding a title helps identify the chart. This chart is known as an **embedded** chart because it's inserted directly in the current worksheet. The **sizing handles**, the small series of dots at the corners and sides of the chart's border, indicate that the chart is selected. See Figure D-5. Your chart might be in a different location on the worksheet and may look slightly different; you will move and resize it in the next lesson. Any time a chart is selected, as it is now, a blue border surrounds the worksheet data range, a purple border surrounds the row labels, and a green border surrounds the column labels. Embedding a chart in the current sheet is the default selection when creating a chart, but you can also place a chart on a different sheet in the workbook, or on a newly created chart sheet. A **chart sheet** is a sheet in a workbook that contains only a chart, which is linked to the workbook data.

8. **Save your work**

FIGURE D-3: Column chart palette

Clustered Column chart type

Column chart types

FIGURE D-4: Clustered Column chart with rows and columns switched

Undo button

Switch Row/Column button

Column labels

Row labels

Data range

Selected chart object

Chart Tools tabs

Legend

Quarter labels on horizontal axis

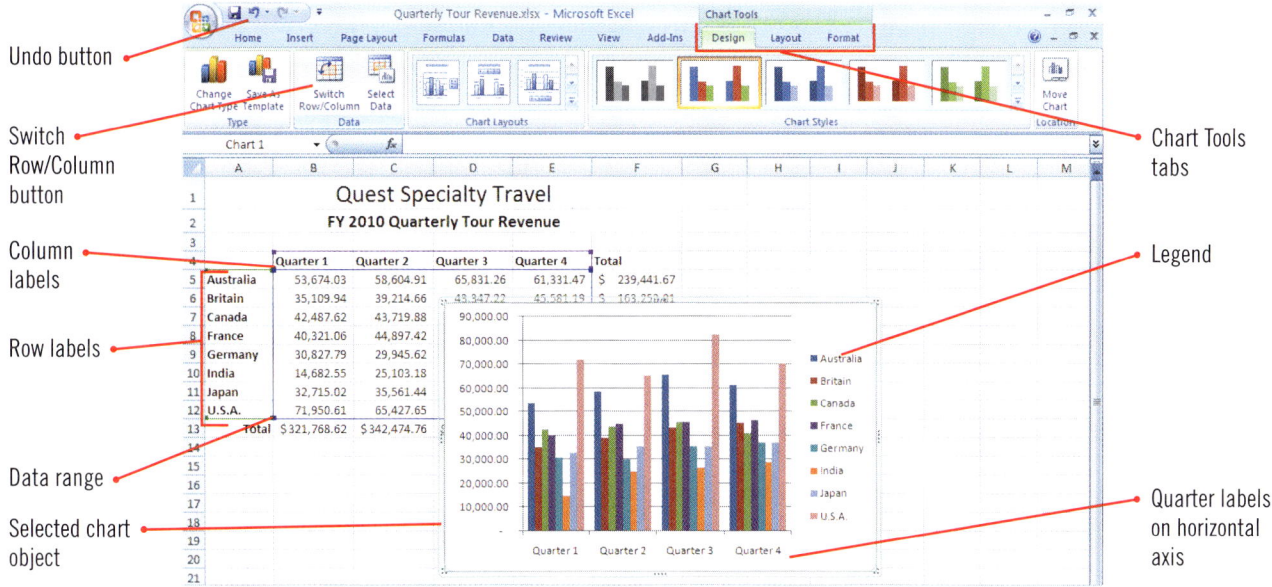

FIGURE D-5: Chart with rows and columns restored and title added

Title

Sizing handles

Country labels on horizontal axis

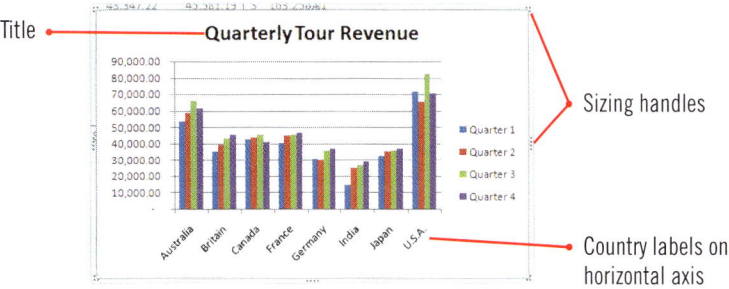

Using the contextual Chart Tools tabs

When a chart is selected, the three contextual Chart Tools tabs (Design, Layout, and Format) appear on the Ribbon. These tabs help guide you through developing and perfecting your chart. Using the Design tab, you can change overall color schemes and positioning of objects within the chart as well as the data range and configuration used for the chart. The Layout tab is used to add and modify chart elements, such as titles and labels, and for adding graphics, such as pictures, shapes, and text boxes. The Format tab lets you format objects such as shapes and text, arrange multiple objects so they are layered attractively, and resize any object to exact specifications. While these tabs organize chart tools in a logical order, it is not necessary to use them in the order in which they appear. In other words, you can jump from the Design tab to the Format tab, back to Design, then to Layout, if you wish.

Moving and Resizing a Chart

Charts are graphics, or drawn objects, and are not located in a specific cell or at a specific range address. An **object** is an independent element on a worksheet. You can select an object by clicking within its borders; sizing handles around the object indicate it is selected. You can move a selected chart object anywhere on a worksheet without affecting formulas or data in the worksheet. However, any data changed in the worksheet is automatically updated in the chart. You can resize a chart to improve its appearance by dragging its sizing handles. You can even move a chart to a different sheet, and it will still reflect the original data. Chart objects contain other objects, such as a title and legend, which you can move and resize. In addition to repositioning chart elements to set locations using commands on the Layout tab, you can freely move any object using the mouse. Simply select it, then drag it or cut and paste it to a new location. When the mouse pointer hovers over any chart object, the name of the selected object appears on screen as a ScreenTip. You want to resize the chart, position it below the worksheet data, and move the legend.

STEPS

1. **Make sure the chart is still selected, then position the pointer over the chart**

   The pointer shape ⌖ indicates that you can move the chart object or use a sizing handle to resize it. For a table of commonly used graphic object pointers, refer to Table D-2.

QUICK TIP

If you want to delete a chart, select it, then press [Delete].

2. **Position ⌖ on a blank area near the top left edge of the chart, press and hold the left mouse button, drag the chart until its upper left corner is at the upper left corner of cell A16, then release the mouse button**

   As you drag the chart, you can see an outline representing the chart's perimeter. The chart appears in the new location.

TROUBLE

If you do not drag a blank area on the chart, you might inadvertently move a chart element instead of the whole chart; if this happens, undo the action and try again.

3. **Position the pointer on the right-middle sizing handle until it changes to ⟷, then drag the right edge of the chart to the right edge of column G**

   The chart is widened. See Figure D-6.

4. **Position the pointer over the upper-middle sizing handle until it changes to ↕, then drag it to the top edge of row 15**

QUICK TIP

To resize a chart object to exact specification, select the object, click the Chart Tools Format tab on the Ribbon, then enter the desired height and width in the Size group.

5. **Scroll down if necessary so row 26 is visible, position the pointer over the lower-middle sizing handle until it changes to ↕, then drag the bottom border of the chart to the bottom border of row 26**

   You can move any object on a chart. You want to align the top of the legend with the top of the plot area.

QUICK TIP

Although the sizing handles on objects within a chart look different from the sizing handles that surround a chart, they function the same way.

6. **Click the legend to select it, press and hold [Shift], drag the legend up using ⌖ so the dotted outline is approximately ¼" above the top of the plot area, then release [Shift]**

   When you click the legend, sizing handles appear around it and "Legend" appears as a ScreenTip when the pointer hovers over the object. As you drag, a dotted outline of the legend border appears. Pressing and holding the [Shift] key holds the horizontal position of the legend as you move it vertically.

7. **Click cell A12, type United States, click the Enter button ✓ on the formula bar, use AutoFit to resize column A, then press [Ctrl][Home]**

   The axis label changes to reflect the updated cell contents, as shown in Figure D-7. Changing any data in the worksheet modifies corresponding text or values in the chart. Because the chart is no longer selected, the Chart Tools tabs no longer appear on the Ribbon.

8. **Save your work**

FIGURE D-6: Moved and resized chart

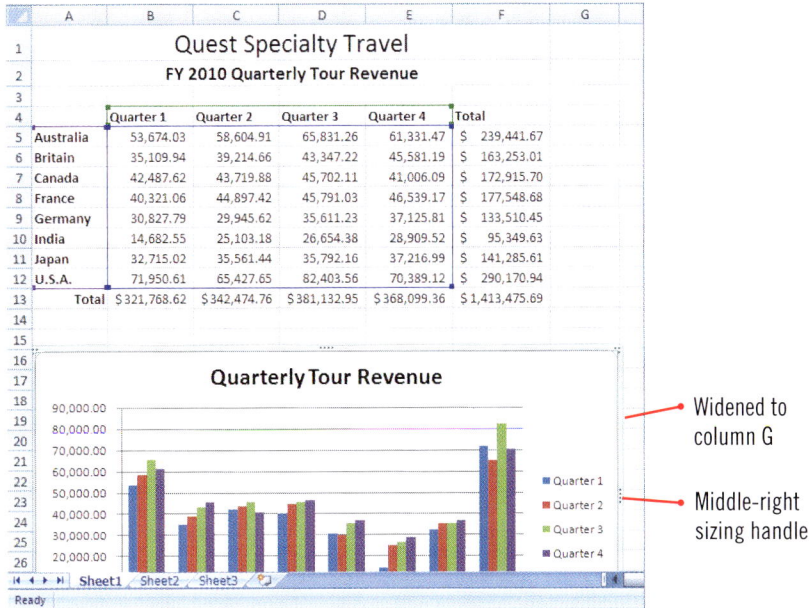

Widened to column G

Middle-right sizing handle

FIGURE D-7: Worksheet with modified legend and label

Modified text

Plot area

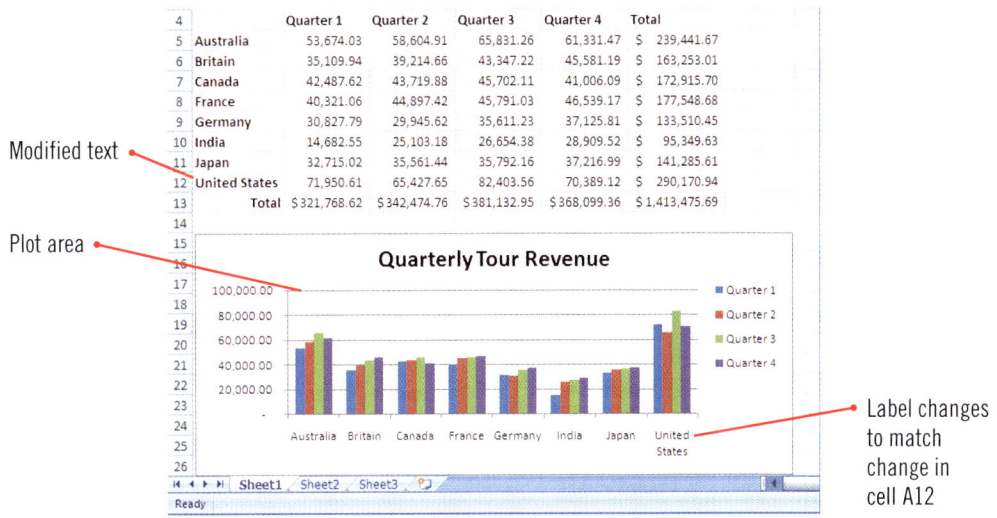

Label changes to match change in cell A12

TABLE D-2: Common graphic object pointers

name	pointer	use	name	pointer	use
Diagonal resizing	⤢ or ⤡	Change chart shape	I-beam	I	Edit chart text from corners
Draw	+	Create shapes	Move chart	✛	Change chart location
Horizontal resizing	⇐	Change chart shape from left to right	Vertical resizing	↕	Change chart shape from top to bottom

Moving an embedded chart to a sheet

Suppose you have created an embedded chart that you decide would look better on a chart sheet. You can make this change without recreating the entire chart. To do so, first select the chart, click the Chart Tools Design tab, then click the Move Chart button in the Location group. The Move Chart dialog box opens. If the chart is embedded, click the New sheet option button, then click OK. If the chart is on its own sheet, click the Object in option button, then click OK.

Changing the Chart Design

Once you've created a chart, it's easy to modify the design. You can change data values in the worksheet, and the chart is automatically updated to reflect the new data. Each of the Chart Tools tabs can be used to make specific changes in a chart. Using the Chart Tools Design tab, you can change the chart type in the Type group, modify the data range and configuration in the Data group, change the layout of objects in the Chart Layouts group, choose from coordinating color schemes in the Chart Styles group, and move the location of the chart in the Location group. The layouts in the Chart Styles group offer preconfigured arrangements of objects in your chart, such as a legend, title, or gridlines; these layouts offer an alternative to manually making formatting and design changes. ![icon] You look over your worksheet and realize the data for the United States in Quarter 2 and Quarter 4 is incorrect. After you correct this data, you want to see how the same data looks using different chart layouts and types.

STEPS

1. **Click cell C12, type 75432.29, press [Tab] twice, type 84295.27, then press [Enter]**
   In the worksheet, the United States entries for Quarter 2 and Quarter 4 reflect the increased sales figures. See Figure D-8. The totals in column F and row 13 are also updated.

QUICK TIP
You can see more layout choices by clicking the More button in the Chart Layouts group.

2. **Select the chart by clicking a blank area within the chart border, click the Chart Tools Design tab on the Ribbon, then click the Layout 3 button in the Chart Layouts group**
   The legend moves to the bottom of the chart. You prefer the original layout.

3. **Click the Undo button ↺ on the Quick Access toolbar, then click the Change Chart Type button in the Type group**
   The Change Chart Type dialog box opens, as shown in Figure D-9, where you can choose from all available chart type categories and types. The left pane lists the available categories, and the right pane shows the individual chart types. An orange border surrounds the currently selected chart type.

QUICK TIP
If you plan to print a chart on a black-and-white printer, you may wish to change to a black-and-white chart style, so you can see how the output will look as you work.

4. **Click Bar in the left pane of the Change Chart Type dialog box, confirm that the Clustered Bar chart type is selected, then click OK**
   The column chart changes to a clustered bar chart. See Figure D-10. You look at the bar chart, then decide to see if the large increase in sales is more apparent if you use a three-dimensional column chart.

5. **Click the Change Chart Type button in the Type group, click Column in the left pane of the Change Chart Type dialog box, click 3-D Clustered Column (fourth from the left in the first row), then click OK**
   A three-dimensional column chart appears. You notice that the three-dimensional column format is more crowded than the two-dimensional format, but it gives you a sense of volume.

QUICK TIP
You can also use the Undo button on the Quick Access toolbar to return to a previous chart type.

6. **Click the Change Chart Type button in the Type group, click the Clustered Column button (first from the left, first row), then click OK**

7. **Click the Style 3 button in the Chart Styles group**
   The columns change to shades of blue. You prefer the previous color scheme.

8. **Click ↺ in the Quick Access toolbar, then save your work**

Creating a Combination Chart

You can apply a chart type to an existing data series in a chart, to create a combination chart. In the existing chart, select the data series that you want plotted on a secondary axis, then open the Format dialog box (use the shortcut menu, or click Format Selection in the Current Selection group of the Format tab on the Ribbon). In the Format dialog box, click Series Options, if necessary, click the Secondary Axis option button under Plot Series On, then click Close. Click the Layout tab on the Ribbon, click Axes in the Axes group, then click the type of secondary axis you want and where you want it to appear. To finish, click the Change Chart Type button in the Type group on the Design tab, then select a chart type for the secondary axis.

FIGURE D-8: Worksheet with modified data

Modified data

Adjusted data points

FIGURE D-9: Change Chart Type dialog box

Currently selected chart type

Bar category

Chart type categories

FIGURE D-10: Column chart changed to bar chart

Change Chart Type button

Move Chart button

Click More button to see additional chart layouts

Working with a 3-D chart

Excel includes true 3-D chart types as well as chart types formatted in 3-D. In a true 3-D chart, a third axis, called the **z-axis**, lets you compare data points across both categories and values. The z-axis runs along the depth of the chart, so it appears to advance from the back of the chart. To create a true 3-D chart, look for chart subtypes that begin with "3-D," such as 3-D Column. Charts that are formatted in 3-D contain only two axes but their graphics give the illusion of three-dimensionality. For example, the Clustered Column in 3-D chart displays columns in a 3-D format, but does not include a z-axis that you can modify. To create a chart that is only formatted in 3-D, look for chart subtypes that end with "in 3-D." In a 3-D chart, other data series in the same chart can sometimes obscure columns or bars, but you can rotate the chart to obtain a better view. Right-click the chart, then click 3-D Rotation. The Format Chart Area dialog box opens, with the 3-D Rotation category active. This dialog box can also be used to modify fill, line, line style, shadow, and 3-D format. The 3-D Rotation options let you choose the orientation and perspective of the chart area, plot area, walls, and floor for a 3-D chart. You can use these rotation options to improve the appearance of plotted data within a chart. The 3-D Format options let you choose what three-dimensional effects you would like to apply to select chart elements. (Not all 3-D Format options are available on all charts.)

Changing the Chart Layout

Changing chart layout involves adding, removing, and modifying individual chart elements such as the chart title, plot area, gridlines, and data series. While the Chart Tools Design tab includes preconfigured chart layouts you can apply, the Chart Tools Layout tab makes it easy to create and modify individual chart objects. Using buttons on this tab, you can also add shapes and additional text to a chart, add and modify labels, change the display of axes, and modify the fill behind the plot area. You can also eliminate or change the look of gridlines. **Gridlines** are the horizontal and vertical lines in the chart that enable the eye to follow the value on an axis. You can create titles for the horizontal and vertical axes, add graphics, or add background color. You can even format the text you use in a chart. You want to make some layout changes in the chart, to make sure it's easy to interpret and improve its general appearance.

STEPS

QUICK TIP

The Chart Tools tabs appear on the Ribbon only when a chart or one of its objects is selected.

1. **With the chart still selected, click the Chart Tools Layout tab on the Ribbon, click the Gridlines button in the Axes group, point to Primary Horizontal Gridlines, then click None**

   The gridlines that extend from the value axis tick marks across the chart's plot area are removed from the chart, as shown in Figure D-11.

2. **Click the Gridlines button in the Axes group, point to Primary Horizontal Gridlines, then click Major & Minor Gridlines**

   Both major and minor gridlines now appear in the chart. **Minor gridlines** show the values between the tick marks. You can change the color of the columns to better distinguish the data series.

3. **Click the Axis Titles button in the Labels group, point to Primary Horizontal Axis Title, click Title Below Axis, triple-click the axis title, then type Tour Countries**

   Descriptive text on the category axis helps readers understand the chart.

QUICK TIP

You can also edit text in a chart element by positioning the pointer over the selected text box until it changes to ⊥, click the text box, then edit the text.

4. **Click the Axis Titles button in the Labels group, point to Primary Vertical Axis Title, then click Rotated Title**

   A placeholder for the vertical axis title is added to the left of the vertical axis.

5. **Triple-click the vertical axis title, then type Revenue (in $)**

   The text "Revenue (in $)" appears to the left of the vertical axis, as shown in Figure D-12.

QUICK TIP

You can move any title to a new position by clicking an edge of the object then dragging it.

6. **Right-click the horizontal axis labels ("Australia", "Britain", etc.), click the Font list on the Mini toolbar, click Times New Roman, click the Font Size list on the Mini toolbar, then click 8**

   The font of the horizontal axis text changes to Times New Roman, and the font size decreases, making more of the plot area visible.

7. **Right-click the vertical axis labels, click the Font list on the Mini toolbar, click Times New Roman, click the Font Size list on the Mini toolbar, then click 8**

8. **Right-click the chart title ("Quarterly Tour Revenue"), click Format Chart Title on the shortcut menu, click Border Color in the left pane, then click the Solid line option button in the right pane**

   Adding a solid border is the first step to creating a shadow box that surrounds the title. You can only add a shadow to a text box that has a border.

9. **Click Shadow in the left pane, click the Presets list arrow, click the Offset Diagonal Bottom Right (first row, first from the left) style in the Outer group, click Close, then save your work**

   A border with a drop shadow surrounds the title. Compare your work to Figure D-13.

FIGURE D-11: Gridlines removed from chart

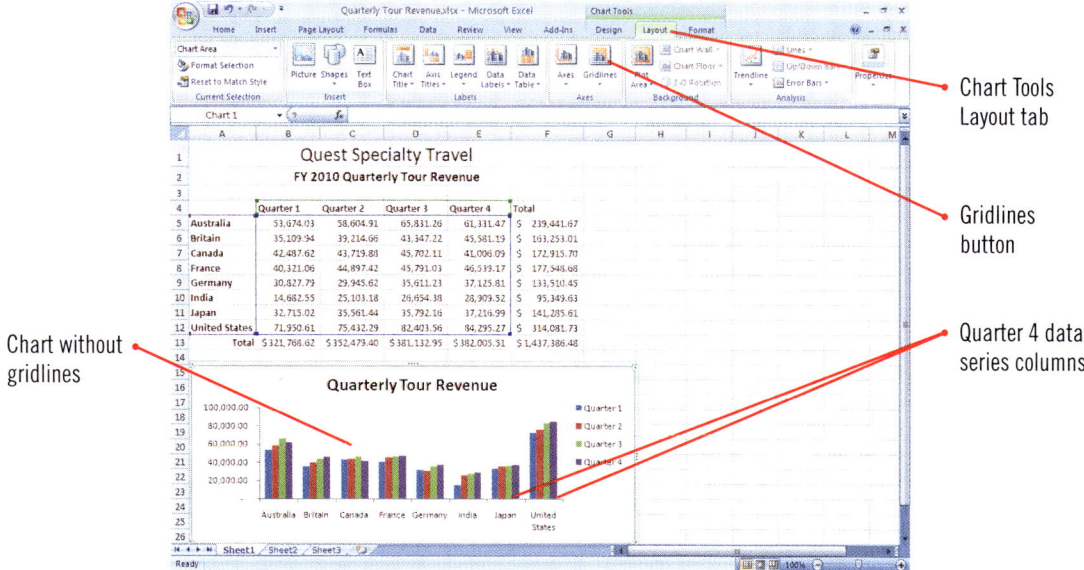

Chart Tools Layout tab

Gridlines button

Quarter 4 data series columns

Chart without gridlines

FIGURE D-12: Axes titles added to chart

Chart Elements list arrow

Axis Titles button

Vertical axis title

Vertical axis labels

Chart title

Horizontal axis labels

Horizontal axis title

FIGURE D-13: Enhanced chart

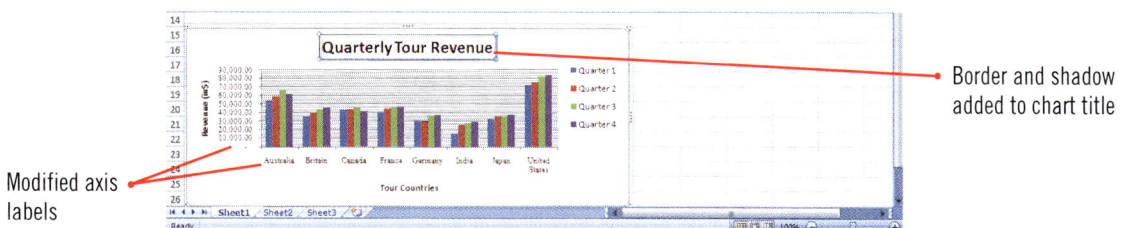

Modified axis labels

Border and shadow added to chart title

Adding data labels to a chart

There are times when your audience might benefit by seeing data labels on a chart. These labels can indicate the series name, category name, and/or the value of one or more data points. Once your chart is selected, you can add this information to your chart by clicking the Data Labels button in the Labels group in the Chart Tools Layout tab on the Ribbon. Once you have added the data labels, you can apply formatting to them or delete individual data labels. Delete individual data labels by clicking them until handles surround the set you want to delete, then press [Delete].

Formatting a Chart

Formatting a chart can make it easier to read and understand. Many formatting enhancements can be made using the Chart Tools Format tab. You can change colors in a specific data series or you can apply a style to a series using the Shape Styles group. Styles make it possible to apply multiple formats, such as an outline, fill color, and text color, all with a single click. You can also make individual selections of fill color, outline, and other effects using the Shape Styles group. WordArt, which lets you create curved or stylized text, can be created using the WordArt Styles group. You want to improve the appearance of the chart by creating titles for the horizontal and vertical axes and adding a drop shadow to the chart title.

STEPS

1. **With the chart selected, click the Chart Tools Format tab on the Ribbon, then click any column in the Quarter 4 data series**

   The Chart Tools Format tab opens, and handles surround each column in the Quarter 4 data series, indicating that the entire series is selected.

2. **Click the Format Selection button in the Current Selection group**

3. **Click Fill in the left pane of the Format Data Series dialog box, then click the Solid fill option button**

4. **Click the Color list arrow, click Orange, Accent 6 (first row, tenth from the left) as shown in Figure D-14, then click Close**

   All the columns for the series become orange, and the legend changes to match the new color. You can also change the color of selected objects by applying a shape style.

5. **Click any column in the Quarter 3 data series**

   Handles surround each column in the Quarter 3 data series.

6. **Click the More button on the Shape Styles gallery, then hover the pointer over the Moderate Effect – Accent 3 button (fifth row, fourth from the left) as shown in Figure D-15**

7. **Click the Subtle Effect – Accent 3 button (fourth row, fourth from the left) in the palette**

   The color for the data series changes, as shown in Figure D-16.

8. **Save your work**

Changing alignment in axis text and titles

The buttons on the Chart Tools Layout tab provide a few options for aligning axis text and titles, but you can customize the position and rotation to exact specifications using the Format dialog box. You can modify the alignment of axis text to make it fit better within the plot area. With a chart selected, right-click the axis text you want to modify, then click Format Axis on the shortcut menu. The Format Axis dialog box opens for the selected element. Click Alignment, then select the appropriate option. You can create a custom angle by clicking the Text direction list arrow, clicking Horizontal, then selecting the number of degrees from the Custom angle text box. When you have made the desired changes, click Close.

FIGURE D-14: Format Data Series dialog box

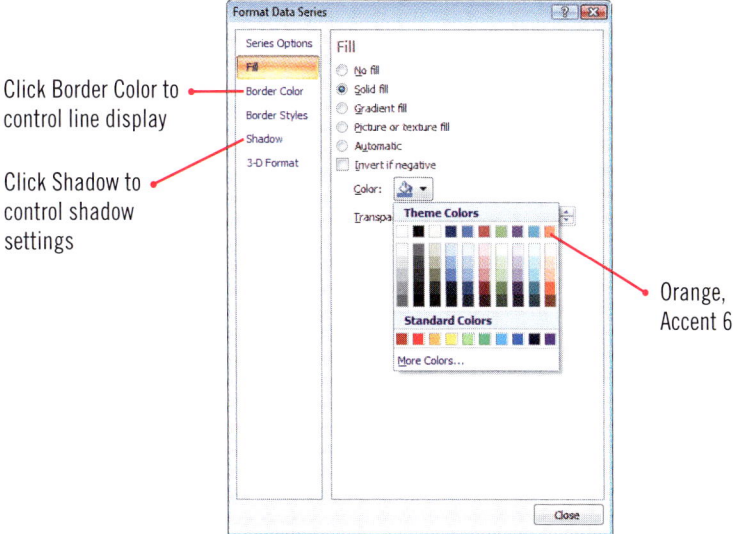

Click Border Color to control line display

Click Shadow to control shadow settings

Orange, Accent 6

FIGURE D-15: Chart with formatted data series

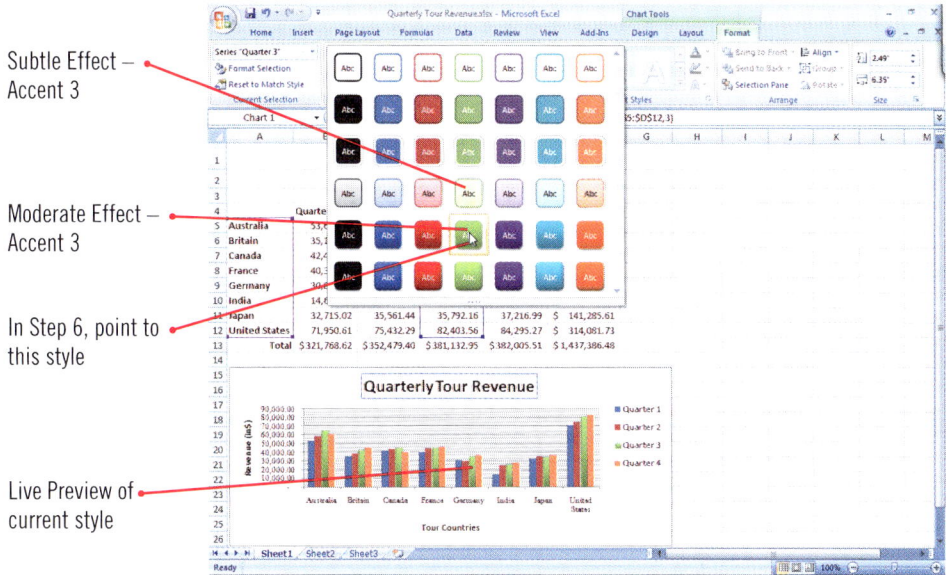

Subtle Effect – Accent 3

Moderate Effect – Accent 3

In Step 6, point to this style

Live Preview of current style

FIGURE D-16: Color of data series changed

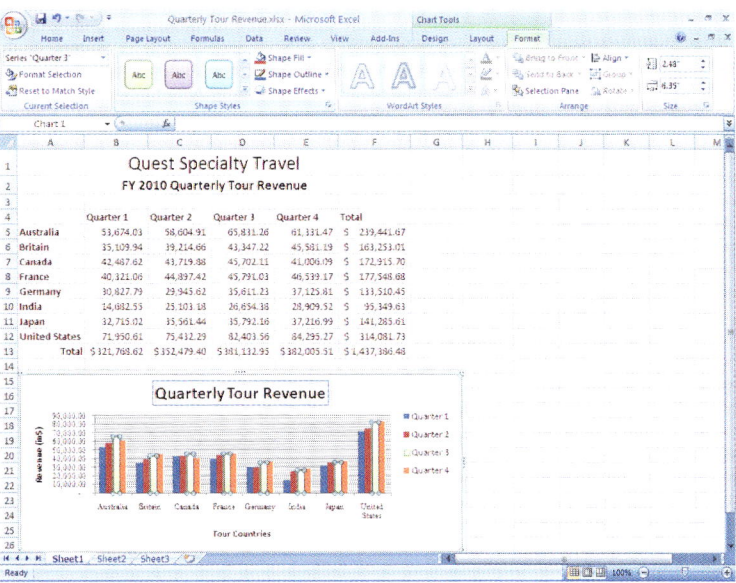

Annotating and Drawing on a Chart

You can add text annotations and graphics to a chart to point out critical information. **Text annotations** are labels that further describe your data. You can also draw lines and arrows that point to the exact locations you want to emphasize. Shapes such as arrows and boxes can be added from the Illustrations group on the Insert tab or from the Insert group on the Chart Tools Layout group on the Ribbon. These groups are also used to Insert pictures and clip art. 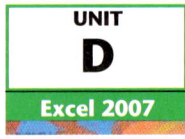 You want to call attention to the India tour revenue increases, so you decide to add a text annotation and an arrow to this information in the chart.

STEPS

1. **Make sure the chart is selected, click the Chart Tools Layout tab, click the Text Box button in the Insert group, then move the pointer over the worksheet**
   The pointer changes to ↧, indicating that you can begin typing text by clicking.

QUICK TIP
You can also insert text by clicking the Text Box button in the Text group in the Insert tab.

2. **Click to the right of the chart (anywhere *outside* the chart boundary)**
   A text box is added to the worksheet, and the Drawing Tools Format tab opens, so that you can format the new object. First you need to type the text.

3. **Type Great improvement**
   The text appears in a selected text box on the worksheet and the chart is no longer selected, as shown in Figure D-17. Your text box may be in a different location; this is not important, because you'll move the annotation in the next step.

4. **Point to an edge of the text box so that the pointer changes to ⁺⁺⃗, drag the text box into the chart to the left of the chart title, as shown in Figure D-18, then release the mouse button**
   You want to add a simple arrow shape in the chart.

QUICK TIP
To annotate a chart, you can also use the Callouts category of the Shapes palette in either the Illustrations group on the Insert tab or the Insert group on the Chart Tools Layout tab.

5. **Click the chart to select it, click the Chart Tools Layout tab, click the Shapes button in the Insert group, click the Arrow shape in the Lines category, then move the pointer over the chart**
   The pointer changes to ┼, and the status bar displays "Click and drag to insert an AutoShape." When you draw an arrow, the point farthest from where you start has the arrowhead. When ┼ is near the text box handles, the handles turn red. The red handles act as an anchor for the arrow.

6. **Position ┼ at the red square to the right of the t in the word "improvement" (in the text box), press and hold the left mouse button, drag the line to the Quarter 2 column in the India series, then release the mouse button**
   An arrow points to India's second quarter revenue, and the Drawing Tools Format tab displays options for working with this new object. You can resize, format, or delete it just like any other object in a chart.

7. **Click the Shape Outline list arrow in the Shape Styles group, point to Weight, then click 1½ pt**
   Compare your finished chart to Figure D-19.

8. **Save your work**

FIGURE D-17: Text box added

Drawing Tools
Format tab

Text
annotation

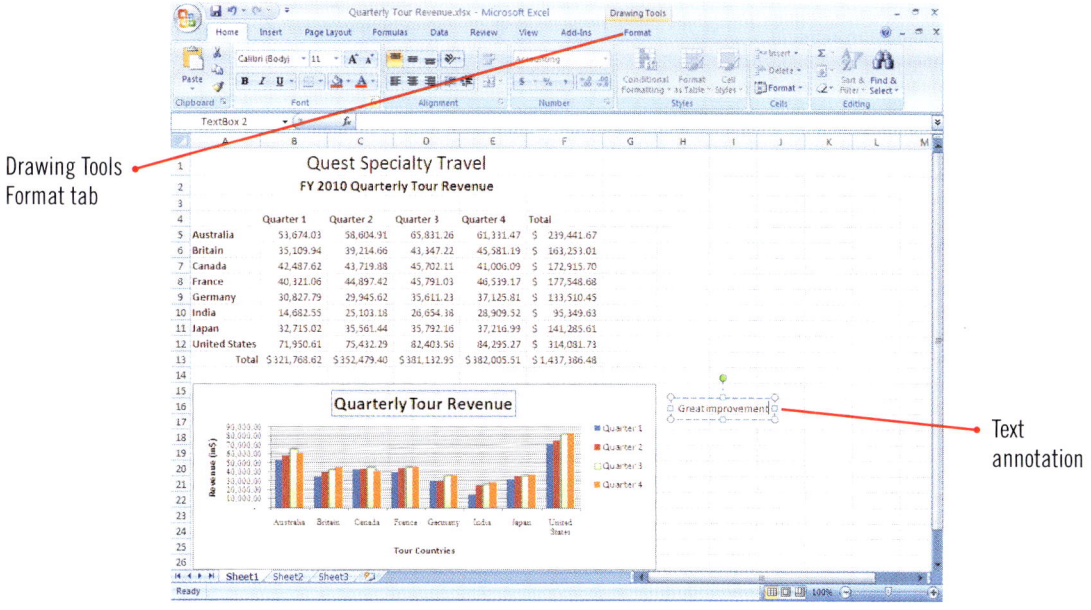

FIGURE D-18: Text annotation on chart

Text annotation

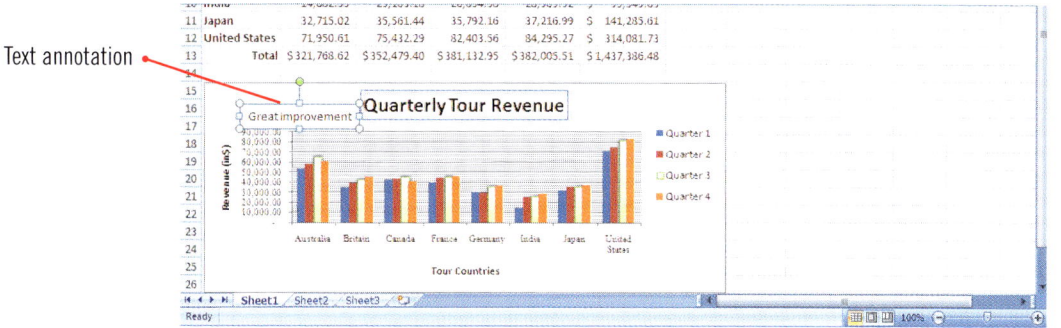

FIGURE D-19: Drawn object added to chart

Arrow added and
formatted

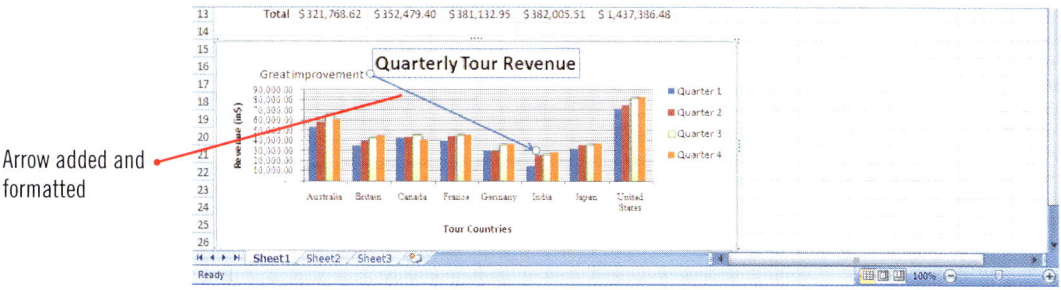

Adding SmartArt graphics

In addition to charts, annotations, and drawn objects, you can create a variety of diagrams using SmartArt. Diagram types include List, Process, Cycle, Hierarchy, Relationship, Matrix, and Pyramid. To insert SmartArt, click the SmartArt button in the Illustrations group on the Insert tab on the Ribbon. Click the category of SmartArt you want to create from the left panel, then click the style from the center panel. The right panel shows a sample of the selection you've chosen, as shown in Figure D-20. The diagram appears on the worksheet as an embedded object with sizing handles. An additional window opens where you can enter the diagram text.

FIGURE D-20: Choose a SmartArt Graphic dialog box

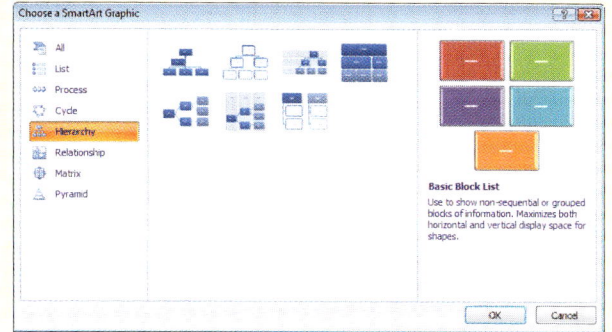

Creating a Pie Chart

You can create multiple charts based on the same worksheet data. While a column chart may illustrate certain important aspects of your worksheet data, you may find you want to create an additional chart to emphasize a different point. Depending on the type of chart you create, you have additional options for calling attention to trends and patterns. For example, if you create a pie chart, you can emphasize one data point by **exploding**, or pulling that slice away from, the pie chart. When you're ready to print a chart, you can preview it just as you do a worksheet, to check the output before committing it to paper. You can print a chart by itself or as part of the worksheet. 🎨 At an upcoming meeting, Grace plans to discuss the total tour revenue and which countries need improvement. You want to create a pie chart she can use to illustrate total revenue. Finally, you want to print the worksheet and the charts.

STEPS

> **QUICK TIP**
> The Exploded Pie in 3-D button creates a pie chart in which all slices are exploded.

1. **Select the range A5:A12, press and hold [Ctrl], select the range F5:F12, click the Insert tab, click the Pie button in the Charts group, then click the Pie in 3-D button in the gallery**

    The new chart appears in the center of the worksheet. You can move the chart and quickly format it using a Chart Layout.

2. **Drag the chart so its top left corner is at the top left corner of cell G1, then click the Layout 2 button in the Chart Layouts group**

> **QUICK TIP**
> If the Format Data Series command displays instead of Format Data Point, double-click the data point for the slice you want exploded before right-clicking.

3. **Click the slice for the India data point, click again so it is the only data point selected, right-click, then click Format Data Point**

    The Format Data Point dialog box opens, as shown in Figure D-21. You can use the Point Explosion slider to control the distance a pie slice moves or you can type a value in the Point Explosion text box.

4. **Double-click 0 in the Point Explosion text box, type 40, then click Close**

    Compare your chart to Figure D-22. You decide to preview the chart and data before you print.

5. **Drag the bottom edge of the chart so it is close to the top of row 15, if necessary**

6. **Click cell A1, switch to Page Layout view, type Your Name in the left-hand header box, then click cell A1**

    You decide the chart and data would fit better on the page if they were printed in **landscape** orientation—that is, with the text running the long way on the page.

7. **Click the Page Layout tab, click the Orientation button in the Page Setup group, then click Landscape**

> **QUICK TIP**
> To preview only a chart, select the chart, click the Office button 🔵, point to Print, then click Print Preview.

8. **Open the Print Preview window, click the Page Setup button on the Print Preview tab, click the Fit to option button, make sure the contents are set to fit to 1 page wide by 1 page tall, then click OK**

    The data and chart are positioned horizontally on a single page. See Figure D-23. The printer you have selected may affect the appearance of your preview screen, and if you do not have a color printer installed, the image will appear in black & white.

9. **Click the Print button on the Print Preview tab, print one copy of the page, save and close the workbook, then exit Excel**

FIGURE D-21: Format Data Point dialog box

Point Explosion slider

Point Explosion text box

FIGURE D-22: Exploded pie slice

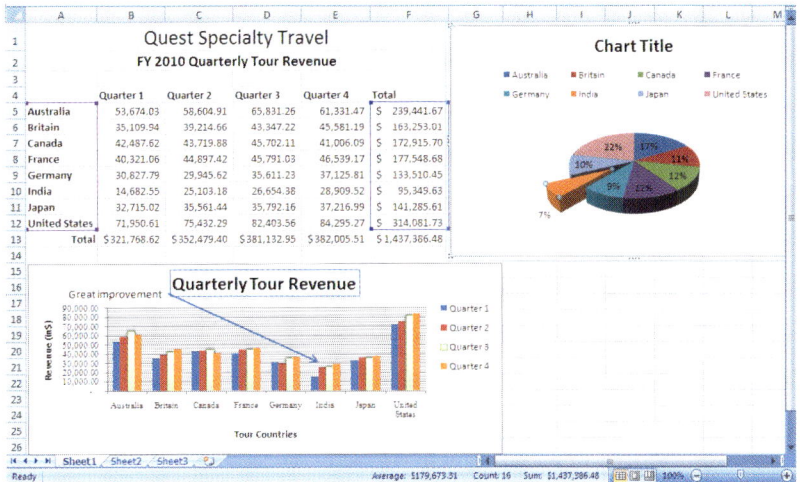

FIGURE D-23: Landscape view of completed charts

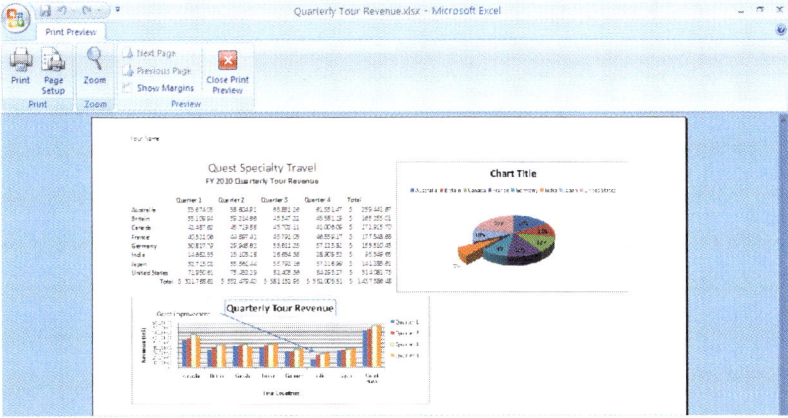

Using the Page Setup dialog box for a chart

When a chart is selected (or a chart sheet is active) and the Print Preview window is open, you can make modifications by clicking Page Setup in the Print group on the Print Preview tab. The Page Setup dialog box does not display all the options normally available. For example, the Center on page options (in the Margins tab) are not always available, and the Scaling options (in the Page tab) are grayed out.

You can also use the Show Margins checkbox in the Preview group of the Print Preview tab to accurately position a chart on the page. Margin lines appear on the screen and show you exactly how the margins appear on the page. The exact placement appears in the status bar when you press and hold the mouse button on the margin line. You can drag the lines to the exact settings you want.

Practice

▼ CONCEPTS REVIEW

Label each element of the Excel chart shown in Figure D-24.

FIGURE D-24

Handwritten annotations:
- 1 — column label
- 2 — Row label
- 3 — Title
- 6 — text annotation
- 5 — legend
- 4 — horizontal axis title

The chart spreadsheet shows "Quest Specialty Travel", "FY 2010 Quarterly Tour Revenue" with a column chart titled "Quarterly Tour Revenue" and text annotation "Great improvement".

	Quarter 1	Quarter 2	Quarter 3	Quarter 4	Total
Australia	53,674.03	58,604.91	65,831.26	61,331.47	$ 239,441.67
Britain	35,109.94	39,214.66	43,347.22	45,581.19	$ 163,253.01
Canada	42,487.62	43,719.88	45,702.11	41,006.09	$ 172,915.70
France	40,321.06	44,897.42	45,791.03	46,539.17	$ 177,548.68
Germany	30,827.79	29,945.62	35,611.23	37,125.81	$ 133,510.45
India	14,682.55	25,103.18	26,654.38	28,909.52	$ 95,349.63
Japan	32,715.02	35,561.44	35,792.16	37,216.99	$ 141,285.61
United States	71,950.61	75,432.29	82,403.56	84,295.27	$ 314,081.73
Total	$321,768.62	$352,479.40	$381,132.95	$382,005.51	$1,437,386.48

Match each chart type with the statement that best describes it.

7. Line   A
8. Pie   e
9. Area   b
10. Column   c
11. Combination   d

a. Compares trends over even time intervals
b. Shows how volume changes over time
c. Compares data over time the Excel default
d. Displays a column and line chart using different scales of measurement
e. Compares data as parts of a whole

Select the best answer from the list of choices.

12. **Which tab on the Ribbon do you use to create a chart?**

    a. Design

    b. Insert

    c. Page Layout

    d. Format

13. **Which tab appears only when a chart is selected?**

    a. Insert

    b. Chart Tools Format

    c. Review

    d. Page Layout

14. **Which pointer do you use to resize a chart object?**

    a. +

    b. I

    c. ↓

    d. ↕

15. **How do you move an embedded chart to a chart sheet?**

    a. Click a button on the Chart Tools Design tab.

    b. Drag the chart to the sheet tab.

    c. Delete the chart, switch to a different sheet, then create a new chart.

    d. Use the Copy and Paste buttons on the Ribbon.

16. **The object in a chart that identifies patterns used for each data series is a(n):**

    a. Data marker.

    b. Data point.

    c. Organizer

    d. Legend.

17. **A collection of related data points in a chart is called a:**

    a. Data series.

    b. Data tick.

    c. Cell address.

    d. Value title.

▼ SKILLS REVIEW

1. **Plan a chart.**

    a. Start Excel, open the Data File EX D-2.xlsx from the drive and folder where you store your Data Files, then save it as **Departmental Software Usage**.

    b. Describe the type of chart you would use to plot this data.

    c. What chart type would you use to compare total company expenses by department?

    d. What term is used to describe each value in a worksheet range selected for a chart?

2. **Create a chart.**

    a. In the worksheet, select the range containing all the data and headings.

    b. Click the Insert tab, if necessary.

    c. Create a clustered column chart, then add the chart title **Software Usage, by Department** above the chart.

    d. Save your work.

3. **Move and resize a chart.**

    a. Make sure the chart is still selected.

    b. Move the chart beneath the data.

    c. Resize the chart so it extends to the left edge of column I.

    d. Use the Chart Tools Layout tab to move the legend below the charted data.

    e. Resize the chart so its bottom edge is at the top of row 25.

    f. Save your work.

4. **Change the chart design.**

    a. Change the value in cell B3 to **25**. Observe the change in the chart.

    b. Select the chart.

    c. Use the Chart Layouts group on the Chart Tools Design tab to change to Layout 7, then undo the change.

    d. Use the Change Chart Type button on the Chart Tools Design tab to change the chart to a clustered bar chart.

    e. Change the chart to a 3-D clustered column chart , then change it back to a clustered column chart.

    f. Save your work.

5. **Change the chart layout.**
   a. Use the Layout tab to turn off the displayed gridlines in the chart.
   b. Change the font used in the horizontal and vertical axes labels to Times New Roman.
   c. Turn on the major gridlines for both the horizontal and vertical axes.
   d. Change the chart title's font to Times New Roman, with a font size of 20.
   e. Enter **Departments** as the horizontal axis title.
   f. Enter **Number of Users** as the vertical axis title. (*Hint*: Use a rotated title)
   g. Change the font size of the horizontal axis to 10, if necessary, and the font to Times New Roman.
   h. Change the font size of the vertical axis labels to 10, if necessary, and the font to Times New Roman.
   i. Change Personnel in the column heading to **Human Resources**. (*Hint*: Change the label in the worksheet, then resize the column.)
   j. Change the font size of the legend to 14.
   k. Add an offset diagonal bottom-right outer drop shadow to the chart title. (*Hint*: Use a solid line border in the default color.)
   l. Save your work.

6. **Format a chart.**
   a. Make sure the chart is selected, then select the Format tab, if necessary.
   b. Change the color of the Excel data series to Olive Green, Accent 3 Darker 50%.
   c. Change the shape effect of the Excel data series to Bevel – Circle.
   d. Save your work.

7. **Annotate and draw on a chart.**
   a. Make sure the chart is selected, then create the text annotation **Needs more users**.
   b. Position the text annotation so the 'N' in 'Needs' is positioned approximately below the 't' in 'Software'.
   c. Use the Shapes group on the Insert tab to create a 1½ pt weight arrow that points to the Excel users in the Design Department.
   d. Deselect the chart.
   e. Save your work.

8. **Create a pie chart.**
   a. Select the range A1:F2, then create a 3-D pie chart.
   b. Drag the 3-D pie chart beneath the existing chart.
   c. Change the chart title to **Excel Users**.
   d. Apply Chart Style 26 to the chart.
   e. Explode the Human Resources slice from the pie chart at 25%.
   f. In the worksheet, enter your name in the left section of the header.

g. View the worksheet and charts in the Print Preview window, make sure all the contents fit on one page, then compare your work to Figure D-25.

h. Save your work.

i. Close the workbook, then exit Excel.

FIGURE D-25

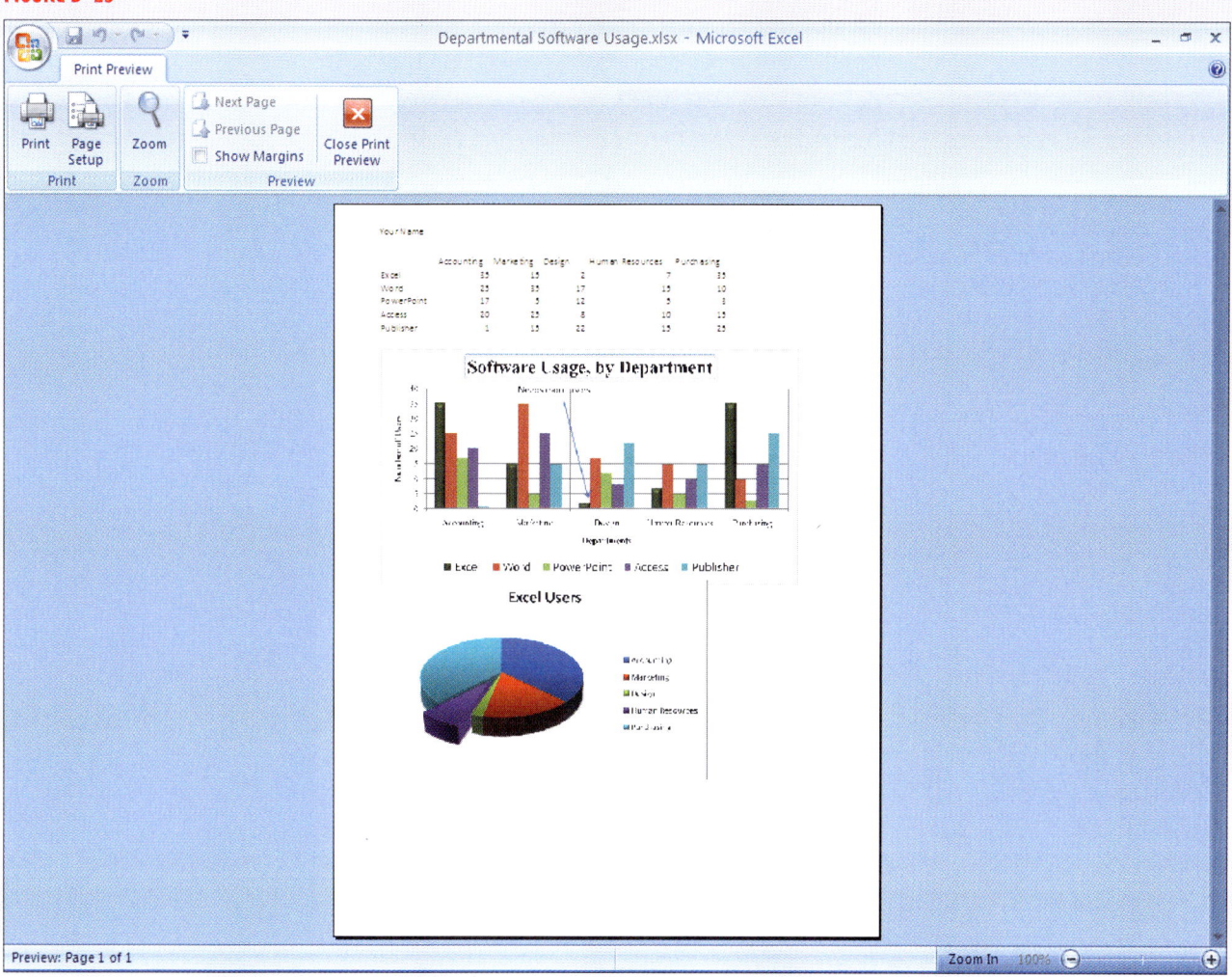

▼ INDEPENDENT CHALLENGE 1

You are the operations manager for the Springfield Theater Group in Massachusetts. Each year the group applies to various state and federal agencies for matching funds. For this year's funding proposal, you need to create charts to document the number of productions in previous years.

a. Start Excel, open the file EX D-3.xlsx from the drive and folder where you store your Data Files, then save it as **Springfield Theater Group**.

b. Take some time to plan your charts. Which type of chart or charts might best illustrate the information you need to display? What kind of chart enhancements do you want to use? Will a 3-D effect make your chart easier to understand?

Excel 2007

c. Create a clustered column chart for the data.

d. If you wish, change at least one of the colors used in a data series.

e. Make the appropriate modifications to the chart to make it easy to read and understand, and visually attractive. Include chart titles, legends, and value and category axis titles, using the suggestions in Table D-3.

TABLE D-3

suggested chart enhancements for a column chart	
Title	Types and Number of Plays
Legend	Year 1, Year 2, Year 3, Year 4
Vertical axis title	Number of Plays
Horizontal axis title	Play Types

f. Create at least two additional charts for the same data to show how different chart types display the same data. Place each new chart on its own sheet in the workbook, and name the sheet according to the type of chart you created. One of the additional charts should be a pie chart; the other is up to you. Modify each new chart as necessary to improve its appearance and effectiveness. Compare your chart to the sample in Figure D-26.

FIGURE D-26

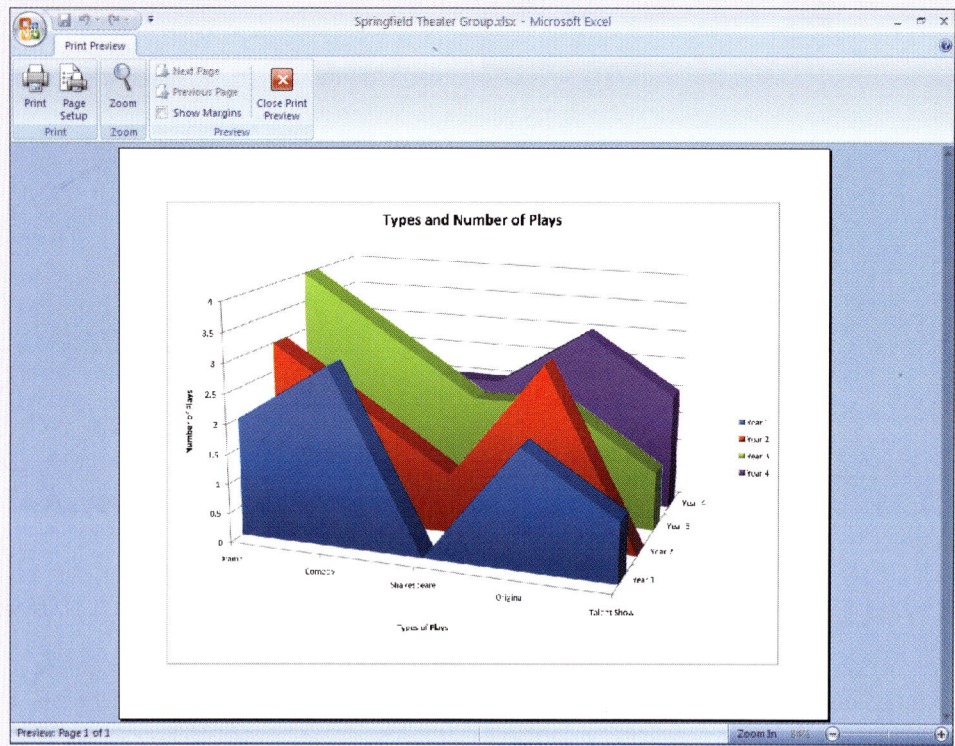

g. Enter your name in the worksheet header.

h. Save your work. Before printing, preview the workbook in Print Preview, then adjust any items as necessary.

i. Print the worksheet (charts and data).

j. Close the workbook, then exit Excel.

▼ INDEPENDENT CHALLENGE 2

FIGURE D-27

You work at Three Dog Bakery, a locally-owned bakery for dogs. One of your responsibilities at the bakery is to manage the company's sales and expenses using Excel. Another is to convince the current staff that Excel can help them make daily operating decisions more easily and efficiently. To do this, you've decided to create charts using the previous year's operating expenses, including rent, utilities, and payroll. The manager will use these charts at the next monthly meeting.

a. Start Excel, open the Data File EX D-4.xlsx from the drive and folder where you store your Data Files, then save it as **Three Dog Bakery Analysis**.

b. Decide which data in the worksheet should be charted. What type of chart or charts are best suited for the information you need to show? What kinds of chart enhancements are necessary?

c. Create a 3-D column chart (with the data series in rows) on the worksheet, showing the expense data for all four quarters. (*Hint*: Do not include the totals.)

d. Change the scale of the vertical axis (Expense data) so no decimals are displayed. (*Hint*: Right-click the scale you want to modify, click Format Axis, click Number category, change the number of decimal places, then click Close.)

e. Using the sales data, create two charts on this worksheet that illustrate trends in the data. (*Hint*: Move each chart to a new location on the worksheet, then deselect it before creating the next one.)

f. In one chart of the sales data, add data labels, then add chart titles as you see fit.

g. Make any necessary formatting changes to make the charts look more attractive, then enter your name in a worksheet cell.

h. Save your work.

i. Before printing, preview each chart, and adjust any items as needed. Fit the charts to a single page, then print one copy. Compare your work to the sample in Figure D-27.

j. Close the workbook, then exit Excel.

▼ INDEPENDENT CHALLENGE 3

FIGURE D-28

You are working as an account representative at the Inspiration Ad Agency. You have been examining the expenses charged to clients of the firm. The board of directors wants to examine certain advertising expenses and has asked you to prepare charts that can be used in this evaluation. In particular, you want to see how dollar amounts compare among the different expenses, and you also want to see how expenses compare with each other proportional to the total budget.

a. Start Excel, open the Data File EX D-5.xlsx from the drive and folder where you store your Data Files, then save it as **Ad Agency Expenses**.

b. Choose three types of charts that seem best suited to illustrate the data in the range A16:B24. What kinds of chart enhancements are necessary?

c. Create at least two different types of charts that show the distribution of advertising expenses. (*Hint*: Move each chart to a new location on the same worksheet.) One of the charts should be a 3-D pie chart.

d. Add annotated text and arrows highlighting important data, such as the largest expense.

e. Change the color of at least one data series in at least one of the charts.

f. Add chart titles and category and value axis titles where appropriate. Format the titles with a font of your choice. Place a drop shadow around the chart title in at least one chart.

g. Add your name to a section of the header, then save your work.

h. View the file in Print Preview. Adjust any items as needed. Be sure the charts are all visible on the page. Compare your work to the sample in Figure D-28.

Advanced Challenge Exercise

■ Explode a slice from the 3-D pie chart.

■ Add a data label to the exploded pie slice.

■ Change the number format of labels in the non-pie charts so no decimals are displayed.

■ Modify the scale of the vertical axis in one of the charts. (*Hint*: Right-click the vertical axis, click Format Axis, then click Axis Options.)

■ Save your work, then view it in Print Preview.

i. Print the charts, close the workbook, then exit Excel.

▼ REAL LIFE INDEPENDENT CHALLENGE

FIGURE D-29

Note: This project requires an Internet connection.

A cash inheritance from a distant relative has finally been deposited in your bank account, and you have decided to quit your job and relocate to the town of your dreams. You have a good idea where you'd like to live and decide to use the Web to see what sort of houses are currently available.

a. Start Excel, then save a new, blank workbook as **My Dream House** to the drive and folder where you save your Data Files.

b. Decide on where you would like to live, and use your favorite search engine to find information sources on homes for sale in that area.

c. Determine a price range and features within the home. Find data for at least five homes that meet your location and price requirements, and enter them in the worksheet. See Table D-4 below for suggested data layout.

d. Format the data so it looks attractive and professional.

e. Create any type of column chart, using only the House and Asking Price data. Place it on the same worksheet as the data. Include a descriptive title.

f. Change the colors in the chart, using the Chart Style of your choice.

g. Enter your name in a section of the header.

TABLE D-4

location					
price range					
	House 1	House 2	House 3	House 4	House 5
Asking price					
Bedrooms					
Bathrooms					
Year built					
Size (in sq. ft.)					

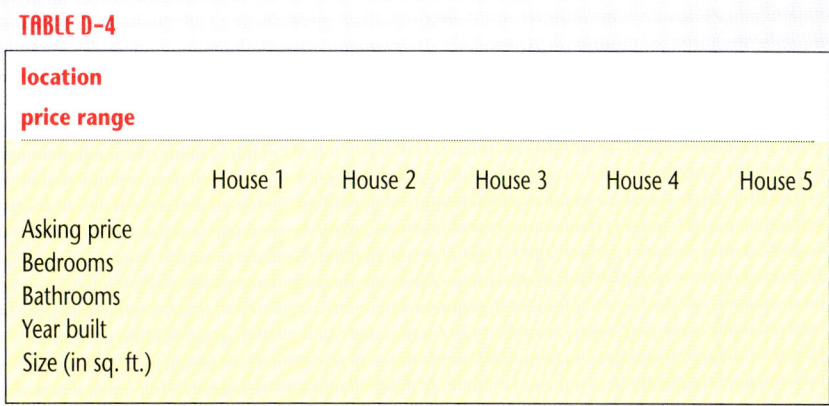

h. Save the workbook. Preview the chart(s) and change margins and/or orientation as necessary. Compare your work to the sample chart shown in Figure D-29.

i. Print your worksheet(s), including the data and chart(s), making setup modifications as necessary.

Advanced Challenge Exercise

- Change the chart type to a Clustered Column chart.
- Create a combination chart that plots the asking price on one axis and the size of the home on the other axis.
   (*Hint*: Use Help to get tips on how to chart with a secondary axis.)

j. Close the workbook, then exit Excel.

▼ VISUAL WORKSHOP

Open the Data File EX D-6.xlsx from the drive and folder where you store your Data Files, then save it as **Projected Project Revenue**. Modify the worksheet data so it looks like Figure D-30, then create and modify two charts to match the ones shown in the figure. You will need to make formatting, layout, and design changes once you create the charts. Enter your name in the left section of the header, then save, preview, and print your results.

FIGURE D-30

Analyzing Data Using Formulas

Files You Will Need:

EX E-1.xlsx

EX E-2.xlsx

EX E-3.xlsx

EX E-4.xlsx

EX E-5.xlsx

EX E-6.xlsx

EX E-7.xlsx

As you have learned, formulas and functions help you to analyze worksheet data. As you learn how to use different types of formulas and functions, you will discover more valuable uses for Excel. In this unit, you will gain a deeper understanding of Excel formulas and learn how to use several Excel functions. Kate Morgan, QST's vice president of sales, uses Excel formulas and functions to analyze sales data for the U.S. region and to consolidate sales data from several worksheets. Because management is considering adding a new regional branch, Kate asks you to estimate the loan costs for a new office facility and to compare tour sales in the existing U.S. offices.

OBJECTIVES

Format data using text functions

Sum a data range based on conditions

Consolidate data using a formula

Check formulas for errors

Construct formulas using named ranges

Build a logical formula with the IF function

Build a logical formula with the AND function

Calculate payments with the PMT function

Formatting Data Using Text Functions

Often, data you import needs restructuring or reformatting to be understandable and attractive, or to match the formatting of other data in your worksheet. Instead of handling these tasks manually in each cell, you can use Excel conversion tools and text functions to perform these tasks automatically for a range of cell data. The Convert Text to Columns feature breaks data fields in one column into separate columns. Your data elements should be separated by a **delimiter**, or separator, such as a space, comma, or semicolon. The text function PROPER capitalizes (converts to a proper noun) the first letter in a string of text as well as any text following a space. For example, if cell A1 contains the text string marketing department, then =PROPER(A1) would display Marketing Department. The CONCATENATE function is used to join two or more strings into one text string. Kate has received the U.S. sales representatives' data from the human resources department. She asks you to use text formulas to format the data into a more useful layout.

STEPS

1. Start Excel, open the file EX E-1.xlsx from the drive and folder where you store your Data Files, then save it as Sales Data

2. On the Sales Reps sheet, select the range A4:A15, click the Data tab, then click the Text to Columns button in the Data Tools group

   The Convert Text to Columns Wizard opens, as shown in Figure E-1. The data fields on your worksheet are separated by commas, which will act as delimiters.

3. If necessary, click the Delimited option button to select it, click Next, in the Delimiters area of the dialog box click the Comma check box to select it if necessary, click any other selected check boxes to deselect them, then click Next

   You instructed Excel to separate your data at the comma delimiter.

> **QUICK TIP**
>
> You can move the Function Arguments dialog box if it overlaps a cell or range that you need to click. You can also click the Collapse Dialog Box button ⊞, select the cell or range, then click the Expand Dialog box button ⊞ to return to the Function Arguments dialog box.

4. Click the Text option button in the Column data format area, click the General column to select it in the Data preview area, click the Text option button in the Column data format area, then click Finish

   The data are separated into three columns of text. You want to format the letters to the correct cases.

5. Click cell D4, click the Formulas tab, click the Text button in the Function Library group, click PROPER, with the insertion point in the Text text box, click cell A4, then click OK

   The name is copied from cell A4 to cell D4 with the correct uppercase letters for proper names. The remaining names and the cities are still in lowercase letters.

6. Drag the fill handle to copy the formula in cell D4 to cell E4, then copy the formulas in cells D4:E4 into the range D5:E15

   You want to format the years data to be more descriptive.

> **QUICK TIP**
>
> Excel automatically inserts quotation marks to enclose the space and the Years text.

7. Click cell F4, click the Text button in the Function Library group, click CONCATENATE, with the insertion point in the Text1 text box, click cell C4, press [Tab], with the insertion point in the Text2 text box, press [Spacebar], type Years, then click OK

8. Copy the formula in cell F4 into the range F5:F15, click the Insert tab, click the Header & Footer button in the Text group, click the Go to Footer button in the Navigation group, enter your name in the center text box, click cell A1, then click the Normal button ⊞ in the status bar

9. Save your file, then print the worksheet and compare your work to Figure E-2

FIGURE E-1: Convert Text to Columns dialog box

Preview of data with delimiters

FIGURE E-2: Worksheet with data formatted in columns

			United States Sales Representatives		
			Name	Office	Years of Service
rafal sanchez	new york	2	Rafal Sanchez	New York	2 Years
anthony dolongi	new york	5	Anthony Dolongi	New York	5 Years
gregor blake	new york	8	Gregor Blake	New York	8 Years
lin guan	new york	10	Lin Guan	New York	10 Years
joyce kuang	chicago	4	Joyce Kuang	Chicago	4 Years
garrin cunha	chicago	7	Garrin Cunha	Chicago	7 Years
cathy jaques	chicago	5	Cathy Jaques	Chicago	5 Years
alyssa maztta	chicago	4	Alyssa Maztta	Chicago	4 Years
april radka	miami	6	April Radka	Miami	6 Years
jose costello	miami	7	Jose Costello	Miami	7 Years
joyce haddad	miami	4	Joyce Haddad	Miami	4 Years
summer zola	miami	7	Summer Zola	Miami	7 Years

Using text functions

Other commonly used text functions include UPPER, LOWER, and SUBSTITUTE. The UPPER function converts text to all uppercase letters, the LOWER function converts text to all lowercase letters, and SUBSTITUTE replaces text in a text string. For example, if cell A1 contains the text string Today is Wednesday, then =LOWER(A1) would produce today is wednesday, =UPPER(A1) would produce TODAY IS WEDNESDAY, and =SUBSTITUTE(A1, "Wednesday", "Tuesday") would result in Today is Tuesday.

If you want to copy and paste data formatted using text functions, you need to select Values Only from the Paste Options drop-down list to paste the cell values rather than the text formulas.

Summing a Data Range Based on Conditions

You have learned how to use the SUM, COUNT, and AVERAGE functions for data ranges. You can also use Excel functions to sum, count, and average data in a range based on criteria, or conditions, you set. The SUMIF function conditionally totals cells in a sum range that meet given criteria. For example, you can total the values in a column of sales where a sales rep name equals Joe Smith (the criterion). Similarly, the COUNTIF function counts cells and the AVERAGEIF function averages cells in a range based on a specified condition. The format for the SUMIF function appears in Figure E-3. Kate asks you to analyze the New York branch's January sales data to provide her with information about each tour.

STEPS

1. **Click the NY sheet tab, click cell G7, click the Formulas tab, click the More Functions button in the Function Library group, point to Statistical, then click COUNTIF**

   The Function Arguments dialog box opens, as shown in Figure E-4. You want to count the number of times Pacific Odyssey appears in the Tour column. The formula you use will say, in effect, "Examine the range I specify, then count the number of cells in that range that contain "Pacific Odyssey." You will specify absolute addresses for the range so you can copy the formula.

2. **With the insertion point in the Range text box, select the range A6:A25, press [F4], press [Tab], with the insertion point in the Criteria text box, click cell F7, then click OK**

   The number of Pacific Odyssey tours, 4, appears in cell G7. You want to calculate the total sales revenue for the Pacific Odyssey tours.

3. **Click cell H7, click the Math & Trig button in the Function Library group, scroll down the list of functions, then click SUMIF**

   The Function Arguments dialog box opens. You want to enter two ranges and a criterion; the first range is the one where you want Excel to search for the criteria entered. The second range contains the corresponding cells that will be totaled when the criterion you want Excel to search for in the first range is met.

   QUICK TIP
   You can also sum, count, and average ranges with multiple criteria using the functions SUMIFS, COUNTIFS, and AVERAGEIFS

4. **With the insertion point in the Range text box, select the range A6:A25, press [F4], press [Tab], with the insertion point in the Criteria text box, click cell F7, press [Tab], with the insertion point in the Sum_range text box, select the range B6:B25, press [F4], then click OK**

   Your formula asks Excel to search the range A6:A25, and where it finds the value shown in cell F7 (that is, when it finds the value Pacific Odyssey), add the corresponding amounts from column B. The revenue for the Pacific Odyssey tours, 12403, appears in cell H7. You want to calculate the average price paid for the Pacific Odyssey tours.

5. **Click cell I7, click the More Functions button in the Function Library group, point to Statistical, then click AVERAGEIF**

6. **With the insertion point in the Range text box, select the range A6:A25, press [F4], press [Tab], with the insertion point in the Criteria text box, click cell F7, press [Tab], with the insertion point in the Average_range text box, select the range B6:B25, press [F4], then click OK**

   The average price paid for the Pacific Odyssey tours, 3101, appears in cell I7.

7. **Select the range G7:I7, then drag the fill handle to fill the range G8:I10**

   Compare your results with those in Figure E-5.

8. **Add your name to the center of the footer, save the workbook, then preview and print the worksheet**

SUMIF(range, criteria, [sum_range])

The range the function searches

The condition that must be satisfied in the range

The range where the cells that meet the condition will be totaled

FIGURE E-4: COUNTIF function in the Function Arguments dialog box

FIGURE E-5: Worksheet with conditional statistics

UNIT
E

Excel 2007

Consolidating Data Using a Formula

When you want to summarize similar data that exists in different sheets or workbooks, you can **consolidate**, or combine and display, the data in one sheet. For example, you might have entered departmental sales figures on four different store sheets that you want to consolidate on one summary sheet, showing total departmental sales for all stores. The best way to consolidate data is to use cell references to the various sheets on a consolidation, or summary, sheet. Because they reference other sheets that are usually behind the summary sheet, such references effectively create another dimension in the workbook and are called **3-D references**, as shown in Figure E-6. You can reference, or **link** to, data in other sheets and in other workbooks. Linking to a worksheet or workbook is a better method than retyping calculated results from the worksheet or workbook because the data values on which calculated totals depend might change. If you reference the values, any changes to the original values are automatically reflected in the consolidation sheet. Kate asks you to prepare a January sales summary sheet comparing the total U.S. revenue for the tours sold in the month.

STEPS

QUICK TIP

You can also consolidate data using named ranges. For example, you might have entered team sales figures using the names team1, team2, and team3 on different sheets that you want to consolidate on one summary sheet. As you enter the summary formula you can click the Formulas tab, click the Use in Formula button in the Defined Names group, and select the range name.

1. **Click the US Summary Jan sheet tab**

   Because the US Summary Jan sheet (which is the consolidation sheet) will contain the reference to the data in the other sheets, the cell pointer must reside there when you initiate the reference.

2. **Click cell B7, click the Formulas tab, click the AutoSum button in the Function Library group, click the NY sheet tab, press and hold [Shift] and click the Miami sheet tab, click cell G7, then click the Enter button ☑ on the formula bar**

   The US Summary Jan sheet becomes active, and the formula bar reads =SUM(NY:Miami!G7), as shown in Figure E-7. NY:Miami references the NY, Chicago, and Miami sheets. The ! (exclamation point) is an **external reference indicator**, meaning that the cells referenced are outside the active sheet; G7 is the actual cell reference you want to total in the external sheets. The result, 12, appears in cell B7 of the US Summary Jan sheet; it is the sum of the number of Pacific Odyssey tours sold and referenced in cell G7 of the NY, Chicago, and Miami sheets. Because the Revenue data is in the column to the right of the Tours Sold column on the NY, Chicago, and Miami sheets, you can copy the tours sold summary formula, with its relative addresses, into the cell that holds the revenue summary information.

3. **Drag the fill handle to copy the formula in cell B7 to cell C7**

   The result, 37405, appears in cell C7 of the US Summary Jan sheet, showing the sum of the Pacific Odyssey tour revenue referenced in cell H7 of the NY, Chicago, and Miami sheets.

QUICK TIP

You can also use a summary worksheet to consolidate yearly sales figures. Place data for each quarter on a separate sheet. On a summary sheet, use a row for each quarter that references each quarter's sales. Then sum the quarterly information to display total yearly sales.

4. **In the US Summary Jan sheet, with the range B7:C7 selected, drag the fill handle to fill the range B8:C10**

   You can test a consolidation reference by changing one cell value on which the formula is based and seeing if the formula result changes.

5. **Click the Chicago sheet tab, edit cell A6 to read Pacific Odyssey, then click the US Summary Jan sheet tab**

   The number of Pacific Odyssey tours sold is automatically updated to 13 and the revenue is increased to 40280, as shown in Figure E-8.

6. **Click the Insert tab, click the Header & Footer button in the Text group, click the Go to Footer button, enter your name in the center text box, click cell A1, then click the Normal button ⊞ in the status bar**

FIGURE E-6: Consolidating data from three worksheets

FIGURE E-7: Worksheet showing total Pacific Odyssey tours sold

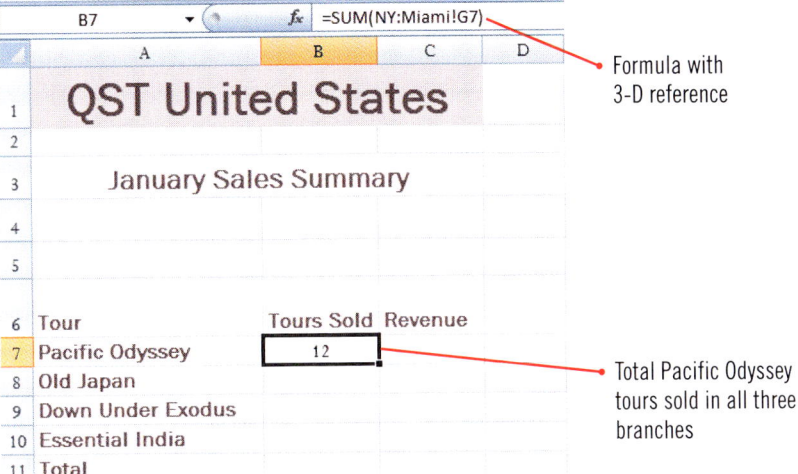

Formula with 3-D reference

Total Pacific Odyssey tours sold in all three branches

FIGURE E-8: US Summary Jan worksheet with updated totals

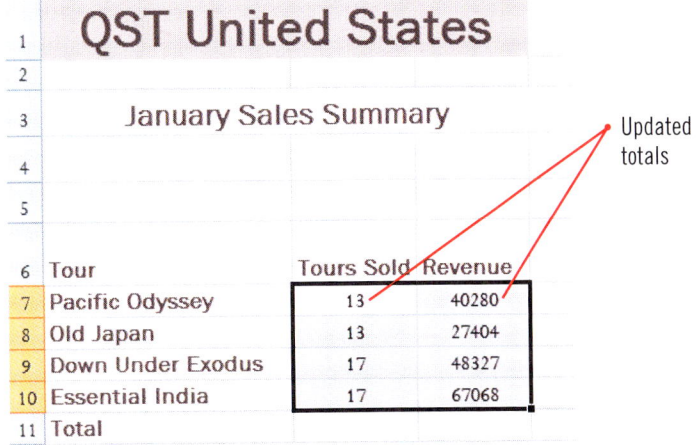

Updated totals

Linking data between workbooks

Just as you can link data between cells in a worksheet and between sheets in a workbook, you can link workbooks so that changes made in referenced cells in one workbook are reflected in the consolidation sheet in the other workbook. To link a single cell between workbooks, open both workbooks, select the cell to receive the linked data, type = (the equal sign), select the cell in the other workbook containing the data to be linked, then press [Enter]. Excel automatically inserts the name of the referenced workbook in the cell reference. For example, if the linked data is contained in cell C7 of worksheet New in the Products workbook, the cell entry reads ='[Product.xlsx]New'!C7. To perform calculations, enter formulas on the consolidation sheet using cells in the supporting sheets. If you are linking more than one cell, you can copy the linked data to the Clipboard, select the upper left cell in the workbook to receive the link, click the Home tab, click the Paste list arrow, then click Paste Link.

Checking Formulas for Errors

When formulas result in errors, Excel displays an error value based on the error type. See Table E-1 for a description of the error types and error codes that might appear in worksheets. The IFERROR function simplifies the error-checking process for your worksheets. This function displays a message or value that you specify, rather than the one automatically generated by Excel, if there is an error in a formula. Kate asks you to use formulas to compare the tour revenues for January. You will use the IFERROR function to help catch formula errors.

STEPS

1. **Click cell B11, click the Formulas tab, click the AutoSum button in the Function Library group, then click the Enter button ☑ on the formula bar**

   The number of tours sold, 60, appears in cell B11.

2. **Drag the fill handle to copy the formula in cell B11 into cell C11**

   The tour revenue total of 183079 appears in cell C11. You decide to enter a formula to calculate the percentage of revenue the Pacific Odyssey tour represents by dividing the individual tour revenue figures by the total revenue figure. To help with error checking, you decide to enter the formula using the IFERROR function.

3. **Click cell B14, click the Logical button in the Function Library group, click IFERROR, with the insertion point in the Value text box, click cell C7, type /, click cell C11, press [Tab], in the Value_if_error text box, type ERROR, then click OK**

   The percentage of Pacific Odyssey tour revenue of 22.00% appears in cell B14. You want to be sure that your error message will display properly, so you decide to test it by intentionally creating an error. You copy and paste the formula—which has a relative address in the denominator, where an absolute address should be used.

4. **Drag the fill handle to copy the formula in cell B14 into the range B15:B17**

   The ERROR value appears in cells B15:B17, as shown in Figure E-9. The errors are a result of the relative address for C11 in the denominator of the copied formula. Changing the relative address of C11 in the copied formula to an absolute address of C11 will correct the errors.

   QUICK TIP
   You can also check formulas for errors using the buttons in the Formula Auditing group on the Formulas tab.

5. **Double-click cell B14, select C11 in the formula, press [F4], then click ☑ on the formula bar**

   The formula now contains an absolute reference to cell C11.

6. **Copy the corrected formula in cell B14 into the range B15:B17**

   The tour revenue percentages now appear in all four cells, without error messages, as shown in Figure E-10.

7. **Save the workbook, print the worksheet, then close the workbook**

Correcting circular references

A cell with a circular reference contains a formula that refers to its own cell location. If you accidentally enter a formula with a circular reference, a warning box opens, alerting you to the problem. Click OK to open a Help window explaining how to find the circular reference. In simple formulas, a circular reference is easy to spot. To correct it, edit the formula to remove any reference to the cell where the formula is located.

FIGURE E-9: Worksheet with error codes

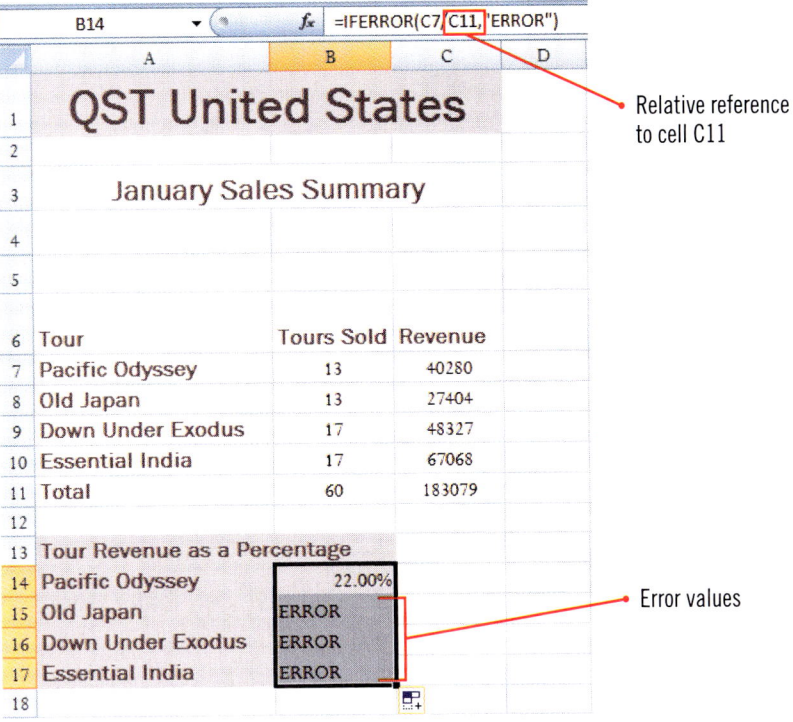

Relative reference to cell C11

Error values

FIGURE E-10: Worksheet with tour percentages

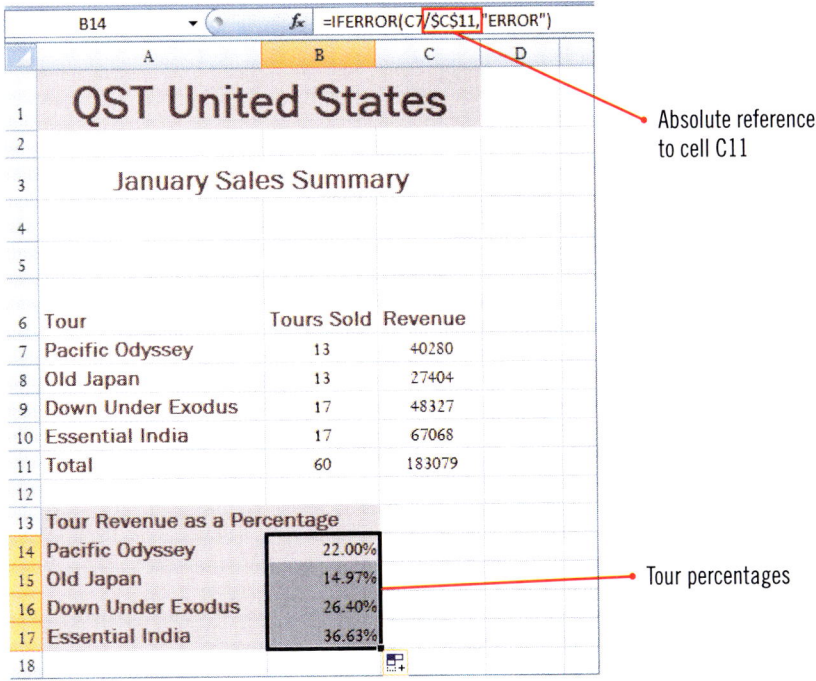

Absolute reference to cell C11

Tour percentages

TABLE E-1: Understanding error values

error value	cause of error	error value	cause of error
#DIV/0!	A number is divided by 0	#NAME?	Formula contains text error
#NA	A value in a formula is not available	#NULL!	Invalid intersection of areas
#NUM!	Invalid use of a number in a formula	#REF!	Invalid cell reference
#VALUE!	Wrong type of formula argument or operand	#####	Column is not wide enough to display data

Constructing Formulas Using Named Ranges

To make your worksheet easier to follow, you can assign names to cells and ranges. You can also use names in formulas to make them easier to build and to reduce formula errors. For example, a formula named revenue-cost is easier to understand than the formula A5-A8. Names can use uppercase or lowercase letters as well as digits, but cannot have spaces. After you name a cell or range, you can define its **scope**, or the worksheets where it can be used. When defining a name's scope, you can limit its use to a worksheet or make it available to the entire workbook. If you move a named cell or range, its name moves with it, and if you add or remove rows or column to the worksheet the ranges are adjusted to their new position in the worksheet. When used in formulas, names become absolute cell references by default. Kate asks you to calculate the number of days before each tour departs. You will use range names to construct the formula.

STEPS

1. Open the file **EX E-2.xlsx** from the drive and folder where you store your Data Files, then save it as **Tours**

2. Click cell **B4**, click the **Formulas tab** if necessary, click the **Define Name button** in the Defined Names group

   The New Name dialog box opens, as shown in Figure E-11. You can name ranges containing dates to make formulas that perform date calculations easier to build.

   > **QUICK TIP**
   > Because names can not contain spaces, underscores are often used between words to replace spaces, making names with multiple words easier to read.

3. Type **current_date** in the Name text box, click the **Scope list arrow**, click **April Tours**, then click **OK**

   The name assigned to cell B4, current_date, appears in the Name box. Because its scope is the April Tours worksheet, the range name current_date will appear on the name list on that worksheet only. You can also name ranges that contain dates.

4. Select the range **B7:B13**, click the **Define Name button** in the Defined Names group, enter **tour_date** in the Name text box, click the **Scope list arrow**, click **April Tours**, then click **OK**

   Now you can use the named range and named cell in a formula. The formula =tour_date–current_date is easier to understand than =B7-B4.

   > **QUICK TIP**
   > Named cells and ranges can be used as a navigational tool in a worksheet by selecting the name in the Name box. The named cell or range becomes active.

5. Click cell **C7**, type **=**, click the **Use in Formula button** in the Defined Names group, click **tour_date**, type **–**, click the **Use in Formula button**, click **current_date**, then click the **Enter button** ✔ on the formula bar

   The number of days before the Pacific Odyssey tour departs, 10, appears in cell C7. You can use the same formula to calculate the number of days before the other tours depart.

6. Drag the fill handle to copy the formula in cell C7 into the range **C8:C13**, then compare your formula results with those in Figure E-12

7. Save the workbook

FIGURE E-11: New Name dialog box

Enter cell or range name here

FIGURE E-12: Worksheet with days before departure

Name box

Formula using names rather than cell references

Days before departure

Managing workbook names

You can use the Name Manager to create, delete, and edit names in a workbook. Click the Name Manager button in the Defined Names group on the Formulas tab to open the Name Manager dialog box, as shown in Figure E-13. Click the New button to create a new named cell or range, click Edit to change a highlighted cell name, and click Delete to remove a highlighted name. Click Filter to see options for displaying specific criteria for displaying names.

FIGURE E-13: Name Manager dialog box

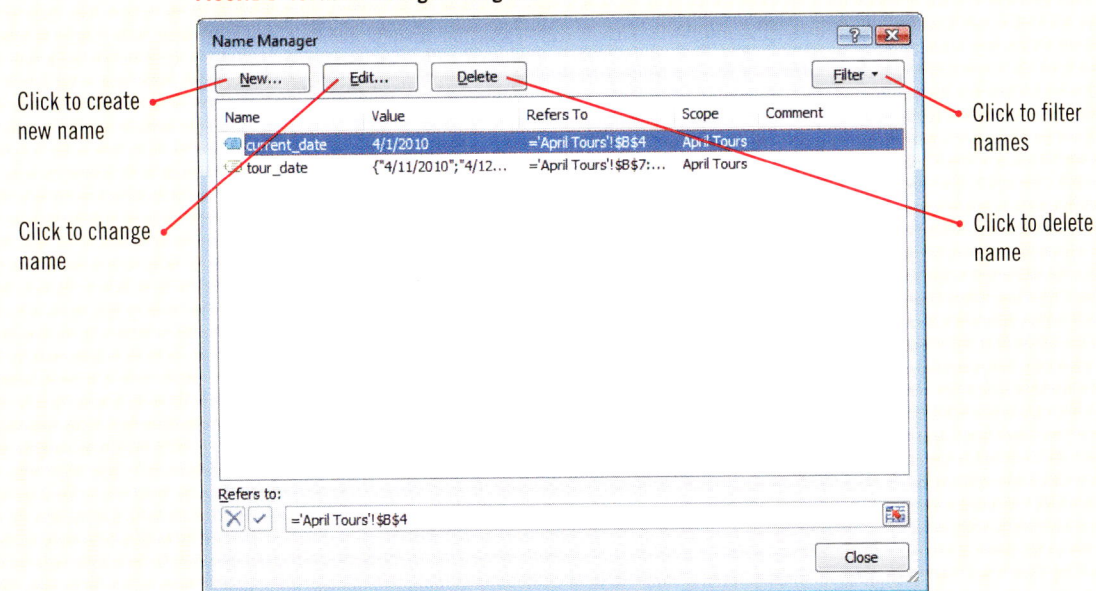

Click to create new name

Click to change name

Click to filter names

Click to delete name

Building a Logical Formula with the IF Function

You can build a logical formula using an IF function. A **logical formula** makes calculations based on criteria that you create, called **stated conditions**. For example, you can build a formula to calculate bonuses based on a person's performance rating. If a person is rated a 5 (the stated condition) on a scale of 1 to 5, with 5 being the highest rating, he or she receives an additional 10% of his or her salary as a bonus; otherwise, there is no bonus. A condition that can be answered with a true or false response is called a **logical test**. The IF function has three parts, separated by commas: a condition or logical test, an action to take if the logical test or condition is true, and an action to take if the logical test or condition is false. Another way of expressing this is: IF(test_cond,do_this,else_this). Translated into an Excel IF function, the formula to calculate bonuses might look like this: IF(Rating=5,Salary*0.10,0). In other words, if the rating equals 5, multiply the salary by 0.10 (the decimal equivalent of 10%), then place the result in the selected cell; if the rating does not equal 5, place a 0 in the cell. When entering the logical test portion of an IF statement, you typically use some combination of the comparison operators listed in Table E-2. Kate asks you to use an IF function to calculate the number of seats available for each tour in April.

STEPS

1. **Click cell F7, on the Formulas tab, click the Logical button in the Function Library group, then click IF**

   The Function Arguments dialog box opens. You want the function to calculate the seats available as follows: If the seat capacity is greater than the number of seats reserved, calculate the number of seats that are available (capacity–number reserved), and place the result in cell F7; otherwise, place the text "None" in the cell.

2. **With the insertion point in the Logical_test text box, click cell D7, type >, click cell E7, then press [Tab]**

   The symbol (>) represents "greater than." So far, the formula reads "If the seating capacity is greater than the number of reserved seats,". The next part of the function tells Excel the action to take if the capacity exceeds the reserved number of seats.

3. **With the insertion point in the Value_if_true text box, click cell D7, type –, click cell E7 , then press [Tab]**

   This part of the formula tells the program what you want it to do if the logical test is true. Continuing the translation of the formula, this part means "Subtract the number of reserved seats from the seat capacity." The last part of the formula tells Excel the action to take if the logical test is false (that is, if the seat capacity does not exceed the number of reserved seats).

4. **Enter None in the Value_if_false text box, then click OK**

   The function is complete, and the result, None (the number of available seats), appears in cell F7, as shown in Figure E-14.

5. **Drag the fill handle to copy the formula in cell F7 into the range F8:F13**

   Compare your results with Figure E-15.

6. **Save the workbook**

FIGURE E-14: Worksheet with IF function

	A	B	C	D	E	F	G
F7			=IF(D7>E7,D7-E7,"None")				
1			QST				
2			April Tours				
3							
4	Report Date	4/1/2010					
5							
6	Tour	Tour Date	Days Before Departure	Seat Capacity	Seats Reserved	Seats Available	Qualify for Discount
7	Pacific Odyssey	4/11/2010	10	50	50	None	
8	Old Japan	4/12/2010	11	47	41		
9	Down Under Exodus	4/18/2010	17	30	28		
10	Essential India	4/20/2010	19	51	40		
11	Amazing Amazon	4/23/2010	22	43	38		
12	Wild River Escape	4/27/2010	26	21	21		
13	Cooking in France	4/29/2010	28	18	15		
14							

IF function   Seats available

FIGURE E-15: Worksheet showing seats available

	A	B	C	D	E	F	G
F7			=IF(D7>E7,D7-E7,"None")				
1			QST				
2			April Tours				
3							
4	Report Date	4/1/2010					
5							
6	Tour	Tour Date	Days Before Departure	Seat Capacity	Seats Reserved	Seats Available	Qualify for Discount
7	Pacific Odyssey	4/11/2010	10	50	50	None	
8	Old Japan	4/12/2010	11	47	41	6	
9	Down Under Exodus	4/18/2010	17	30	28	2	
10	Essential India	4/20/2010	19	51	40	11	
11	Amazing Amazon	4/23/2010	22	43	38	5	
12	Wild River Escape	4/27/2010	26	21	21	None	
13	Cooking in France	4/29/2010	28	18	15	3	
14							

Seats available

TABLE E-2: Comparison operators

operator	meaning	operator	meaning
<	Less than	<=	Less than or equal to
>	Greater than	>=	Greater than or equal to
=	Equal to	<>	Not equal to

Building a Logical Formula with the AND Function

You can also build a logical function using the AND function. The AND function evaluates all of its arguments and **returns**, or displays, TRUE if every logical test in the formula is true. The AND function returns a value of FALSE if one or more of its logical tests is false. The AND function arguments can include text, numbers, or cell references. Kate wants you to analyze the tour data to find tours that qualify for discounting. You will use the AND function to check for tours with seats available and that depart within 21 days.

STEPS

1. **Click cell G7, click the Logical button in the Function Library group, then click AND**

   The Function Arguments dialog box opens. You want the function to evaluate the discount qualification as follows: There must be seats available and the tour must depart within 21 days.

2. **With the insertion point in the Logical1 text box, click cell F7, type < >, type "None", then press [Tab]**

   The symbol (<>) represents "not equal to." So far, the formula reads "If the number of seats available is not equal to None,"—in other words, if it is an integer. The next logical test checks the number of days before the tour departs.

3. **With the insertion point in the Logical2 text box, click cell C7, type <21, then click OK**

   The function is complete, and the result, FALSE, appears in cell G7, as shown in Figure E-16.

4. **Drag the fill handle to copy the formula in cell G7 into the range G8:G13**

   Compare your results with Figure E-17.

5. **Click the Insert tab, click the Header & Footer button in the Text group, click the Go to Footer button, enter your name in the center text box, click cell A1, then click the Normal button in the status bar**

6. **Save the workbook, then preview and print the worksheet**

Using the OR and NOT logical functions

The OR logical function has the same syntax as the AND function, but rather than returning TRUE if every argument is true, the OR function will return TRUE if any of its arguments are TRUE. It will only return FALSE if all of its arguments are FALSE. The NOT logical function reverses the value of its argument. For example NOT(TRUE) reverses its argument of TRUE and returns FALSE. This can be used in a worksheet to ensure that a cell is not equal to a particular value. See Table E-3 for examples of the AND, OR, and NOT functions.

TABLE E-3: Examples of AND, OR, and NOT functions with cell values A1=10 and B1=20

function	formula	result
AND	=AND(A1>5,B1>25)	FALSE
OR	=OR(A1>5,B1>25)	TRUE
NOT	=NOT(A1=0)	TRUE

FIGURE E-16: Worksheet with AND function

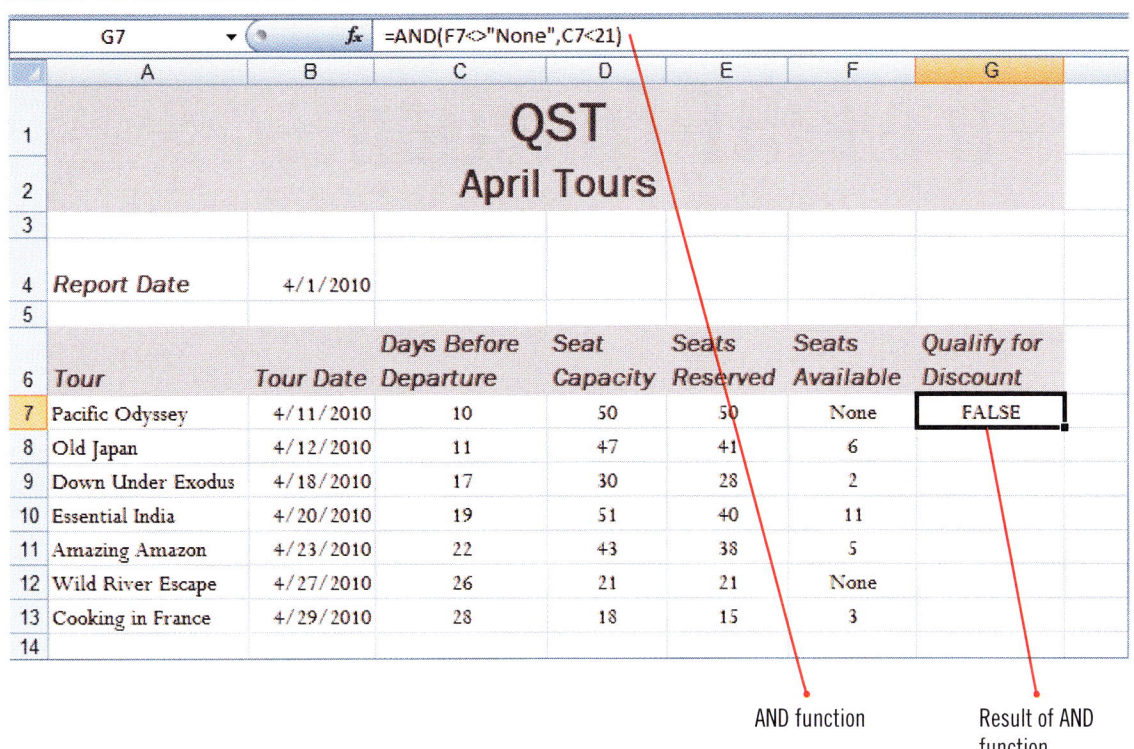

AND function

Result of AND function

FIGURE E-17: Worksheet with discount status evaluated

Calculating Payments with the PMT Function

PMT is a financial function that calculates the periodic payment amount for money borrowed. For example, if you want to borrow money to buy a car, and you know the principal amount, interest rate, and loan term, the PMT function can calculate your monthly payment. Say you want to borrow $20,000 at 6.5% interest and pay the loan off in five years. The Excel PMT function can tell you that your monthly payment will be $391.32. The main parts of the PMT function are: PMT(rate, nper, pv). See Figure E-18 for an illustration of a PMT function that calculates the monthly payment in the car loan example. 🎨 For several months, QST's United States region has been discussing opening a new branch in San Francisco. Kate has obtained quotes from three different lenders on borrowing $259,000 to begin the expansion. She obtained loan quotes from a commercial bank, a venture capitalist, and an investment banker. She wants you to summarize the information using the Excel PMT function.

STEPS

1. **Click the Loan sheet tab, click cell F5, click the Formulas tab, click the Financial button in the Function Library group, scroll down the list of functions, then click PMT**

2. **With the insertion point in the Rate text box, click cell D5 on the worksheet, type /12, then press [Tab]**

   You must divide the annual interest by 12 because you are calculating monthly, not annual, payments.

3. **With the insertion point in the Nper text box, click cell E5; click the Pv text box, click cell B5, then click OK**

   The payment of (5445.81) in cell F5 appears in red, indicating that it is a negative amount. Excel displays the result of a PMT function as a negative value to reflect the negative cash flow the loan represents to the borrower. To show the monthly payment as a positive number, you can place a minus sign in front of the Pv cell reference in the function. The Fv and Type arguments are optional: The argument Fv is the future value, or the total amount you want to obtain after all payments. If you omit it, Excel assumes the Fv is 0. The Type argument indicates when the payments are made; 0 is the end of the period, and 1 is the beginning of the period. The default is the end of the period.

4. **Double-click cell F5 and edit it so it reads =PMT(D5/12,E5,-B5), then click the Enter button ☑ on the formula bar**

   A positive value of $5,445.81 now appears in cell F5, as shown in Figure E-19. You can use the same formula to generate the monthly payments for the other loans.

5. **With cell F5 selected, drag the fill handle to fill the range F6:F7**

   A monthly payment of $8,266.30 for the venture capitalist loan appears in cell F6. A monthly payment of $11,826.41 for the investment banker loan appears in cell F7. The loans with shorter terms have much higher payments. You will not know the entire financial picture until you calculate the total payments and total interest for each lender.

6. **Click cell G5, type =, click cell E5, type *, click cell F5, then press [Tab], in cell H5, type =, click cell G5, type –, click cell B5, then click ☑**

7. **Copy the formulas in cells G5:H5 into the range G6:H7, then click cell A1**

   Your worksheet appears as shown in Figure E-20. You can experiment with different interest rates, loan amounts, or terms for any one of the lenders; the PMT function generates a new set of values automatically.

8. **Add your name to the center section of the footer, save the workbook, preview and print the worksheet, then close the workbook and exit Excel**

FIGURE E-18: Example of PMT function for car loan

$$PMT(0.065/12, 60, 20000) = \$391.32$$

Interest rate per period (rate)

Number of payments (nper)

Present value of loan amount (pv)

Monthly payment calculated

FIGURE E-19: PMT function calculating monthly loan payment

F5   =PMT(D5/12,E5,-B5)

QST
Expansion Loan Summary

Lender	Loan Amount	Term (Years)	Interest Rate	Term (Months)	Monthly Payment	Total Payments	Total Interest
Commercial Bank	$ 259,000	5	9.55%	60	$5,445.81		
Venture Capitalist	$ 259,000	3	9.25%	36			
Investment Banker	$ 259,000	2	8.95%	24			

Minus sign before present value displays payment as a positive amount

Monthly payment calculated

FIGURE E-20: Completed worksheet

QST
Expansion Loan Summary

Lender	Loan Amount	Term (Years)	Interest Rate	Term (Months)	Monthly Payment	Total Payments	Total Interest
Commercial Bank	$ 259,000	5	9.55%	60	$5,445.81	$ 326,748.77	$ 67,748.77
Venture Capitalist	$ 259,000	3	9.25%	36	$8,266.30	$ 297,586.78	$ 38,586.78
Investment Banker	$ 259,000	2	8.95%	24	$11,826.41	$ 283,833.78	$ 24,833.78

Copied formula calculates total payments and interest for remaining two loan options

Excel 2007

Calculating future value with the FV function

You can use the FV (Future Value) function to determine the amount of money a given monthly investment will amount to, at a given interest rate, after a given number of payment periods. The syntax is similar to that of the PMT function: FV(rate,nper,pmt,pv,type). The rate is the interest paid by the financial institution, the nper is the number of periods, and the pmt is the amount that you deposit. For example, suppose you want to invest $1000 every month for the next 12 months into an account that pays 12% a year, and you want to know how much you will have at the end of 12 months (that is, its future value). You enter the function FV(.01,12,-1000), and Excel returns the value $12,682.50 as the future value of your investment. As with the PMT function, the units for the rate and nper must be consistent. If you made monthly payments on a three-year loan at 6% annual interest, you use the rate .06/12 and 36 periods (12*3). The arguments pv and type are optional; pv is the present value, or the total amount the series of payments is worth now. If you omit it, Excel assumes the pv is 0. The "type" argument indicates when the payments are made; 0 is the end of the period, and 1 is the beginning of the period. The default is the end of the period.

Practice

▼ CONCEPTS REVIEW

FIGURE E-21

1. Which element points to the area where the name of a selected cell or range is displayed? *C*
2. Which element points to a logical formula? *e*
3. Which element do you click to add a statistical function to a worksheet? *f*
4. Which element do you click to name a cell or range? *G*
5. Which element do you click to insert an IF function into a worksheet? *A*
6. Which element do you click to add a PMT function to a worksheet? *B*
7. Which element do you click to add a SUMIF function to a worksheet? *D*

Match each term with the statement that best describes it.

8. SUMIF *d*
9. PROPER *A*
10. test_cond *e*
11. FV *b*
12. PV *C*

   a. Function used to change the first letter of a string to uppercase
   b. Function used to determine the future amount of an investment
   c. Part of the PMT function that represents the loan amount
   d. Part of the IF function in which the conditions are stated
   e. Function used to conditionally total cells

Select the best answer from the list of choices.

13. **When you enter the rate and nper arguments in a PMT function, you must:**
    a. Use monthly units instead of annual units.
    b. Multiply both units by 12.
    c. Divide both values by 12.
    d. Be consistent in the units used.

14. **To express conditions such as less than or equal to, you can use a(n):**
    a. Statistical function.
    b. PMT function.
    c. Text formula.
    d. Comparison operator.

15. **Which of the following statements is false?**
    a. If you move a named cell or range, its name moves with it.
    b. Named ranges make formulas easier to build.
    c. Names cannot contain spaces.
    d. When used in formulas, names become relative cell references by default.

16. **Which of the following is an external reference indicator in a formula?**
    a. :
    b. &
    c. !
    d. =

▼ SKILLS REVIEW

1. **Format data using text functions.**
   a. Start Excel, open the file EX E-3.xlsx from the drive and folder where you store your Data Files, then save it as **Reviews**.
   b. On the Managers worksheet, select the range A2:A9 and, using the Text to Columns button on the Data tab, separate the names into two text columns. (*Hint*: The delimiter is a space.)
   c. In cell D2, enter the text formula to convert the first letter of the department in cell C2 to uppercase, then copy the formula in cell D2 into the range D3:D9.
   d. In cell E2, enter the text formula to convert all letters of the department in cell C2 to uppercase, then copy the formula in cell E2 into the range E3:E9.
   e. In cell F2, use the text formula to convert all letters of the department in cell C2 to lowercase, then copy the formula in cell F2 into the range F3:F9.
   f. In cell G2, use the text formula to substitute "Human Resources" for "hr" in cell F2. (*Hint*: In the Function Arguments dialog box, Text is F2, Old_text is hr, and New_text is Human Resources.) Copy the formula in cell G2 into the range G3:G9 to change the other cells containing hr to Human Resources. (Note that the marketing and sales entries will not change because the formula searches for the text hr).
   g. Save your work, then enter your name in the worksheet footer. Compare your screen to Figure E-22.
   h. Display the formulas in the worksheet, then print the worksheet.
   i. Redisplay the formula results.

FIGURE E-22

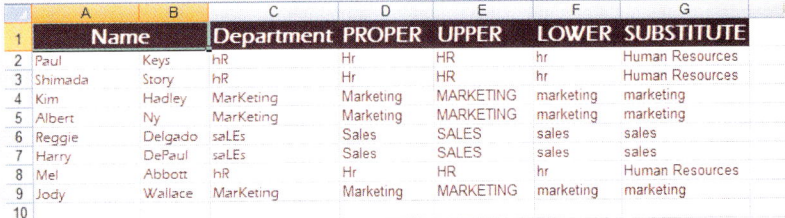

	A	B	C	D	E	F	G
1	Name		Department	PROPER	UPPER	LOWER	SUBSTITUTE
2	Paul	Keys	hR	Hr	HR	hr	Human Resources
3	Shimada	Story	hR	Hr	HR	hr	Human Resources
4	Kim	Hadley	MarKeting	Marketing	MARKETING	marketing	marketing
5	Albert	Ny	MarKeting	Marketing	MARKETING	marketing	marketing
6	Reggie	Delgado	saLEs	Sales	SALES	sales	sales
7	Harry	DePaul	saLEs	Sales	SALES	sales	sales
8	Mel	Abbott	hR	Hr	HR	hr	Human Resources
9	Jody	Wallace	MarKeting	Marketing	MARKETING	marketing	marketing
10							

2. **Sum a range of data conditionally.**
   a. Make the HR sheet active.
   b. In cell B20, use the COUNTIF function to count the number of employees with a rating of 5.
   c. In cell B21, use the AVERAGEIF function to average the salaries of employees with a rating of 5.
   d. In cell B22, enter the SUMIF function that totals the salaries of employees with a rating of 5.
   e. Format cells B21 and B22 with the Number format using commas and no decimals. Save your work.

3. Consolidate data using a formula.

   a. Make the Summary sheet active.

   b. In cell B4, use the AutoSum function to total cell F15 on the HR and Accounting sheets.

   c. Format cell B4 with the Accounting number format.

   d. Enter your name in the worksheet footer, then save your work. Compare your screen to Figure E-23.

   e. Display the formula in the worksheet, then print the worksheet.

   f. Redisplay the formula results in the worksheet.

FIGURE E-23

	A	B
1	**Payroll Summary**	
2		
3		**Salary**
4	**TOTAL**	$ 565,787.00
5		
6		

4. Check formulas for errors.

   a. Make the HR sheet active.

   b. In cell I6, use the IFERROR function to display "ERROR" in the event that the formula F6/F15 results in a formula error. (*Note*: This formula will generate an intentional error, which you will correct in a moment.)

   c. Copy the formula in cell I6 into the range I7:I14.

   d. Correct the formula in cell I6 by making the denominator, F15, an absolute address.

   e. Copy the new formula in cell I6 into the range I7:I14.

   f. Format the range I6:I14 as percentage with two decimal places.

   g. Save your work.

5. Construct formulas using named ranges.

   a. On the HR sheet, name the range C6:C14 **review_date** and limit the scope of the name to the HR worksheet.

   b. In cell E6, enter the formula **=review_date+183**, using the Use in Formula button to enter the cell name.

   c. Copy the formula in cell E6 into the range E7:E14.

   d. Use the Name Manager to add a comment of "Date of last review" to the review_date name. (*Hint*: In the Name Manager dialog box, click the review_date name, then click Edit to enter the comment.)

   e. Save your work.

6. Build a logical formula with the IF function.

   a. In cell G6, use the Function Arguments dialog box to enter the formula **=IF(D6=5,F6*0.05,0)**

   b. Copy the formula in cell G6 into the range G7:G14.

   c. In cell G15, use AutoSum to total the range G6:G14.

   d. Format the range G6:G15 with the Currency number format, using the $ symbol and no decimal places.

   e. Save your work.

7. Build a logical formula with the AND function.

   a. In cell H6, use the Function Arguments dialog box to enter the formula **=AND(G6>0,B6>5)**.

   b. Copy the formula in cell H6 into the range H7:H14.

   c. Enter your name in the worksheet footer, save your work, compare your worksheet to Figure E-24, then print the worksheet.

   d. Make the Accounting sheet active.

   e. In cell H6, indicate if the employee needs more development hours to reach the minimum of 5: Use the Function Arguments dialog box for the NOT function to enter **B6>5** in the Logical text box. Copy the formula in cell H6 into the range H7:H14.

   f. In cell I6, indicate if the employee needs to enroll in a quality class, as indicated by a rating less than 5 and having less than 5 development hours: Use the Function Arguments dialog box for the OR function to enter **D6<>5** in the Logical1 text box and **B6<=5** in the Logical2 text box. Copy the formula in cell I6 into the range I7:I14.

FIGURE E-24

	A	B	C	D	E	F	G	H	I
1			**Human Resources Department**						
2			**Merit Pay**						
3									
4									
5	**Last Name**	**Professional Development Hours**	**Review Date**	**Rating**	**Next Review**	**Salary**	**Bonus**	**Pay Bonus**	**Percentage of Total**
6	Barry	5	2/1/2010	4	8/3/2010	19,840	$0	FALSE	7.21%
7	Gray	8	3/1/2010	5	8/31/2010	26,700	$1,335	TRUE	9.71%
8	Greenwood	1	7/1/2010	3	12/31/2010	33,200	$0	FALSE	12.07%
9	Hemsley	3	4/1/2010	5	10/1/2010	25,500	$1,275	FALSE	9.27%
10	Kim	9	3/1/2010	3	8/31/2010	37,500	$0	FALSE	13.63%
11	Manchevski	8	5/1/2010	5	10/31/2010	36,500	$1,825	TRUE	13.27%
12	Marley	10	6/1/2010	4	12/1/2010	37,500	$0	FALSE	13.63%
13	Smith	6	1/1/2010	3	7/3/2010	28,600	$0	FALSE	10.40%
14	Storey	1	9/1/2010	5	3/3/2011	29,700	$1,485	FALSE	10.80%
15					Total	$ 275,040	$5,920		
16									
17									
18	**Department Statistics**								
19		**Rating of 5**							
20	Number		4						
21	Average Salary	29,600							
22	Total Salary	118,400							
23									

▼ SKILLS REVIEW (CONTINUED)

g. Enter your name in the worksheet footer, save your work, compare your screen to Figure E-25, then print the worksheet.

8. **Calculate payments with the PMT function.**

a. Make the Loan sheet active.

b. In cell B9, determine the monthly payment using the loan information shown: Use the Function Arguments dialog box to enter the formula **=PMT(B5/12,B6,-B4)**.

c. In cell B10, enter the formula **=B9*B6**.

d. In cell B11, enter the formula **=B10-B4**, then compare your screen to Figure E-26.

e. Enter your name in the worksheet footer, save the workbook, then print the worksheet.

f. Close the workbook, then exit Excel.

FIGURE E-25

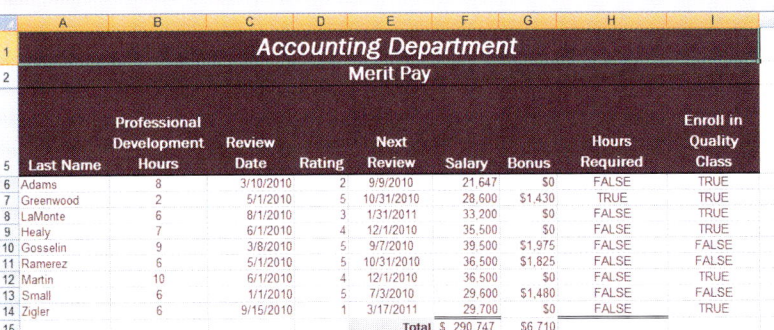

Last Name	Professional Development Hours	Review Date	Rating	Next Review	Salary	Bonus	Hours Required	Enroll in Quality Class
Adams	8	3/10/2010	2	9/9/2010	21,647	$0	FALSE	TRUE
Greenwood	2	5/1/2010	5	10/31/2010	28,600	$1,430	TRUE	TRUE
LaMonte	6	8/1/2010	3	1/31/2011	33,200	$0	FALSE	TRUE
Healy	7	6/1/2010	4	12/1/2010	35,500	$0	FALSE	TRUE
Gosselin	9	3/8/2010	5	9/7/2010	39,500	$1,975	FALSE	FALSE
Ramerez	6	5/1/2010	5	10/31/2010	36,500	$1,825	FALSE	FALSE
Martin	10	6/1/2010	4	12/1/2010	36,500	$0	FALSE	TRUE
Small	6	1/1/2010	5	7/3/2010	29,600	$1,480	FALSE	FALSE
Zigler	6	9/15/2010	1	3/17/2011	29,700	$0	FALSE	TRUE
				Total	$ 290,747	$6,710		

Accounting Department — Merit Pay

FIGURE E-26

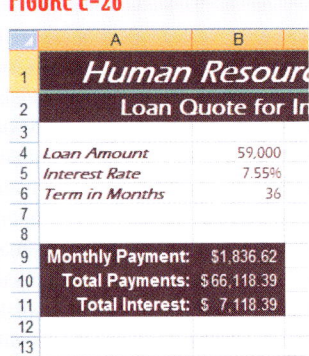

	A	B
1	Human Resour	
2	Loan Quote for In	
4	Loan Amount	59,000
5	Interest Rate	7.55%
6	Term in Months	36
9	Monthly Payment:	$1,836.62
10	Total Payments:	$66,118.39
11	Total Interest:	$ 7,118.39

▼ INDEPENDENT CHALLENGE 1

As the accounting manager of Travel Well, a travel insurance company, you are reviewing the accounts payable information for your advertising accounts and prioritizing the overdue invoices for your collections service. You will analyze the invoices and use logical functions to emphasize priority accounts.

a. Start Excel, open the file EX E-4.xlsx from the drive and folder where you store your Data Files, then save it as **Ad Accounts**.

b. Name the range B7:B13 **invoice_date** and give the name a scope of the accounts payable worksheet.

c. Name the cell B4 **current_date** and give the name a scope of the accounts payable worksheet.

d. Enter a formula using the named range invoice_date in cell E7 that calculates the invoice due date by adding 30 to the invoice date.

e. Copy the formula in cell E7 to the range E8:E13.

f. In cell F7, enter a formula using the named range invoice_date and the named cell current_date that calculates the invoice age by subtracting the invoice date from the current date.

g. Copy the formula in cell F7 to the range F8:F13.

h. In cell G7, enter an IF function that calculates the number of days an invoice is overdue, assuming that an invoice must be paid in 30 days. (*Hint*: The Logical_test should check to see if the age of the invoice is greater than 30, the Value_if_true should calculate the current date minus the invoice due date, and the Value_if_false should be 0). Copy the IF function into the range G8:G13.

i. In cell H7, enter an AND function to prioritize the overdue invoices that are more than $1000 for collection services. (*Hint:* The Logical1 condition should check to see if the number of days overdue is more than 0 and the Logical2 condition should check if the amount is more than 1000). Copy the AND function into the range H8:H13.

j. Enter your name in the worksheet footer, then save, preview, and print the worksheet.

k. Close the workbook, then exit Excel.

Advanced Challenge Exercise

■ Use the "Refers to:" text box in the Name Manager dialog box to verify that the names in the worksheet refer to the correct ranges.

■ Use the filter in the Name Manager dialog box to verify that your names are scoped to the worksheet and not the workbook.

■ Use the filter in the Name Manager dialog box to verify that your names are defined, free of errors, and not part of a table.

▼ INDEPENDENT CHALLENGE 2

You are an auditor with a certified public accounting firm. Goals, a manufacturer of ice skating products based in Quebec, has contacted you to audit its first-quarter sales records. The management at Goals is considering opening a branch in Great Britain and needs its sales records audited to prepare the business plan. Specifically, they want to show what percent of annual sales each category represents. You will use a formula on a summary worksheet to summarize the sales for January, February, and March and to calculate the overall first-quarter percentage of the sales categories.

a. Start Excel, open the file EX E-5.xlsx from the drive and folder where you store your Data Files, then save it as **Goals Sales**.

b. In cell B10 of the Jan, Feb, and Mar sheets, enter the formulas to calculate the sales totals for the month.

c. For each month, in cell C5, create a formula calculating the percent of sales for the Sticks sales category. Use a function to display "ERROR" if there is a mistake in the formula. Verify that the percent appears with two decimal places. Copy this formula as necessary to complete the % of Sales data for all sales categories on all sheets. If any cells display "ERROR", fix the formulas in those cells.

d. In column B of the Summary sheet, use formulas to total the sales categories for the Jan, Feb, and Mar worksheets.

e. Locate the first-quarter sales total in cell B10 of the Summary sheet. Calculate the percent of each sales category on the Summary sheet. Use a function to display "ERROR" if there is a mistake in the formula. Copy this formula as necessary. If any cells display "ERROR", fix the formulas in those cells.

f. Enter your name in the Summary worksheet footer, then save, preview, and print the worksheet.

g. On the Products sheet, separate the product list in cell A1 into separate columns of text data. (*Hint*: The products are delimited with commas.) Widen the columns as necessary. Use the second row to display the products with the first letter of each word in uppercase, as shown in Figure E-27.

h. Enter your name in the Products worksheet footer, then save, preview, and print the worksheet.

i. Close the workbook, then exit Excel.

FIGURE E-27

	A	B	C	D	E	F
1	sticks	ice skates	apparel	pads	equipment bags	
2	Sticks	Ice Skates	Apparel	Pads	Equipment Bags	
3						

▼ INDEPENDENT CHALLENGE 3

As the owner of Best Dressed, a clothing boutique with a growing clientele, you are planning to expand your business into a neighboring city. Because you will have to purchase additional inventory and renovate your new rental space, you decide to take out a $20,000 loan to finance your expansion expenses. You check three loan sources: the Small Business Administration (SBA), your local bank, and a consortium of investors. The SBA will lend you the money at 7.5% interest, but you have to pay it off in three years. The local bank offers you the loan at 8.25% interest over four years. The consortium offers you a 7% loan, but they require you to pay it back in two years. To analyze all three loan options, you decide to build a loan summary worksheet. Using the loan terms provided, build a worksheet summarizing your options.

a. Start Excel, open a new workbook, then save it as **Dress Shop Loan**.

b. Using Figure E-28 as a guide, enter labels and worksheet data for the three loan sources. (*Hint*: The Aspect theme is used with Orange Accent 1 as the fill color in the first two rows and Orange, Accent 1, Darker 25% as the text color in the calculation area.)

c. Enter the monthly payment formula for your first loan source (making sure to show the payment as a positive amount), copy the formula as appropriate, then name the range containing the monthly payment formulas **Monthly_Payment** with a scope of the workbook.

FIGURE E-28

	A	B	C	D	E	F	G
1				Best Dressed			
2				Loan Options			
3							
4	Loan Source	Loan Amount	Interest Rate	# Payments	Monthly Payment	Total Payments	Total Interest
5	SBA	20,000	7.50%	36			
6	Bank	20,000	8.25%	48			
7	Investors	20,000	7.00%	24			
8							

▼ INDEPENDENT CHALLENGE 3 (CONTINUED)

d. Name the cell range containing the number of payments **Number_Payments** with the scope of the workbook.

e. Enter the formula for total payments for your first loan source using the named ranges Monthly_Payment and Number_Payments, then copy the formula as necessary.

f. Name the cell range containing the formulas for Total payments **Total_Payments**. Name the cell range containing the loan amounts **Loan_Amount**.

g. Enter the formula for total interest for your first loan source using the named ranges Total_Payments and Loan_Amount, then copy the formula as necessary.

h. Format the worksheet using formatting appropriate to the worksheet purpose, then enter your name in the worksheet footer.

i. Save, preview, and print the worksheet in landscape orientation, on a single page.

Advanced Challenge Exercise

- Turn on the print gridlines option for the worksheet.
- Turn on the printing of row and column headings.
- Print the worksheet formulas with the worksheet gridlines and headings on one page.
- Display the worksheet values.

j. Close the workbook then exit Excel.

▼ REAL LIFE INDEPENDENT CHALLENGE

You decide to create a weekly log of your daily aerobic exercise. As part of this log, you record your aerobic activity along with the number of minutes spent working out. If you do more than one activity in a day, for example, if you bike and walk, record each as a separate event. Along with each activity, you record the location where you exercise. For example, you may walk in the gym or outdoors. You will use the log to analyze the amount of time that you spend on each type of exercise.

a. Start Excel, open the file EX E-6.xlsx from the drive and folder where you store your Data Files, then save it as **Workout**.

b. Use the structure of the worksheet to record your aerobic exercise activities. Change the data in columns A, B, C, D, and F to reflect your activities, locations, and times. If you do not have any data to enter, use the provided worksheet data.

c. Use a SUMIF function in the column G cells to calculate the total minutes spent on each activity.

d. Enter an AVERAGEIF function in the column H cells to average the number of minutes spent on each activity.

e. Enter a COUNTIF function in the column I cells to calculate the number of sessions spent on each activity.

Advanced Challenge Exercise

- Enter one of your activities with a specific location, such as Walk Outdoors, in a column F cell, then enter the SUMIFS function in the adjacent column G cell that calculates the total number of minutes spent on that activity in the specific location (such as walking ...outdoors).
- Enter the AVERAGEIFS function in the corresponding column H cell that calculates the average number of minutes spent on the activity in the specified location.
- Enter the COUNTIFS function in the corresponding column I cell that calculates the number of days spent on the activity in the specific location.

f. Enter your name in the worksheet footer, then save, preview, and print the worksheet.

g. Close the workbook, then exit Excel.

▼ VISUAL WORKSHOP

Open the file EX E-7.xlsx from the drive and folder where you store your Data Files, then save it as **Quarterly Sales Summary**. Create the worksheet shown in Figure E-29 using the data in columns B, C, and D. (*Hints:* Use AND formulas to determine if a person is eligible for a bonus, and use IF formulas to enter the bonus amounts. An employee with a performance rating of seven or higher and who meets the sales quota receives a bonus of one percent of the sales. If the rating is less than seven, or if the sales amounts are less than the quota, no bonus is awarded.) Enter your name in the worksheet footer, then preview and print the worksheet.

FIGURE E-29

	A	B	C	D	E	F
1			Bonus Pay Summary			
2						
3	Last Name	Quota	Sales	Performance Rating	Eligible	Bonus Amount
4	Allen	$100,000	$125,400	7	TRUE	$1,254
5	Gray	$80,000	$75,420	3	FALSE	$0
6	Greenwood	$90,000	$83,540	9	FALSE	$0
7	Hanson	$120,000	$132,980	5	FALSE	$0
8	Kerns	$150,000	$147,650	8	FALSE	$0
9	Maloney	$140,000	$149,800	5	FALSE	$0
10	Martin	$135,000	$132,200	7	FALSE	$0
11	Smith	$100,000	$98,650	3	FALSE	$0
12	Storey	$90,000	$96,700	9	TRUE	$967
13						

Appendix
A
Appendix

Restoring Defaults in Windows Vista and Disabling and Enabling Windows Aero

Files You Will Need:

No files needed.

Windows Vista is the most recent version of the Windows operating system. An operating system controls the way you work with your computer, supervises running programs, and provides tools for completing your computing tasks. After surveying millions of computer users, Microsoft incorporated their suggestions to make Windows Vista secure, reliable, and easy to use. In fact, Windows Vista is considered the most secure version of Windows yet. Other improvements include a powerful new search feature that lets you quickly search for files and programs from the Start menu and most windows, tools that simplify accessing the Internet, especially with a wireless connection, and multimedia programs that let you enjoy, share, and organize music, photos, and recorded TV. Finally, Windows Vista offers lots of visual appeal with its transparent, three-dimensional design in the Aero experience. This appendix explains how to make sure you are using the Windows Vista default settings for appearance, personalization, security, hardware, and sound and to enable and disable Windows Aero. For more information on Windows Aero, go to *www.microsoft.com/windowsvista/experiences/aero.mspx*.

OBJECTIVES

Restore the defaults in the Appearance and Personalization section

Restore the defaults in the Security section

Restore the defaults in the Hardware and Sound section

Disable Windows Aero

Enable Windows Aero

Restoring the Defaults in the Appearance and Personalization Section

The following instructions require a default Windows Vista Ultimate installation and the student logged in with an Administrator account. All of the following settings can be changed by accessing the Control Panel.

STEPS

- To restore the defaults in the Personalization section

  1. Click Start, and then click Control Panel. Click Appearance and Personalization, click Personalization, and then compare your screen to Figure A-1

  2. In the Personalization window, click Windows Color and Appearance, select the Default color, and then click OK

  3. In the Personalization window, click Mouse Pointers. In the Mouse Properties dialog box, on the Pointers tab, select Windows Aero (system scheme) in the Scheme drop-down list, and then click OK

  4. In the Personalization window, click Theme. Select Windows Vista from the Theme drop-down list, and then click OK

  5. In the Personalization window, click Display Settings. In the Display Settings dialog box, drag the Resolution bar to 1024 by 768 pixels, and then click OK

FIGURE A-1

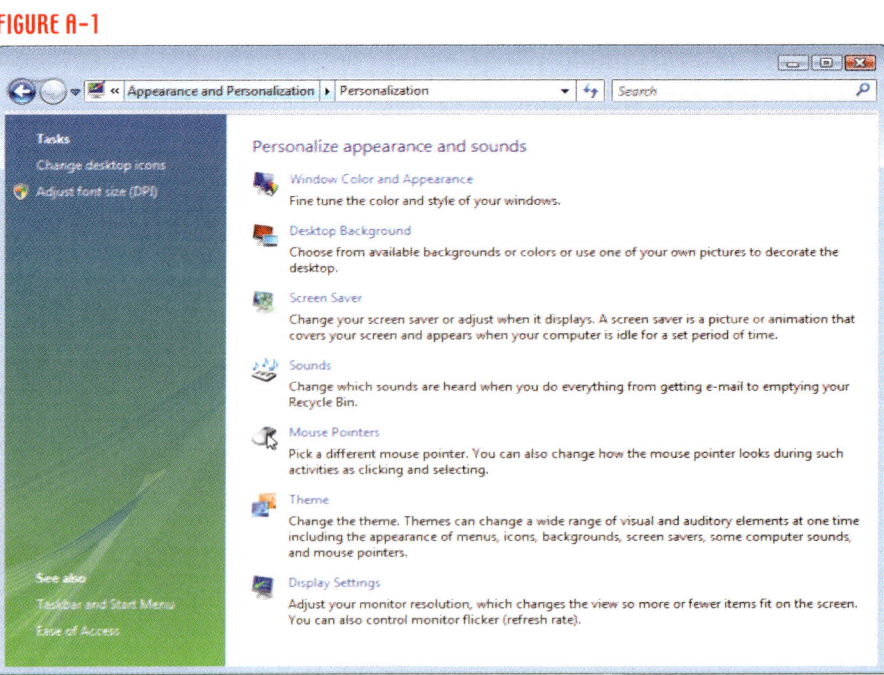

- **To restore the defaults in the Taskbar and Start Menu section**
    1. Click Start, and then click Control Panel. Click Appearance and Personalization, click Taskbar and Start Menu, and then compare your screen to Figure A-2
    2. In the Taskbar and Start Menu Properties dialog box, on the Taskbar tab, click to select all checkboxes except for "Auto-hide the taskbar"
    3. On the Start Menu tab, click to select the Start menu radio button and check all items in the Privacy section
    4. In the System icons section on the Notification Area tab, click to select all of the checkboxes except for "Power"
    5. On the Toolbars tab, click to select Quick Launch, none of the other items should be checked
    6. Click OK to close the Taskbar and Start Menu Properties dialog box

- **To restore the defaults in the Folder Options section**
    1. Click Start, and then click Control Panel. Click Appearance and Personalization, click Folder Options, and then compare your screen to Figure A-3
    2. In the Folder Options dialog box, on the General tab, click to select Show preview and filters in the Tasks section, click to select Open each folder in the same window in the Browse folders section, and click to select Double-click to open an item (single-click to select) in the Click items as follows section
    3. On the View tab, click the Reset Folders button, and then click Yes in the Folder views dialog box. Then click the Restore Defaults button
    4. On the Search tab, click the Restore Defaults button
    5. Click OK to close the Folder Options dialog box

- **To restore the defaults in the Windows Sidebar Properties section**
    1. Click Start, and then click Control Panel. Click Appearance and Personalization, click Windows Sidebar Properties, and then compare your screen to Figure A-4
    2. In the Windows Sidebar Properties dialog box, on the Sidebar tab, click to select Start Sidebar when Windows starts. In the Arrangement section, click to select Right, and then click to select 1 in the Display Sidebar on monitor drop-down list
    3. Click OK to close the Windows Sidebar Properties dialog box

FIGURE A-3

FIGURE A-4

FIGURE A-2

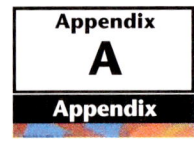

Restoring the Defaults in the Security Section

The following instructions require a default Windows Vista Ultimate installation and the student logged in with an Administrator account. All of the following settings can be changed by accessing the Control Panel.

STEPS

- **To restore the defaults in the Windows Firewall section**

  1. Click Start, and then click Control Panel. Click Security, click Windows Firewall, and then compare your screen to Figure A-5

  2. In the Windows Firewall dialog box, click Change settings. If the User Account Control dialog box appears, click Continue

  3. In the Windows Firewall Settings dialog box, click the Advanced tab. Click Restore Defaults, then click Yes in the Restore Defaults Confirmation dialog box

  4. Click OK to close the Windows Firewall Settings dialog box, and then close the Windows Firewall window

- **To restore the defaults in the Internet Options section**

  1. Click Start, and then click Control Panel. Click Security, click Internet Options, and then compare your screen to Figure A-6

  2. In the Internet Properties dialog box, on the General tab, click the Use default button. Click the Settings button in the Tabs section, and then click the Restore defaults button in the Tabbed Browsing Settings dialog box. Click OK to close the Tabbed Browsing Settings dialog box

  3. On the Security tab of the Internet Properties dialog box, click to uncheck the Enable Protected Mode checkbox, if necessary. Click the Default level button in the Security level for this zone section. If possible, click the Reset all zones to default level button

  4. On the Programs tab, click the Make default button in the Default web browser button for Internet Explorer, if possible. If Office is installed, Microsoft Office Word should be selected in the HTML editor drop-down list

  5. On the Advanced tab, click the Restore advanced settings button in the Settings section. Click the Reset button in the Reset Internet Explorer settings section, and then click Reset in the Reset Internet Explorer Settings dialog box

  6. Click Close to close the Reset Internet Explorer Settings dialog box, and then click OK to close the Internet Properties dialog box

FIGURE A-5

FIGURE A-6

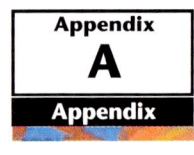

Appendix
A
Appendix

Restoring the Defaults in the Hardware and Sound Section

The following instructions require a default Windows Vista Ultimate installation and the student logged in with an Administrator account. All of the following settings can be changed by accessing the Control Panel.

STEPS

- To restore the defaults in the Autoplay section
    1. Click Start, and then click Control Panel. Click Hardware and Sound, click Autoplay, and then compare your screen to Figure A-7. Scroll down and click the Reset all defaults button in the Devices section at the bottom of the window, and then click Save

- To restore the defaults in the Sound section
    1. Click Start, and then click Control Panel. Click Hardware and Sound, click Sound, and then compare your screen to Figure A-8
    2. In the Sound dialog box, on the Sounds tab, select Windows Default from the Sound Scheme drop-down list, and then click OK

- To restore the defaults in the Mouse section
    1. Click Start, and then click Control Panel. Click Hardware and Sound, click Mouse, and then compare your screen to Figure A-9
    2. In the Mouse Properties dialog box, on the Pointers tab, select Windows Aero (system scheme) from the Scheme drop-down list
    3. Click OK to close the Mouse Properties dialog box

FIGURE A-7

FIGURE A-8

FIGURE A-9

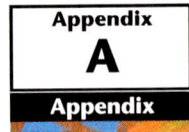
Disabling and Enabling Windows Aero

Unlike prior versions of Windows, Windows Vista provides two distinct user interface experiences: a "basic" experience for entry-level systems and more visually dynamic experience called Windows Aero. Both offer a new and intutive navgation experience that helps you more easily find and organize your applications and files, but Aero goes further by delivering a truly next-generation desktop experience.

Windows Aero builds on the basic Windows Vista user experience and offers Mircosoft's best-designed, highest-preforming desktop experience. Using Aero requires a PC with compatible graphics adapter and running a Premium or Business edition of Windows Vista.

The following instructions require a computer capable of running Windows Aero, with a default Windows Vista Ultimate installation and student logged in with an Administrator account.

STEPS

- **To Disable Windows Aero**

We recommend that students using this book disable Windows Aero and restore their operating systems default settings (instructions to follow).

1. Right-click the desktop, select Personalize, and then compare yor screen in Figure A-10. Select Window Color and Appearance, and then select Open classic appeareance properties for more color options. In Appearance Settings dialong box, on the Appearance tab, select any non-Aero scheme (such as Windows Vista Basic or Windows Vista Standard) in the Color Scheme list, and then click OK Figure A-11 compares Windows Aero to other color schemes. Note that this book uses Windows Vista Basic as the color scheme

- **To Enable Windows Aero**

1. Right-click the desktop, and then select Personalize. Select Window Color and Appearance, then select Windows Aero in the Color scheme list, and then click OK in the Appearance Settings dialog box

FIGURE A-10

FIGURE A-11

Select other color schemes

Windows Aero color scheme applied

3-D reference A reference that uses values on other sheets or workbooks, effectively creating another dimension to a workbook.

Absolute cell reference In a formula, type of cell address that does not change when you copy the formula; indicated by a dollar sign before the column letter and/or row number. *See also* Relative cell reference.

Accessories Simple programs to perform specific tasks that come with Windows Vista, such as the Calculator for performing calculations.

Active The currently available document, program, or object; on the taskbar, the button of the active document appears in a darker shade while the buttons of other open documents are dimmed.

Active cell The cell in which you are currently working.

Active window The window you are currently using.

Add-in A supplementary program that provides additional program features; for example, the Solver add-in enables you to find a solution to a calculation that has several inputs; the Analysis ToolPak provides optional Excel features. To activate an add-in, click the Office button, click Excel options, click Add-Ins, then click Go. Select or deselect add-ins from the list.

Address Bar A horizontal box near the top of a window that shows your current location in the computer's file hierarchy as a series of links separated by arrows; used to navigate to other locations on your computer.

Alignment The placement of cell contents; for example, left, center, or right.

AND condition A filtering feature that searches for records by specifying that all entered criteria must be matched.

Apply (a template) To open a document based on an Excel template.

Argument In the Visual Basic for Applications (VBA) programming language, variable used in procedures that a main procedure might run. *See also* Main procedure.

Arithmetic operators In a formula, symbols that perform mathematical calculations, such as plus (+), minus (–), multiplication (*), division (/), or exponentiation (^).

Ascending order In sorting worksheet records, the lowest value (the beginning of the alphabet, or the earliest date) appears at the beginning of the sorted data.

ASCII file A text file that contains data but no formatting; instead of being divided into columns, ASCII file data are separated, or delimited, by tabs or commas.

Attributes Styling characteristics such as bold, italic, and underlining that you can apply to change the way text and numbers look in a worksheet or chart. In XML, the components that provides information about the document's elements.

Auditing An Excel feature that helps track errors and check worksheet logic.

AutoComplete In the Visual Basic for Applications (VBA) programming language, a list of words that appears as you enter code; helps you automatically enter elements with the correct syntax.

AutoFill Options button Feature that lets you fill cells with specific elements (such as formatting) of the copied cell.

AutoFilter A table feature that lets you click a list arrow and select criteria by which to display certain types of records; *also called* filter.

AutoFilter list arrows List arrows that appear next to field names in an Excel table; used to display portions of your data. *Also called* filter list arrows.

AutoFit A feature that automatically adjusts the width of a column or the height of a row to accommodate its widest or tallest entry.

Backsolving A problem-solving method in which you specify a solution and then find the input value that produces the answer you want; sometimes described as a what-if analysis in reverse. In Excel, the Goal Seek feature performs backsolving.

Backup A duplicate copy of a file that is stored in another location.

Backward-compatible Software feature that enables documents saved in an older version of a program to be opened in a newer version of the program.

Banding Worksheet formatting in which adjacent rows and columns are formatted differently.

Boolean filter A word or symbol for locating programs, folders, and files by specifying one or more criteria so that you have a greater chance of finding what you need.

Booting A process that Windows steps through to get the computer up and running.

Bug In programming, an error that causes a procedure to run incorrectly.

Byte One character of storage space on disk or in RAM.

Calculated columns In a table, a column that uses one formula that automatically adjusts to accommodate additional rows.

Calculation operators Symbols that indicate what type of calculation to perform on the cells, ranges or values.

Category axis Horizontal axis of a chart, usually containing the names of data groups; in a 2-dimensional chart, also known as the x-axis.

Cell The intersection of a column and a row in a worksheet, datasheet, or table.

Cell address The location of a cell, expressed by cell coordinates; for example, the cell address of the cell in column A, row 1 is A1.

Cell comments Notes you've written about a workbook that appear when you place the pointer over a cell.

Cell pointer A dark rectangle that outlines the active cell.

Cell styles Predesigned combinations of formatting attributes that can be applied to selected cells, to enhance the look of a worksheet.

Change history A worksheet containing a list of changes made to a shared workbook.

Changing cells In what-if analysis, cells that contain the values that change in order to produce multiple sets of results.

Chart sheet A separate sheet in a workbook that contains only a chart, which is linked to the workbook data.

Charts Pictorial representations of worksheet data that make it easier to see patterns, trends, and relationships; *also called* graphs.

Check box A box that turns an option on when checked or off when unchecked.

Click To quickly press and release the left button on the pointing device; also called single-click.

Clip A media file, such as art, sound, animation, or a movie.

Clip art A graphic image, such as a corporate logo, a picture, or a photo, that can be inserted into a document.

Clipboard Temporary storage area in Windows.

Code *See* Program code.

Code window In the Visual Basic Editor, the window that displays the selected module's procedures, written in the Visual Basic programming language.

Collapse button A button that shrinks a portion of a dialog box to hide some settings.

Color scale In conditional formatting, a formatting scheme that uses a set of two, three, or four fill colors to convey relative values of data.

Column heading Identifies the column letter, such as A, B, etc.; located above each column in a worksheet.

Command An instruction to perform a task.

Command button A button that completes or cancels an operation.

Comments In a Visual Basic procedure, notes that explain the purpose of the macro or procedure; they are preceded by a single apostrophe and appear in green. *See also* Cell comments.

Comparison operators In a calculation, symbols that compare values for the purpose of true/false results.

Compatible The capability of different programs to work together and exchange data.

Complex formula A formula that uses more than one arithmetic operator.

Compress To reduce the size of file so that it takes up less storage space on a disk.

Computer window The window shows the drives on your computer as well as other installed hardware components.

Conditional format A type of cell formatting that changes based on the cell's value or the outcome of a formula.

Consolidate To combine data on multiple worksheets and display the result on another worksheet.

Constraints Limitations or restrictions on input data in what-if analysis.

Contextual tab Tab on the Ribbon that appears when needed to complete a specific task; for example, if you select a chart in an Excel workbook, three contextual Chart Tool tabs (Design, Layout, and Format) appear.

Copy To make a duplicate copy of a file that is stored in another location.

Criteria range In advanced filtering, a cell range containing one row of labels (usually a copy of column labels) and at least one additional row underneath it that contains the criteria you want to match.

Custom chart type A specially formatted Excel chart.

Data entry area The unlocked portion of a worksheet where users are able to enter and change data.

Data label Descriptive text that appears above a data marker in a chart.

Data marker A graphical representation of a data point, such as a bar or column.

Data point Individual piece of data plotted in a chart.

Data series A column or row in a datasheet. Also, the selected range in a worksheet that Excel converts into a chart.

Data source Worksheet data used to create a chart or a PivotTable.

Data table A range of cells that shows the resulting values when one or more input values are varied in a formula; when one input value is changed, the table is called a one-input data table, and when two input values are changed, it is called a two-input data table. In a chart, it is a grid containing the chart data.

Data validation A feature that allows you to specify what data is allowable (valid) for a range of cells.

Database An organized collection of related information. In Excel, a database is called a table.

Debug In programming, to find and correct an error in code.

Declare In the Visual Basic programming language, to assign a type, such as numeric or text, to a variable.

Default A setting that is built into a program that is used by that program until you change the setting.

Delete To remove a folder or file.

Delimiter A separator such as a space, comma, or semicolon between elements in imported data.

Dependent cell A cell, usually containing a formula, whose value changes depending on the values in the input cells. For example, a payment formula or function that depends on an input cell containing changing interest rates is a dependent cell.

Descending order In sorting an Excel table, the order that begins with the letter Z or the highest number in a table.

Desktop The graphical user interface (GUI) displayed on your screen after you start Windows that you use to interact with Windows and other software on your computer.

Destination program In a data exchange, the program that will receive the data.

Details Pane A pane located at the bottom of a window that displays information about the selected disk, drive, folder, or file.

Device A hardware component in your computer system.

Dialog box A type of window in which you specify how you want to complete an operation.

Dialog box launcher An icon available in many groups on the Ribbon that you can click to open a dialog box or task pane, offering an alternative way to choose commands.

Document To make notes about basic worksheet assumptions, complex formulas, or questionable data. In a macro, to insert comments that explain the Visual Basic code.

Document window The portion of a program window that displays all or part of an open document.

Documents folder The folder on your hard drive used to store most of the files you create or receive from others.

Double-click To quickly click the left button on the pointing device twice.

Drag To point to an object, press and hold the left button on the pointing device, move the object to a new location, and then release the left button.

Drag and drop To use a pointing device to move or copy a file or folder to a new location.

Drive A physical location on your computer where you can store files.

Drive name A name for a drive that consists of a letter followed by a colon, such as C: for the hard disk drive.

Drop-down list button A button that opens a list with one or more options from which you can choose.

Dynamic page breaks In a larger workbook, horizontal or vertical dashed lines that represent the place where pages print separately. They also adjust automatically when you insert or delete rows or columns, or change column widths or row heights.

Edit (Excel) To make a change to the contents of an active cell. (Windows) To make changes to a file.

Electronic spreadsheet A computer program that performs calculations and presents numeric data.

Element An XML component that defines the document content.

Embed To insert a copy of data into a destination document; you can double-click the embedded object to modify it using the tools of the source program.

Embedded chart A chart displayed as an object in a worksheet.

Expand button A button that extends a dialog box to display additional settings.

Exploding pie slice A slice of a pie chart that has been pulled away from the whole pie, in order to add emphasis.

Extensible Markup Language (XML) A system for defining languages using tags to structure data.

External reference indicator The exclamation point (!) used in a formula to indicate that a referenced cell is outside the active sheet.

Extract To place a copy of a filtered table in a range you specify in the Advanced Filter dialog box.

Field In a table (an Excel database), a column that describes a characteristic about records, such as first name or city.

Field name A column label that describes a field.

File A collection of stored electronic data, such as text, pictures, video, music, and programs.

File extension Additional characters assigned by a program added to the end of a filename to identify the type of file.

File hierarchy The structure for organizing folders and files; describes the logic and layout of the folder structure on a disk.

File management A strategy for organizing folders and files.

Filename A unique, descriptive name for a file that identifies the file's content. A filename can be no more than 255 characters, including spaces, and can include letters, numbers, and certain symbols.

Filter To display data in an Excel table that meet specified criteria. *See also* AutoFilter.

Filter arrows *See* AutoFilter list arrows.

Folder A container for a group of related files. A folder may contain subfolders for organizing files into smaller groups.

Folder name A unique, descriptive name for a folder that identifies what you store in that folder.

Font The typeface or design of a set of characters (letters, numerals, symbols, and punctuation marks).

Font size The size of characters, measured in units called points (pts).

Format (n.) The appearance of text and numbers, including color, font, attributes, borders, and shading. *See also* Number format. (v.) To enhance or improve the appearance of a document.

Format bar A toolbar in the WordPad window that displays buttons for formatting, or enhancing, the appearance of a document.

Formula bar The area above the worksheet grid where you enter or edit data in the active cell.

Formula A set of instructions used to perform one or more numeric calculations, such as adding, multiplying, or averaging, on values or cells.

Formula prefix An arithmetic symbol, such as the equal sign (=), used to start a formula.

Freeze To hold in place selected columns or rows when scrolling in a worksheet that is divided in panes. *See also* Panes.

Function (Excel) A built-in formula that includes the information necessary to calculate an answer; for example, SUM (for calculating a sum) or FV (for calculating the future value of an investment) (Visual Basic) In the Visual Basic for Applications (VBA) programming language, a predefined procedure that returns a value, such as the InputBox function that prompts the user to enter information.

Gadget A mini-program on the Windows Sidebar for performing an every day task, such as the Clock gadget for viewing the current time.

Gallery A collection of choices you can browse through to make a selection. Often available with Live Preview.

Gigabyte (GB or G) One billion bytes (or one thousand megabytes).

Goal cell In backsolving, a cell containing a formula in which you can substitute values to find a specific value, or goal.

Goal Seek A problem-solving method in which you specify a solution and then find the input value that produces the answer you want; sometimes described as a what-if analysis in reverse; also called backsolving.

Gridlines Evenly spaced horizontal and/or vertical lines used in a worksheet or chart to make it easier to read.

Group On the Ribbon, a set of related commands on a tab.

Hard copy A paper copy of a file.

Hard disk A built-in, high-capacity, high-speed storage medium for all the software, folders, and files on a computer.

Header row In a table, the first row that contains the field names.

Hotspot An object that, when clicked, will run a macro or open a file.

HTML Hypertext Markup Language, the format of pages that a Web browser can read.

Hyperlink An object (a filename, a word, a phrase, or a graphic) in a worksheet that, when you click it, displays another worksheet or a Web page called the target. *See also* Target.

Icon A small image on the desktop or in a window that represents a tool, resource, folder, or file you can open and use.

Icon sets In conditional formatting, groups of images that are used to visually communicate relative cell values based on the values they contain.

If...Then...Else statement In the Visual Basic programming language, a conditional statement that directs Excel to perform specified actions under certain conditions; its syntax is "If *condition* Then *statements* Else [*elsestatements*].

Inactive window An open window you are not currently using.

Input Information that produces desired results, or output, in a worksheet.

Input cells Spreadsheet cells that contain data instead of formulas and that act as input to a what-if analysis; input values often change to produce different results. Examples include interest rates, prices, or other data.

Input values In a data table, the variable values that are substituted in the table's formula to obtain varying results, such as interest rates.

Insertion point A blinking vertical line that appears when you click in the formula bar; indicates where new text will be inserted.

Instance A worksheet in its own workbook window.

Instant Search A Windows tool you use to quickly find a folder or file on your computer.

Integrate To incorporate a document and parts of a document created in one program into another program; for example, to incorporate an Excel chart into a PowerPoint slide, or an Access table into a Word document.

Integration A process in which data is exchanged among Excel and other Windows programs; can include pasting, importing, exporting, embedding, and linking.

Interface The look and feel of a program; for example, the appearance of commands and the way they are organized in the program window.

Intranet An internal network site used by a group of people who work together.

Keyboard shortcut A key or a combination of keys that you press to perform a command.

Keyword (Excel) Terms added to a workbook's Document Properties that help locate the file in a search. (Macros) In a macro procedure, a word that is recognized as part of the Visual Basic programming language. (Windows) A descriptive word or phrase you enter to obtain a list of results that include that word or phrase.

Kilobyte (KB or K) One thousand bytes.

Labels Descriptive text or other information that identifies rows, columns, or chart data, but is not included in calculations.

Landscape orientation Print setting that positions a document so it spans the widest margins of the page, making the page wider than it is tall.

Launch To open or start a program on your computer.

Legend In a chart, information that explains how data is represented by colors or patterns.

Linear trendline In an Excel chart, a straight line representing an overall trend in a data series.

Link (Windows) A shortcut for opening a Help topic or a Web site. (Office) To insert an object into a destination program; the information you insert will be updated automatically when the data in the source document changes.

Linking The dynamic referencing of data in other workbooks, so that when data in the other workbooks is changed, the references in the current workbook are automatically updated.

List arrows *See* AutoFilter list arrows.

List box A box that displays a list of options from which you can choose (you may need to scroll and adjust your view to see additional options in the list).

Live Preview A feature that lets you point to a choice in a gallery or palette and see the results in the document without actually clicking the choice.

Live taskbar thumbnails A Windows Aero feature that displays a small image of the content within open, but not visible windows, including live content such as video.

Live view A file icon that displays the actual content in a file on the icon.

Lock (Windows) To lock your user account, then display the Welcome screen. (Excel) To secure a row, column, or sheet so that data in that location cannot be changed.

Lock button A Start menu option that locks your computer.

Lock menu button A Start menu option that displays a list of shut-down options.

Log Off To close all windows, programs, and documents, then display the Welcome screen.

Logical conditions Using the operators And and Or to narrow a custom filter criteria.

Logical formula A formula with calculations that are based on stated conditions.

Logical test The first part of an IF function; if the logical test is true, then the second part of the function is applied, and if it is false, then the third part of the function is applied.

Macro A set of instructions recorded or written in the Visual Basic programming language; used to automate worksheet tasks.

Main procedure A macro procedure containing several macros that run sequentially.

Manual calculation option An option that turns off automatic calculation of worksheet formulas, allowing you to selectively determine if and when you want Excel to perform calculations.

Map An XML schema that is attached to a workbook.

Map an XML element A process in which XML element names are placed on an Excel worksheet in specific locations.

Maximized window A window that fills the desktop.

Megabyte (MB or M) One million bytes (or one thousand kilobytes).

Menu A list of related commands.

Menu bar A horizontal bar in a window that displays menu names that represent categories of related commands.

Metadata Information that describes data and is used in Microsoft Windows document searches.

Microsoft Windows Vista An operating system.

Minimized window A window that shrinks to a button on the taskbar.

Mixed reference Cell reference that combines both absolute and relative addressing.

Mode In dialog boxes, a state that offers a limited set of possible choices.

Mode indicator An area in the lower-left corner of the status bar that informs you of a program's status. For example, when you are entering or changing the contents of a cell, the word 'Edit' appears.

Model A worksheet used to produce a what-if analysis that acts as the basis for multiple outcomes.

Modeless Describes dialog boxes that, when opened, allow you to select other elements on a chart or worksheet to change the dialog box options and format, or otherwise alter the selected elements.

Module In Visual Basic, a module is stored in a workbook and contains macro procedures.

Move To change the location of a file by physically placing it in another location.

Multilevel sort A reordering of table data using more than one column at a time.

Multitask To perform several tasks at the same time.

Name box Left-most area of the formula bar that shows the cell reference or name of the active cell.

Named range A contiguous group of cells given a meaningful name such as "July Sales"; it retains its name when moved and can be referenced in a formula.

Navigate To move around in a worksheet; for example, you can use the arrow keys on the keyboard to navigate from cell to cell, or press [Page Up] or [Page Down] to move a screen at a time.

Navigation Pane A pane on the left side of a window that contains links to your personal folders, including the Documents, Pictures, and Music folders.

Normal view Default worksheet view that shows the worksheet without features such as headers and footers; ideal for creating and editing a worksheet, but may not be detailed enough when formatting a document.

Notification area An area on the right side of the taskbar that displays the current time as well as icons for open programs, connecting to the Internet, and checking problems identified by Windows Vista.

Number format A format applied to values to express numeric concepts, such as currency, date, and percentage.

Object A chart or graphic image that can be moved and resized and contains handles when selected. In object linking and embedding (OLE), the data to be exchanged between another document or program. In Visual Basic, every Excel element, including ranges.

Object Linking and Embedding (OLE) A Microsoft Windows technology that allows you to transfer data from one document and program to another using embedding or linking.

OLE *See* Object Linking and Embedding.

One-input data table A range of cells that shows resulting values when one input value in a formula is changed.

Online collaboration The ability to incorporate feedback or share information across the Internet or a company network or intranet.

Operating system Software that manages the complete operation of your computer.

Option button A small circle you click to select only one of two or more related options.

Or condition The records in a search must match only one of the criterion.

Outline symbols In outline view, the buttons that, when clicked, change the amount of detail in the outlined worksheet.

Output The end result of a worksheet.

Output values In a data table, the calculated results that appear in the body of the table.

Page Break Preview A worksheet view that displays page break indicators which you can drag to include more or less information on each page in a worksheet.

Page Layout View Provides an accurate view of how a worksheet will look when printed, including headers and footers.

Panes Sections into which you can divide a worksheet when you want to work on separate parts of the worksheet at the same time; one pane freezes, or remains in place, while you scroll in another pane until you see the desired information.

Paste Options button Allows you to paste only specific elements of the copied selection, such as the formatting or values.

Personal macro workbook A workbook that can contain macros that are available to any open workbook. By default, the personal macro workbook is hidden.

PivotChart report An Excel feature that lets you summarize worksheet data in the form of a chart in which you can rearrange, or "pivot," parts of the chart structure to explore new data relationships.

PivotTable Interactive table format that lets you summarize worksheet data.

PivotTable Field List A window containing fields that can be used to create or modify a PivotTable.

PivotTable report An Excel feature that allows you to summarize worksheet data in the form of a table in which you can rearrange, or "pivot," parts of the table structure to explore new data relationships; also called a PivotTable.

Plot The Excel process that converts numerical information into data points on a chart.

Plot area In a chart, the area inside the horizontal and vertical axes.

Point (n.) A unit of measure used for fonts and row height. One inch equals 72 points, or a point is equal to $1/72^{nd}$ of an inch. (v.) To position the tip of the pointer over an object, option, or item.

Pointer A small arrow or other symbol on the screen that moves in the same direction as the pointing device.

Pointing device A hardware device, such as a mouse, trackball, touch pad, or pointing stick, or an onscreen object for interacting with your computer and the software you are using.

Populate a worksheet with XML data The process of importing an XML file and filling the mapped elements on the worksheet with data from the XML file.

Portrait orientation A print setting that positions the document on the page so the page is taller than it is wide.

Post To place an interactive workbook in a shared location.

Power button A Start menu option that puts your computer to sleep (your computer appears off and uses very little power).

Precedents In formula auditing, the cells that are used in the formula to calculate the value of a given cell.

Presentation graphics program A program such as Microsoft PowerPoint that you can use to create slide show presentations.

Preview Pane A pane on the right side of a window that shows the actual contents of a selected file without opening a program. Preview may not work for some types of files.

Previewing Prior to printing, to see onscreen exactly how the printed document will look.

Primary Key The field in a database that contains unique information for each record.

Print area A portion of a worksheet that you can define using the Print Area button on the Page Layout tab; after you select and define a print area, the Quick Print feature prints only that worksheet area.

Print Preview A full-page view of a document that you can use to check its layout before you print.

Print title In a table that spans more than one page, the field names that print at the top of every printed page.

Procedure A sequence of Visual Basic statements contained in a macro that accomplishes a specific task.

Procedure footer In Visual Basic, the last line of a Sub procedure.

Procedure header The first line in a Visual Basic procedure, it defines the procedure type, name, and arguments.

Program code Macro instructions, written in the Visual Basic for Applications (VBA) programming language.

Program tab Single tab on the Ribbon specific to a particular view, such as Print Preview.

Project In the Visual Basic Editor, the equivalent of a workbook; a project contains Visual Basic modules.

Project Explorer In the Visual Basic Editor, a window that lists all open projects (or workbooks) and the worksheets and modules they contain.

Properties 1) Characteristics or settings of a component of the graphical user interface; 2) File characteristics, such as the author's name, keywords, or the title, that help others understand, identify, and locate the file.

Properties window In the Visual Basic Editor, the window that displays a list of characteristics, or properties, associated with a module.

Property In Visual Basic, an attribute of an object that describes its character or behavior.

Publish To place an Excel workbook or worksheet on a Web site or an intranet in HTML format so that others can access it using their Web browsers.

Quick Access toolbar Customizable toolbar that includes buttons for common Office commands, such as saving a file and undoing an action.

Quick Launch toolbar A toolbar on the left side of the taskbar; includes buttons for showing the desktop when it is not currently visible, switching between windows, and starting the Internet Explorer Web browser.

RAM (Random Access Memory) The physical location used to temporarily store open programs and documents.

Range A selection of two or more cells, such as B5:B14.

Range object In Visual Basic, an object that represents a cell or a range of cells.

Read-only format Data that users can view but not change.

Record In a table (an Excel database), data about an object or a person.

Recycle Bin A desktop object that stores folders and files you delete from your hard drive(s) and that enables you to restore them.

Reference operators Mathematical calculations which enable you to use ranges in calculations.

Refresh To update a PivotTable so it reflects changes to the underlying data.

Regression analysis A way of representing data with a mathematically-calculated trendline showing the overall trend represented by the data.

Relative cell reference In a formula, type of cell addressing that automatically changes when the formula is copied or moved, to reflect the new location; default type of referencing used in Excel worksheets. *See also* Absolute cell referencing.

Removable storage Storage media that you can easily transfer from one computer to another, such as DVDs, CDs, or flash drives.

Report filter A feature that allows you to specify the ranges you want summarized in a PivotTable.

Resizing button A button that you use to adjust the size of a window, such as Maximize, Restore Down, and Minimize.

Restart To shut down your computer, then start it again.

Return In a function, to display.

Ribbon Area that displays commands for the current Office program, organized into tabs and groups.

Right-click To quickly press and release the right button on the pointing device.

Ruler A horizontal bar in the WordPad window that marks a document's width in 1/8ths of an inch (also shows one-inch marks).

Run To play, as a macro.

Scenario A set of values you use to forecast results; the Excel Scenario Manager lets you store and manage different scenarios.

Scenario summary An Excel table that compiles data from various scenarios so that you can view the scenario results next to each other for easy comparison.

Schema In an XML document, a list of the fields, called elements or attributes, and their characteristics.

Scope In a named cell or range, the worksheets where the name can be used.

Screen capture A snapshot of your screen, as if you took a picture of it with a camera, which you can paste into a document.

Scroll To adjust your view in a window.

Scroll arrow button A button at each end of a scroll bar for adjusting your view in small increments in that direction.

Scroll bar A vertical or horizontal bar that appears along the right or bottom side of a window when there is more content than can be displayed within the window so that you can adjust your view.

Scroll box A box in a scroll bar that you can drag to display a different part of a window.

Search criteria (Windows) One or more pieces of information that helps Windows identify the program, folder, or file you want to locate. (Excel) In a workbook or table search, the text you are searching for.

Share *See* Shared workbook.

Shared workbook An Excel workbook that several users can open and modify at the same time.

Sheet tab Identifies sheets in a workbook and lets you switch between sheets; sheet tabs are located below the worksheet grid.

Shortcut A link that gives you quick access to a particular folder, file, or Web site.

Shortcut menu A menu of common commands for an object that opens when you right-click that object.

Shut Down To completely shut down your computer.

Sidebar A Windows Vista desktop component that displays gadgets.

Single-click *See* Click.

Single-file Web page A Web page that integrates all of the worksheets and graphical elements from a workbook into a single file in the MHTML file format, making it easier to publish to the Web.

Sizing handles Small dots at the corners and edges of a chart, indicating that the chart is selected.

Sleep To save your work, turn off the monitor, then reduce power consumption to all the hardware components in your computer so it appears off; press any key to use your computer again.

Slider A shape you drag to select a setting that falls within a range, such as between Slow and Fast.

SmartArt Predesigned diagram types for the following types of data: List, Process, Cycle, Hierarchy, Relationship, Matrix, and Pyramid.

Sort To change the order of records in a table according to one or more fields, such as Last Name.

Sort keys Criteria on which a sort, or a reordering of data, is based.

Source program In a data exchange, the program used to create the data you are embedding or linking.

Spin box A text box with up and down arrows; you can type a setting in the text box or click the arrows to increase or a decrease the setting.

Start button The button on the left side of the taskbar that opens the Start menu to start programs, find and open files, access Windows Help and Support, and more.

Stated conditions In a logical formula, criteria you create.

Statement In Visual Basic, a line of code.

Status bar (Windows) A horizontal bar at the bottom of a window that displays simple Help information and tips. (Excel) Bar at the bottom of the Excel window that provides information about various keys, commands, and processes.

Structured reference Allows table formulas to refer to table columns by names that are automatically generated when the table is created.

Sub procedure A series of Visual Basic statements that performs an action but does not return a value.

Subfolder A folder within another folder for organizing sets of related files into smaller groups.

Suite A group of programs that are bundled together and share a similar interface, making it easy to transfer skills and program content among them.

Summary function In a PivotTable, a function that determines the type of calculation applied to the PivotTable data, such as SUM or COUNT.

Switch User To lock your user account and display the Welcome screen so another user can log on.

Syntax In the Visual Basic programming language, the formatting rules that must be followed so that the macro will run correctly.

Tab 1) A set of commands on the Ribbon related to a common set of tasks or features. Tabs are further organized into groups of related commands. 2) A sheet within a dialog box that contains a group of related settings.

Table An organized collection of rows and columns of similarly structured data on a worksheet.

Table styles Preset formatting combinations for a table.

Table total row The area at the bottom of a table used for calculations with the data in the table columns.

Tag A word or phrase assigned to a file that reminds you of a file's content.

Target The location that a hyperlink displays after you click it.

Target cell In what-if analysis (specifically, in Excel Solver), the cell containing the formula.

Taskbar The horizontal bar at the bottom of the desktop; displays the Start button, the Quick Launch toolbar, and the Notification area.

Template A file whose content or formatting serves as the basis for a new workbook; Excel template files have the file extension .xltx.

Terabyte (TB or T) One trillion bytes (or one thousand gigabytes).

Text annotations Labels added to a chart to draw attention to a particular area.

Text box A box in which you type text.

Text concatenation operators Mathematical calculations that join strings of text in different cells.

Themes Predesigned combinations of colors, fonts, and formatting attributes you can apply to a document in any Office program.

Thumbnail A smaller image of the actual contents of a file.

Tick marks Notations of a scale of measure on a chart axis.

Tiled Repeated, like a graphic in a worksheet background.

Title bar Area at the top of every program window that displays the document and program name.

Title bar The top border of a window that displays the name of the window, folder, or file and the program name.

Toggle A button with two settings, on and off.

Toolbar A set of buttons you can click to open menus or select common commands that are also available from a menu bar, such as saving and printing.

ToolTip A label that appears and identifies the purpose of an object when you point to it.

Touch pointer A pointer on the screen for performing pointing operations with a finger if touch input is available on your computer.

Tracers In Excel worksheet auditing, arrows that point from cells that might have caused an error to the active cell containing an error.

Track To identify and keep a record of who makes which changes to a workbook.

Translucency The transparency feature of Windows Aero that enable you to locate content by seeing through one window to the next window.

Trendline A series of data points on a line that shows data values that represent the general direction in a series of data.

Two-input data table A range of cells that shows resulting values when two input values in a formula are changed.

USB flash drive (also called a pen drive, jump drive, keychain drive, and thumb drive) A popular, removable storage device for folders and files that provides ease of use and portability.

User interface A collective term for all the ways you interact with a software program.

Validate A process in which an xml schema makes sure the xml data follows the rules outlined in the schema.

Validation *See* Data Validation.

Value axis In a chart, vertical axis that contains numerical values; in a 2-dimensional chart, also known as the y-axis.

Values Numbers, formulas, and functions used in calculations.

Variable In the Visual Basic programming language, an area in memory in which you can temporarily store an item of information; variables are often declared in Dim statements such as *DimNameAsString*. In an Excel scenario or what-if analysis, a changing input value, such as price or interest rate, that affects a calculated result.

View A set of display or print settings that you can name and save for access at another time. You can save multiple views of a worksheet.

Views Display settings that show or hide selected elements of a document in the document window, to make it easier to focus on a certain task, such as formatting or reading text.

Virus Destructive software that can damage your computer files.

Visual Basic Editor A program that lets you display and edit macro code.

Visual Basic for Applications (VBA) A programming language used to create macros in Excel.

Wallpaper The image that fills the desktop background.

Watermark A translucent background design on a worksheet that is displayed when the worksheet is printed. Watermarks are graphic files that are inserted into the document header. Worksheet backgrounds created with the Background button on the Page Layout tab do not print.

Web query An Excel feature that lets you obtain data from a Web, Internet, or intranet site and places it in an Excel workbook for analysis.

Welcome screen An initial startup screen that displays icons for each user account on the computer.

What-if analysis A decision-making tool in which data is changed and formulas are recalculated in order to predict various possible outcomes.

Wildcard A special symbol that substitutes for unknown characters in defining search criteria in the Find and Replace dialog box. The most common types of wildcards are the question mark (?), which stands for any single character, and the asterisk (*), which represents any group of characters.

Window A rectangular-shaped work area that displays a program or file, folders and files, or Windows tools.

Windows See Microsoft Windows Vista.

Windows 3-D Flip A Windows Aero feature that allows you to display stacked windows at a three-dimensional angle to see even more of the content of all open windows and select the window you want to use.

Windows Aero A Windows Vista feature supported in some editions (or versions) of Windows Vista that enhances the transparency (or translucency) of the Start menu, taskbar, windows, and dialog boxes; enables live taskbar thumbnails, Windows Flip, and Windows 3-D Flip.

Windows Flip A Windows Aero feature that allows you to display a set of thumbnails, or miniature images, of all open windows so that you can select and switch to another window.

WordArt Specially formatted text, created using the WordArt button on the Drawing toolbar.

Workbook A collection of related worksheets contained within a single file.

Worksheet A single sheet within a workbook file; also, the entire area within an electronic spreadsheet that contains a grid of columns and rows.

Worksheet window An area of the program window that displays part of the current worksheet; the worksheet window displays only a small fraction of the worksheet, which can contain a total of 1,048,576 rows and 16,384 columns.

Workspace An Excel file with an .xlw extension containing information about the identity, view, and placement of a set of open workbooks. Instead of opening each workbook individually, you can open the workspace file instead.

X-axis The horizontal axis in a chart; because it often shows data categories, such as months, it is also called the category axis.

XML (Extensible Markup Language) A system for defining languages using tags to structure data.

Y-axis The vertical axis in a chart; because it often shows numerical values in a 2-dimensional chart, it is also called the value axis.

Z-axis The third axis in a true 3-D chart, lets you compare data points across both categories and values.

Zooming in A feature that makes a document appear bigger but shows less of it on screen at once; does not affect actual document size.

Zooming out A feature that shows more of a document on screen at once but at a reduced size; does not affect actual document size.

Index

SPECIAL CHARACTERS

> (greater than operator), EX 117
< (less than operator), EX 117
<> (not equal to operator), EX 117
$ (dollar sign), EX 35, EX 38
% (percent sign), EX 7
* (asterisk), EX 7
+ (plus sign), EX 7
- (minus sign), EX 7
/ (slash), EX 7
= (equal sign), EX 6, EX 12, EX 28, EX 30, EX 117
>= (greater than or equal to operator), EX 117
<= (less than or equal to operator), EX 117
^ (caret), EX 7

A

absolute cell references, EX 34, EX 35
    copying formulas, EX 38-39
.accdb file extension, OFF 8
Access, OFF 2, OFF 3
active cell, EX 4, EX 5
    editing cell entries, EX 10-11
active program, OFF 4
addition operator (+), EX 7
addresses, cells, EX 4, EX 5
alignment
    chart axis text and titles, EX 90
    worksheets, EX 56, EX 57
AND function, building logical formulas with, EX 118–119
annotating charts, EX 92, EX 93
area charts, EX 81
arguments, functions, EX 8
arithmetic operators, EX 12
arrow(s), dialog boxes, OFF 10
arrow keys, navigating worksheets, EX 9
Aspect theme, OFF 7
attributes, worksheets, EX 56, EX 57
Auto Fill, EX 38, EX 39
Auto Fill Options button, EX 38, EX 39
AutoCorrect, customizing, EX 68
AutoFit Column Width command, EX 59
AutoSum, EX 8, EX 9
AVERAGEIF function, EX 108
axes, charts, EX 80, EX 81
    alignment of text and titles, EX 90
    titles, EX 88, EX 89

B

backward compatibility, OFF 11
bar charts, EX 81
Between dialog box, EX 64, EX 65
borders, worksheets, EX 62, EX 63

C

calculation operators, EX 12
category axis, charts, EX 80
cell(s), EX 4, EX 5
    active, EX 4, EX 5
    name ranges, EX 12
    selected, inserting and deleting, EX 33
    selecting ranges, EX 4, EX 5, EX 52
cell addresses, EX 4, EX 5
cell entries
    copying, EX 32, EX 33
    editing, EX 10–11
    indenting, EX 57
    moving, EX 32, EX 33
    rotating, EX 57
cell pointer, EX 4, EX 5
cell ranges, selecting, EX 4, EX 5, EX 52
cell references, EX 12
    absolute, EX 34, EX 35
    adding to formulas, EX 26
    circular, EX 12EX 112
    mixed, EX 35
    relative, EX 34, EX 35
cell styles, worksheets, EX 62, EX 63
Change Chart Type dialog box, EX 86, EX 87
chart(s), EX 79–95
    annotating, EX 92, EX 93
    changing design, EX 86–87
    changing type, EX 86, EX 87
    combination, EX 86
    creating, EX 82–83
    data labels, EX 89
    definition, EX 79
    drawing on, EX 92, EX 93
    elements, EX 80, EX 81
    embedded. See embedded charts
    formatting, EX 90–91
    layout, EX 88–89
    moving, EX 84, EX 85
    Page Setup dialog box, EX 95
    planning, EX 80–81
    resizing, EX 84, EX 85
    SmartArt graphics, EX 93
    types, EX 81. See also specific chart types

chart sheets, EX 82
Choose a SmartArt Graphic dialog box, EX 93
circular references, correcting, EX 112
clip(s), worksheets, EX 55
clip art, worksheets, EX 55
Clipboard. See also Office Clipboard
    screen captures, OFF 13
colors, worksheets, EX 62, EX 63
column(s), worksheets. See worksheet columns
column charts, EX 81
    creating, EX 82, EX 83
column width, worksheets, EX 58–59
Column Width command, EX 59
combination charts, EX 86
commands. See also specific commands
    groups, OFF 6
comment(s), worksheets, EX 60, EX 61
comparison operators, EX 117
compatibility
    backward, OFF 11
    programs, OFF 2
compatibility mode, OFF 11
complex formulas, EX 26–27
CONCATENATE function, EX 106
condition(s)
    stated, EX 116
    summing data ranges based on, EX 108–109
conditional formatting, EX 64–65
consolidating data, using formulas, EX 110–111
contextual Chart Tools tabs, EX 83
contextual tabs, program windows, OFF 6
Convert Text to Columns dialog box, EX 106, EX 107
copy pointer, EX 11
copying
    cell entries, EX 32, EX 33
    formulas. See copying formulas
    worksheets, EX 67
copying and pasting, Office Clipboard, OFF 9
copying formulas
    absolute cell references, EX 38–39
    relative cell references, EX 36–37
correcting errors
    circular references, EX 112
    spelling errors in worksheets, EX 68–69
    Undo button, OFF 6
    COUNTIF function, EX 108, EX 109
customizing
    AutoCorrect, EX 68
    Quick Access toolbar, OFF 7

D

data, consolidating using formulas, EX 110–111
data labels, charts, adding to charts, EX 89
data markers, charts, EX 80, EX 81
data points, charts, EX 80, EX 81
data series, charts, EX 80, EX 81
database(s), file extension, OFF 8
Default Width command, EX 59
deleting selected cells, EX 33
delimiters, EX 106
Design tab, charts, EX 83
diagonal resizing pointer, EX 85
dialog box(es). See also specific dialog boxes
  arrows, OFF 10
  ellipsis, OFF 10
dialog box launcher, OFF 6, OFF 7
division operator (/), EX 7
document(s)
  file extension, OFF 8
  previewing, OFF 12, OFF 13
  printing, OFF 12, OFF 13
Document Recovery task pane, OFF 15
document window, program windows, OFF 6, OFF 7
documentation, tables, EX 55
.docx file extension, OFF 8
dollar sign ($), absolute cell references, EX 35, EX 38
draw pointer, EX 85
drawing on charts, EX 92, EX 93

E

editing
  cell entries, EX 10–11
  comments in worksheets, EX 60, EX 61
  formulas, EX 12, EX 13
  text in charts, EX 88
electronic spreadsheets, EX 2, EX 3
ellipsis, OFF 10
e-mail, sending workbooks, EX 68
embedded charts, EX 82
  moving to sheets, EX 85
equal sign (=)
  equal to operator, EX 117
  formula prefix, EX 6, EX 12, EX 28, EX 30
error(s)
  checking formulas for, EX 112–113
  correcting. See correcting errors
  error values, EX 113
Excel, OFF 2, OFF 3
  uses, EX 2, EX 3
exiting programs, OFF 4, OFF 5
exploding pie charts, EX 94, EX 95
exponent operator (^), EX 7

F

file(s)
  creating, OFF 8, OFF 9
  opening, OFF 10, OFF 11
  recovering, EX 10, OFF 15
  saving, OFF 8, OFF 9, OFF 10, OFF 11
  workbook, recovering, EX 10
file extensions, programs, OFF 8
filenames, Office programs, OFF 8
fill handle, EX 11
  sequential text or values, EX 39
Find and Replace dialog box, EX 68, EX 69
font(s), worksheets, EX 54, EX 55
font size, worksheets, EX 54, EX 55
Format Cells dialog box, EX 52, EX 53, EX 54, EX 55
Format Data Series dialog box, EX 90, EX 91
Format tool, charts, EX 83
formatting
  charts, EX 90–91
  conditional. See conditional formatting
  data using text functions, EX 106–107
  worksheets. See formatting worksheets
formatting worksheets, EX 51–65
  alignment, EX 56, EX 57
  attributes, EX 56, EX 57
  borders, EX 62, EX 63
  clearing formatting for selected range, EX 56
  colors, EX 62, EX 63
  column width, EX 58–59
  conditional formatting, EX 64–65
  deleting columns and rows, EX 60, EX 61
  entire rows, EX 54
  font and font size, EX 54–55
  inserting columns and rows, EX 60, EX 61
  patterns, EX 62, EX 63
  as tables, EX 53
  values, EX 52–53
formula(s), EX 6–7, EX 105–121
  adding cell references, EX 26
  calculating payments with PMT function, EX 120–121
  checking for errors, EX 112–113
  complex, EX 26–27
  consolidating data, EX 110–111
  constructing using names ranges, EX 114–115
  copying. See copying formulas
  editing, EX 12, EX 13
  entering, EX 12, EX 13
  logical, building, EX 116–119
  order of precedence, EX 26
  printing, EX 16
  summing data ranges based on conditions, EX 108–109
  text, formatting data using, EX 106–107
formula prefix (=), EX 6, EX 12, EX 28, EX 30
function(s), EX 8. See also specific functions
  inserting using buttons, EX 28–39
  rounding values, EX 40–41
  typing, EX 30–31
Function Arguments dialog box, EX 28
future value, calculating with FV function, EX 121
FV function, EX 121

G

graphics, charts, EX 93
graphs. See chart(s)
greater than operator (>), EX 117
greater than or equal to operator (>=), EX 117
gridlines, charts, EX 88, EX 89
groups, commands, OFF 6

H

header boxes, EX 14, EX 15
Help system, OFF 14–15
Hide & Unhide command, EX 59
hiding, worksheet columns and rows, EX 60
horizontal axis, charts, EX 80, EX 81
horizontal resizing pointer, EX 85

I

I-beam pointer, EX 11
IF function, building logical formulas, EX 116–117
IFERROR function, EX 112
images. See also graphics
  worksheets, EX 55
indenting cell entries, EX 57
Insert dialog box, EX 60, EX 61
Insert Function dialog box, EX 28, EX 29
integration, OFF 2
interfaces, OFF 2

L

labels, EX 8, EX 9
  alignment in worksheets, EX 56, EX 57
  data. See data labels, charts
landscape orientation, EX 16
launching programs, OFF 4, OFF 5
layout, charts, EX 88–89
Layout tool, charts, EX 83
legends, charts, EX 80, EX 81
less than operator (<), EX 117
less than or equal to operator (<=), EX 117
line charts, EX 81
linking data between workbooks, EX 110, EX 111
Live Preview, OFF 6
  colors in worksheets, EX 62, EX 63
  worksheets, EX 54
logical formulas
  building with AND function, EX 118–119
  building with IF function, EX 116–117
logical tests, EX 116
LOWER function, EX 107

M

Microsoft Access. *See* Access
Microsoft Excel. *See* Excel
mixed references, EX 35
mode indicator, EX 4, EX 5, EX 8
mouse pointers, EX 11, OFF 7
move pointer, EX 11
moving. *See also* navigating
   cell entries, EX 32, EX 33
   charts, EX 84, EX 85
   sheets, EX 66, EX 67
multilevel sorts, EX 65
multiplication operator (*), EX 7

N

name(s)
   files, OFF 8
   sheets, EX 66, EX 67
   workbooks, EX 115
Name box, EX 4, EX 5
named ranges, constructing formulas,
   EX 114–115
navigating worksheets, EX 9
negation operator (–), EX 7
New Name dialog box, EX 114, EX 115
New Workbook dialog box, EX 41
normal pointer, EX 11
Normal view, EX 14
not equal to operator (<>), EX 117
NOT function, EX 118

O

objects. *See also* specific objects
   definition, EX 84
Office 2007, OFF 1–15
   benefits, OFF 1
   component programs, OFF 2, OFF 3. *See also*
      specific programs
Office Clipboard, OFF 9
   copying cell entries, EX 32, EX 33
online collaboration, OFF 2
Open dialog box, OFF 10, OFF 11
   options, OFF 10
opening, files, OFF 11
opening files, OFF 10
operators
   arithmetic, EX 7, EX 12
   calculation, EX 12
   reference, EX 12
   text concatenation, EX 12
OR function, EX 118
order of precedence, EX 26

P

Page Break Preview, EX 14, EX 15
Page Layout tab, EX 16, EX 17
Page Layout View, EX 14, EX 15
Page Setup dialog box, charts, EX 95

Page Setup group, EX 16
paper orientation, EX 16
Paste Options button, EX 38, EX 39
patterns, worksheets, EX 62, EX 63
payments, calculating with PMT function,
   EX 120–121
percent operator (%), EX 7
pie charts, EX 81
   creating, EX 94–95
   exploding, EX 94, EX 95
planning charts, EX 80–81
plot area, charts, EX 80, EX 81
PMT function, EX 120–121
point(s), EX 54
PowerPoint, OFF 2, OFF 3
.pptx file extension, OFF 8
presentation(s), file extension, OFF 8
previewing
   documents, OFF 12, OFF 13
   fonts and font sizes, EX 54
print area, EX 16, EX 17
Print dialog box, EX 16, EX 17, OFF 12, OFF 13
Print Preview, EX 16, EX 17
   worksheets, EX 68, EX 69
printing
   documents, OFF 12, OFF 13
   worksheet formulas, EX 16
   worksheets, EX 16–17
programs. *See also* specific programs
   active, OFF 4
   compatibility, OFF 2
   exiting, OFF 4, OFF 5
   starting, OFF 4, OFF 5
   switching between, OFF 5
PROPER function, EX 106

Q

Quick Access toolbar
   customizing, OFF 7
   program windows, OFF 7

R

ranges
   cell, selecting, EX 4, EX 5, EX 52
   named, EX 12
Recent Documents list, OFF 10
recovering files, EX 10, OFF 15
reference operators, EX 12
relative cell references, EX 34, EX 35
   copying formulas, EX 36–37
resizing, charts, EX 85
resizing charts, EX 84
Ribbon, program windows, OFF 6, OFF 7
rotating, cell entries, EX 57
ROUND function, EX 40
rounding values, EX 40–41
row(s), worksheets. *See* worksheet rows
row height, worksheets, EX 58

S

Save As dialog box, OFF 8, OFF 9, OFF 10,
   OFF 11
saving, files, OFF 8, OFF 9, OFF 10, OFF 11
Scale field, EX 16
scaling to fit, EX 17
scatter charts, EX 81
scope, EX 114
screen captures, OFF 13
ScreenTips, OFF 7, OFF 14
scroll bars, EX 4, EX 5
selecting cell ranges, EX 4, EX 5, EX 52
sequential text or values, fill handle, EX 39
sheet(s)
   linking data between, EX 110
   moving, EX 66, EX 67
   moving embedded charts to, EX 85
   naming, EX 66, EX 67
sheet tabs, EX 4, EX 5
shortcut keys, moving between programs, OFF 5
sizing handles, charts, EX 82
SmartArt graphics, charts, EX 93
spell checking, worksheets, EX 68–69
Spelling dialog box, EX 68, EX 69
spreadsheet software, EX 2–3
Start menu, OFF 4, OFF 5
starting programs, OFF 4, OFF 5
stated conditions, EX 116
status bar, EX 4, EX 5
styles, worksheet cells, EX 62, EX 63
SUBSTITUTE function, EX 107
subtraction operator (–), EX 7
suites, OFF 2
SUM function, EX 28
SUMIF function, EX 108, EX 109
summing data ranges based on conditions,
   EX 108–109
switching
   between programs, OFF 5
   worksheet views, EX 14–15

T

tab(s)
   contextual, OFF 6
   program windows, OFF 7
tables
   documentation, EX 55
   formatting worksheets as, EX 53
templates, EX 2
   creating workbooks, EX 41
text, charts
   alignment, EX 90
   editing, EX 88
text annotations, charts, EX 92, EX 93
text concatenation operators, EX 12
text functions, formatting data using,
   EX 106–107
themes, worksheets, EX 63
3–D charts, EX 87
   axes, EX 80

3–D references, EX 110
tick marks, charts, EX 80, EX 81
title(s)
    chart axes, EX 88, EX 89
    charts, alignment, EX 90
title bar, program windows, OFF 6, OFF 7

▶ U

Undo button, OFF 6
unhiding worksheet columns and rows, EX 60
UPPER function, EX 107
user interface, OFF 6–7

▶ V

value(s)
    alignment in worksheets, EX 56, EX 57
    entering, EX 8, EX 9
    error, EX 113
    formatting in worksheets, EX 52–53
    future, calculating with FV function, EX 121
    rounding, EX 40–41
    sequential, EX 39
value axis, charts, EX 80
vertical axis, charts, EX 80, EX 81

▶ W

what–if analysis, EX 2
Word, OFF 2, OFF 3

workbooks, EX 2
    e–mailing, EX 68
    file extension, OFF 8
    linking data between, EX 110, EX 111
    lost, recovering, EX 10
    names, EX 115
    new, creating using templates, EX 41
    templates. See editing
worksheet(s), EX 2, EX 3
    columns. See worksheet columns
    comments, EX 60, EX 61
    copying, EX 67
    creating charts, EX 82–83
    formatting. See formatting worksheets
    formulas. See formula(s)
    functions. See function(s)
    inserting images, EX 55
    moving sheets, EX 66, EX 67
    naming sheets, EX 66, EX 67
    navigating, EX 9
    previewing, EX 68, EX 69
    printing, EX 16–17
    rows. See worksheet rows
    spell checking, EX 68–69
    themes, EX 63
    what–if analysis. See what–if analysis
worksheet columns
    deleting, EX 60, EX 61
    hiding and unhiding, EX 60
    inserting, EX 60, EX 61

worksheet rows
    deleting, EX 60, EX 61
    height, EX 58
    hiding and unhiding, EX 60
    inserting, EX 60, EX 61
worksheet views, switching, EX 14–15

▶ X

x–axis, charts, EX 80
.xlsx file extension, OFF 8

▶ Y

y–axis, charts, EX 80

▶ Z

z–axis, charts, EX 80
Zoom button, OFF 12, OFF 13
Zoom slider, program windows, OFF 7
zooming in, OFF 12, OFF 13
zooming out, OFF 12, OFF 13